Julianne Smith-Devereaux

I Got Out Alive!

One Woman's Journey Outside of America's Most Dangerous Cult, The Illuminati

Editions Dedicaces

I Got Out Alive!

Published by:
Editions Dedicaces LLC
12759 NE Whitaker Way, Suite D833
Portland, Oregon, 97230
www.dedicaces.us

Library of Congress Cataloging-in-Publication Data
Smith-Devereaux, Julianne.
I Got Out Alive! / by Julianne Smith-Devereaux.
p. cm.
ISBN-13: 978-1-77076-538-2 (alk. paper)
ISBN-10: 1-77076-538-7 (alk. paper)

Julianne Smith-Devereaux

I Got Out Alive!

One Woman's Journey Outside of America's Most Dangerous Cult, The Illuminati

Contents

Chapter 1

My name is Gia Mahari. I was born in Hollywood, California at Kaiser Permanente Hospital. I believe it was on Sunset Blvd. My only birth certificate is fake. I *was* born in Hollywood. At least, that is what I have always been told. To a mother that was, I believe, 16 or 17 years old. When she found out that she was pregnant, she wanted to abort me but my grandfather and grandmother were strict Catholics at that time, so 'no go' for the abortion. Oh boy. I survived. Well, we moved in with my grandparents for a while. My grandmother basically raised me when I was an infant because my mother wasn't done 'partying' yet. Anyway, her sister, my aunt, babysat me for a few bucks on the weekends while my mother went out trolling for men. And believe me. She found some 'Winners!' All I really remember is that my mother would come and go; my grandfather, who had polio from the war, my grandmother would just raise, love, and take care of me. They were like my mother and father. I bonded with them. In fact, if I hadn't had them, I would have either been dead or with a severe emotional disorder called 'Attachment Disorder'. If you do not know what that disorder means, please, by ALL means. Look it up. It's 'quite lovely'. In fact, most known serial killers had/have this disorder when they were young as well as growing into adulthood. One day my mother had a 'talking to' either by my grandparents or she got bored or felt guilty. I don't remember. But I do believe it was the latter. So, she decided to move out of their home and move into her/our own apartment; many apartments. I remember moving constantly when I was very young. And the reason was…my biological father. My mother tried to hide from him, run away from him, and then move once he found out where she was; or, rather, *we* were. Everything she could do to get away from *him*. How did he keep on finding out where we were living or where we were? My mother worked for my grandfather in his Insurance Company. And my grandfather knew nothing about my biological father. *Nothing*. My grandfather owned quite a lot of insurance companies around Southern California. What my father would do is he would call my grandfather's main office and say that he knew my mom as a 'friend', had lost her new address, and 'if he would be so kind to give him her new address'. Well, of course he did! This was in the late 60's. No Stalking was known then…etc. So when she would get home from work one day, the phone would ring and there would be his voice. It scared the living shit out of her. Why did he scare her so much? Well, that's a *whole* different story. No one that my mother was close with, let alone her friends, knew anything at all about him. All anyone knew was that he was the gorgeous, dark-haired, good-looking guy with the fast, sweet Corvette who had *very* wealthy parents. So, of course, my mom wanted to meet him. Her girlfriend in High School had a boyfriend who knew him through the 'car circuit' and set them up. And then as they say…. the rest is history. She fell madly in lust/love, with him. She would do anything for him, including participating in hiding him for a while and protecting him when he was involved in attempted murder. All *he* wanted was a child. A 'white, blue-eyed, girl' to be exact. That was all he wanted from her. Since he is 100% Syrian, he was going to have to hope his genes did not 'overpower' hers. Well, they did not. When I was born, on August 10th, 1956, I was a tiny, blond, blue-eyed, baby girl. I think he would have preferred a boy. Not the normal reasons why men want a son either. After I was born, my mother and I continued living with my grandparents. At around one and a half years old, she took me and moved out (to get away from my father, who obviously knew where her parents lived). Our first apartment was in Monrovia, CA; a suburb of Los Angeles. Back in the 60's it wasn't a bad neighborhood; mostly middle class, young people, families, etc. Now it is filled with gangs I am sure. My mother still worked for my grandfather at his insurance company and I stayed with my grandmother during the day. At least I was SAFE then. Approximately two months after I was born, my grandpa received a phone call from my father, not knowing it was my father, and gave out my mother's new address. Now my father knew where we lived. Again. And it didn't take him long to give her a 'welcome note'. One evening when we were both in the apartment, someone knocked on the door and when my mother answered the door, there he was. She was terrified. To put it mildly. I was only a year and a half – two years old and I still remember how terrified she was. I felt it coming through her body. I hid behind her cotton/linen dress, one hand clenched onto her. I don't remember much about that night, but I do remember his eyes. They were black. At least to me. Like shark's eyes. And all he did, at first, was look right at me. Or through me. I was terrified. Plus, feeling my mother's fear, I instantly started crying. Hysterically. My mom picked me up; my father's eyes never stopped looking away from mine and she took me to 'my room' (which was actually her room as well) and put me in my crib. For the night. I don't remember what happened that evening but, I'm sure, it wasn't 'wonderful' for my mother. I don't remember the next day or much after that. All I *do* remember was that my mother and I moved from apartment to apartment at least six times. Because of 'Him'. My mother, after moving for the 6th time, finally figured out how my father was finding her. She decided to switch jobs. Well, my grandpa was paying her quite a bit of money so she wouldn't have to work more than one job. Well, now she had to work two jobs. But, I guess it was better than being found out where we lived by 'Him'. Her daytime job was a receptionist at an insurance company and her night job was a waitress at a topless bar. Those 2 jobs enabled her to afford her rent, my expenses, and other minor things such as clothes…etc. Plus, my grandparents gave her some extra money and bought her a car too. One night, while I was at my grandma and grandpa's, she went over to a girlfriend's apartment that was in the same complex as ours. That particular night, my father decided to go over to our apartment and start a fire inside it. Before he did that though, he slashed every single piece of clothing my mother owned. Everything! From her work clothes to her panties'. Well, obviously when the fire trucks and the police siren's came closer, my mom's friend looked out of her window and saw that my mom's apartment was practically engulfed in flames. Needless to say, we had to move again. At least, because of my grandpa, my mom had renter's insurance. So she got most everything paid for. But….. we still had to move again. I do not remember this new apartment at all. All I do know is that it was the *last* apartment my mother lived in for the rest of her life. Another evening, my mom had a bad feeling at her day job. She called my grandmother and asked her if she could watch me that evening. Of course she said 'yes' so off I went. I had just turned three at this time I believe. That evening my mother had the night off from her night job. Little did she know that my father had been keeping track of her work schedules by calling her employers. My mom decided to hang out at her girlfriend's apartment; the same girlfriend that witnessed my mother's apartment fire. At some point in the evening, they both were hungry. So, my mom offered to walk next door to a fast food restaurant. On her way back, 'someone' jumped out from a trashcan with a lot of bushes around it and held a knife to her throat. He threatened to kill her and her parent's if she didn't agree to come back to him and give me to him. Yes, *me*. At this point, thank God, some older guy was getting into his car outside of the restaurant and saw what happened. He had a rifle in his car and threatened to shoot my father if he didn't let my mother go. After my father took off; probably to his car that was parked not too far away from the fast food place, the man asked my mother if she wanted him to call the police for her. She declined, saying that her best friend's apartment was just up the street. She got to her friend's house and told her everything. That was when her friend told her that she, my mother, needed to get the Hell out of this area and hide out for a while. Plus, to call the police on this psychopath. Well, my mother agreed. Except for 'calling the police' part. Why? Because he told her if she DID happen to call the police on him. For any reason, he would kill both of her parents and sister. He never threatened to kill me though. Very strange, right? Not so much. Especially once I tell you more about him. My mom, yet again, packed up all of our things, and booked it to Newport Beach, CA. By this time, my grandparents had moved there too. On the beach. Sweet, right?

Chapter 2

My lovely dad. Ok. The next few chapter's is mainly about my father. Yes, it is all real, true, non-fiction. Whatever you want to call it, it happened. My father was born in Syria. He and his parents moved to San Marin, California when he was around five or six years old. I have never asked when he moved, exactly. You really don't 'ask' him anything. My father, starting when he was five up until he was 16 yrs. old, was being molested by his mother. She made him sleep and have sex with her for all of those years. She was a very, very, sick woman, obviously. So, that was the start of his psychopathology. He started using LSD and hallucinogenic drugs at the age of 11 years old and did not stop until he was 29 years old. Let me tell you a bit more about my mother and stepfather before I go into living with my real father. I lived with my grandparents most of the time and spent a night here and there with my mom. One night when I did spend the night with my mom, it was the middle of the night; two-three am. The phone rang; I was about three and a half. Maybe a tad older. It was 'Him'. Next thing I know, my mom has me wrapped up in a blanket and we were driving a long-ass way. All I remember about that particular evening was that I was in the backseat and my mom was driving like a bat out of a Hell in the front. We stopped once, as far as I remember, for some gas. And the next time we stopped, we were in the middle of nowhere. Literally. In the desert it turned out. On the way to Vegas. We were in the front of a gas station. Next thing I know, some dude is sitting next to me. Whom I had never seen him before – and my father was sitting up front with my mother. We drove all the way back to Los Angeles after picking up my father and his 'friend' at that gas station. It turned out that he and his friend that weekend were driving to Vegas and needed gas. Plus, they were either drunk, tired, on drugs, or all of the above. My father, very calmly, told my mother that he had asked the owner of the gas station if he and his friend could spend the night or 'sleep it off' for a while in the back of his station. The owner apparently said 'no' so my father stabbed him multiple times while his friend held him down. According to my mother, my father did have blood all over him. I, being afraid of his presence or aura, whatever you call it, didn't say a damn word. I just sat there, in stony silence. I was hoping that they didn't see me, smell me, etc. Hell! I wish someone would swallow me up! So, my mom drove him and his friend back to Los Angeles. I do not remember where she dropped them off. I guess, at that point, she decided that she 'had' them. She was going to call the police the next morning. Or, later THAT morning. When the 'right' moment came, she dropped me off at my grandmother's house and she went back to our apartment. No, she hadn't gotten a house yet. She called the police and much to her surprise, the owner of that very gas station did not die and he had called the police and was admitted into a hospital. He survived. Well, my mother is thinking, that is still attempted murder, right? Yes it is, said the cop. But, to this day, 2013, I have no idea why he got off on that charge! He wasn't charged with a damn, fucking, thing! So, now, here he is. Not in jail, and he knows that someone called the police on him and he also knows that there could only be one person who would do that. My mom. So, he drove over to her apartment. But……. she was not there. Moved out, actually. That probably saved her life as well as my grandparent's lives. My life? Nope. Well, technically, yes, but he 'needed' me for something. At that point my mother and, obviously I, did not know what that 'something' was. As far as my memory goes, that was pretty much all I remember seeing of my real father. Which is not true, come to find out. My mom always needs one thing in her life. A man. I know there is a word for that in the DSM IV or DSM V, whatever number that book is on now (The DSM books are Psychology books. Definitions of everything from phobias too compulsions to OCD, ADD, ADHD; you get the picture). One day, when I was four, my mother apparently met this man by the name of Richard Fisher. At a bar somewhere. He was single and looking for a woman with, it turned out, a little or young girl, as well. He was 30 years older than her. Nice. He was disgusting to look at and he always smelled of sweat. Anyway, he made decent money, I guess. He was in construction so we were provided for. Monetarily anyway. In the very beginning, he was fine. I was just four years old and had a lot of nightmares. No clue why. Anyway, now that my mother was married to 'a man she could trust' she now could take night classes so she could get a better job. And have my step-father watch me at night.

Chapter 3

It didn't start right away but he didn't waste any time either. Once my mother started night school, she'd be gone for about three to four hours. That was just the perfect amount of time for him to do his sick, perverted shit. The first time I *do* remember. I was asleep in my bed. I heard my bedroom door opening. In my half-awake state, I thought it was my mom who'd come home from night school and coming in my room to give me a goodnight kiss. Wrong. It was my step-father who had snuck in my room, covered my mouth with his huge hand, his breath smelling of beer and whispering, 'Do not make a sound or I will kill your mother.' He then proceeded to rape me vaginally, orally and anally. I was in complete and total shock. I remember looking at my bedside clock and knew my mom would not be home until 12 midnight. It was only 9PM. All I could do was to endure the pain and wait until it was, thankfully, over. Which was an hour and a half later. When it finally was over, he got off of me, went into my restroom, cleaned himself up and walked out into the living room. I laid awake in my bed for at least three hours. Complete pain, humiliation and sadness washed over me as I felt the blood running down my legs and backside. I slowly got out of bed, in the most horrid pain you can imagine, and tried to clean myself up. In the same bathroom as he did. I saw that he had gotten rid of ALL of the 'evidence' quite well too. I knew I could not tell my mother because, for once in her life, she was 'happy', had a home on the beach in Balboa and didn't have to worry about money anymore. These 'lovely' night's happened three times a week. From when I was four years old until I was 13 years old. A long-ass time to endure, I know, but who would believe me? That's what I thought ALL of those years. This went on while my mom was away at night-school. After a while, about nine years of living under the same roof as that monster, my mother knew nothing. One weekend, my step-father wanted to take my mother and me over to meet his parents. I would say I was about five or six at that time. We went to their home (I forget where they lived) and unbeknownst to me, The Monster's father was the town's Child Molester. Nice, huh? I actually didn't find out about that little tidbit until many years later. When my mom and step-father and my stepfather's mother went out to eat for lunch or dinner, I forget which, I was asleep in their bedroom and my stepfather's father said he wouldn't mind babysitting me while they were gone. Well, there he was. 'Doing' me, from behind and telling me how much I loved it and how did I like my new step-dad and all of that kind of crap. I just did what I normally did in 'that situation'. I closed my eyes and pretended I was riding my horse on the beach and feeling the wind in my hair. Well, about an hour and a half later, they all came home from their dinner and we all went home. I believe my stepfather and his mother knew exactly what happened as well. Nice step-grandparents to have, huh? Yeah. I agree. Needless to say, when I was picked up, I didn't say a single thing. I just thought that this was what ALL little girls had to endure at this age. One day, when I came home from playing at the beach, my mom sat me down and told me that we were moving to Northern California. The Monster got transferred there for his job. He was in construction. I wasn't thrilled but I really do not remember what I felt. I do know that I was very sad because I was going to miss my grandparents immensely! Plus, they were not thrilled about this idea either. They were my rock, my safety net and my life….. everything! I didn't know what to do or say. In fact, I couldn't do or say anything. I was only a kid. So, I just smiled and said, 'ok.' And gave a half-assed smile. It was the summer after third grade so I would be going to fourth grade near Sacramento. Or a little town near Sacramento called Roseville. The Monster's boss had a Horse Ranch up there.

Since horses were my favorite animals in the world, and still are, I thought that it would be fun. Boy was I wrong. We found a really nice condo in Roseville. Not too far from The Monster's sister, Marilyn. When The Monster was working, we would hang out with his sister, Marilyn. She lived more in the rural part of Roseville. At the time, most of Roseville was rural. I am sure now it is a lot bigger that it was then. Anyhow, Marilyn had a son who was 17 years old and a senior in High School. I do not remember his name either. What I *do* remember was that one evening, when we were at Marilyn's home having dinner, her son was in his bedroom. I don't remember doing what but he did have school books on his bed. He would sometimes invite me in his room and sometimes ignore me. That night he invited me into his room. He said something to the effect of 'do you want to play doctor?' Typical, yes? Douchebag! I, of course, starving for attention, said 'Yes. How do you play?' Well, he laid me down, on my back and stuck his hands down my pants. I knew exactly where this was going. I struggled and started to make noise so he slapped his hands on my mouth and told me to 'shut up. I will enjoy this.' Well, I did shut up but I sure as shit did *not* enjoy 'this'. I guess we went home that night. I don't remember. The next morning my mother and I woke up to the sound of the phone ringing. It was The Monster. He said one of his work buddy's had died while on the job. He was crushed by a construction tractor. I don't know the name of the machine but it had HUGE-ASS tires. My mother and I went to the construction site and all I remember is that we talked to The Monster and his boss. This was the first time The Monster's boss saw me and vice-versa. After the funeral, we all went to The Monster's bosses' house. While everyone was eating and talking, very quietly, The Monster's son asked me if I wanted to go horseback riding. That was music to my ears! I was so damn excited! We went to the stable, put saddles on two horses and off we went. Everything went fine until when we rode quite a bit far from the house/barn. His and my horse drank some water and then his horse took off running back to the barn. Apparently that was what the bosses' son wanted to do too. Without telling me anything. My horse followed HIS horse as well. When I *wasn't* expecting it. He started bucking and off I went (we weren't using saddles) and landed on my left arm. It hurt like Hell! I got back on my horse, gave him a good yank with the bit in his mouth and took off towards the barn. Once we got there, I tied my horse to the stock pole, and walked into the house, looking for my mother. I remember her sitting at a table with about 10 women there. Including Marilyn. I showed her my arm and part of my bone was sticking out. Needless to say, off to the hospital we went. It turned out to be a compound fracture and the closest child Orthopedist worked out of Arkansas. So, after they took X-rays and doped me up and prepped me for surgery, they found out that the doctor couldn't be there for another eight hours or so. I was starving! I hadn't eaten since breakfast that morning and by this time it was 8pm. I couldn't eat anything because they had already given me knockout, surgery drugs too, where I couldn't eat a damn thing for quite a while. I was basically screwed. So they wheeled me back to my room and I had to wait until the next morning to have my surgery. By this time I was thirsty, hungry and had lost 10 lbs. Yeah, no shit. A great diet if you want to try it. I wouldn't recommend it though. After the surgery, I had a cast with two pins in my arm. I was sort of bummed because it wasn't a plaster cast. It was one of those gauze casts, because of the pins. I wouldn't be able to have anyone from school sign it. Try writing on gauze. After I was released from the hospital, I got to stay home for two weeks. I went back to school and a couple of my friends managed to sign it. I don't really remember school there that much. Nothing exciting, I would think. I didn't care much for the school, didn't have many friends there and missed my grandparents *bad.* I called my grandma and grandpa almost every day. Then, all I remember, was that all of us moved back to Southern California. I think it was because Northern California had a long rain spell. And if you are in construction, you cannot work in the rain. So back to good ole So. Cal! But I didn't care. Not one bit. My grandparents were there and that is all I cared about! It was also decided that I would move in with my grandpa and grandma too. As soon as we got back from 'child molestation city'. I was ecstatic! Back 'home', so to speak, my mother and I continued to live with The Monster for a bit until things were 'worked out', my mother said. I was having nightmares every night, I couldn't sleep in my bed at *all* at night because I was afraid 'he' would come back in my room and 'rape' me again. Finally I had 'an episode', (my mother's word's), where I chased her around our house with a butcher knife. I was five. 'The Monster' was at work. This was after I sat down with my Grandpa and Grandma and told them what was going on at my house. My grandfather was so pissed off and beside himself that he almost couldn't believe it. My grandmother just sat there and had her mouth open the whole time. I swear, if my grandpa didn't have polio and could walk without leg braces and crutches, he would have taken my great, great, grandfather's shotgun and blown 'The Monster's' head off. That was when I finally had a mini-breakdown at the ripe old age of five years old. I was sent to live with my *real* father, who *insisted* that I live with him. I didn't know it at the time, but it was so my mother could divorce 'The Monster'. I lived with my real father from the age of 5 until young adulthood. Everything was fine and normal. For now.

Chapter 4

I continued to live with my father and speak with my grandma and grandfather every weekend. After all, it was their idea that I go and live with him ‘because it would be a much more stable and safe environment’ for me to live in. One weekend, when I did call my grandma, she told me the news about my mother and what she was up to. My grandmother told me that my mother would go out every Thursday through Sunday night. Looking for a man. She went through, I would say, five to seven men until she met this 'older' man (try 36 years older) named Vincent Gomati. She met him at her favorite bar. Some bar in an Expensive Hotel in Newport Beach or Costa Mesa located in Southern California. Right by the beach. I forget the name of the actual hotel and bar and it really doesn't matter. They started dating right away and she did not say a word about him too my grandparents or me for almost a year. When their Year Anniversary of dating came up, they got married at the courthouse in Los Angeles or Southern California. This man was to become my 'stepfather' from the time I was almost 14 years old until the present. My mother came to my grandparent's house to talk to them and myself about her new husband. But, the one detail that she left out was his age. If she did indeed tell them his true age, they would have both dropped dead of a coronary I'm pretty damn sure. I wasn't thrilled, as you could possibly imagine, so I still decided to stay living with my father. Plus, my grandparents insisted as well; especially after what I had been through. After about three or four weeks of 'wedded bliss', Vincent (a former child psychologist), insisted to my mom that he truly wanted to be a part of my life. He wanted to meet me, get to know me, and eventually get me to trust him. Like *that* would ever happen. To this day, I am just starting to 'trust' him. He really wanted me to consider him as my father and to call him as such. Let's just say that I have not gotten *there* yet. At school I did really well. Starting with Kindergarten, I used school as my 'escape' from all the bad things that were happening to me at home. If I had to disassociate from all of the abuse, I really focused on my school work; especially Creative Writing class and horseback riding. When a small child is abused, a lot, especially when he/she is very young and the abuse is so traumatic their minds cannot 'deal with it' or 'have no life-experience' in which to place it/put it, they do what is called 'disassociate' from the whole experience. That's why a lot of abused adults don't remember their abuse until much later in their lives; usually around their 30's or sometimes in their late 20's, depending on who abused them and if they are still involved in that child/adults life at that time; and sometimes at the most unusual places. It was coming up on my 14th birthday and Tony had spoken to my mother about both of them taking me out to dinner at my favorite restaurant. I agreed. I thought, what the hell. I'll give him a chance, plus my mother was going to be there as well. So, they picked me up. Just as we were leaving the driveway, Vincent and I got in a verbal fight. From what I can remember, a pretty combative one at that too. Hell! That was even before we had left the house for two minutes! We eventually got there and had a pretty good time. At least I did. Vincent was pretty quiet and my mother was pretty damn silent too, but pretending to be talkative. If you can even get a clue as to what that is like. I, myself, ignored it. After the dinner, my mom and my new step-father dropped me off at my father's/my house. I guess all in all it was a decent evening. If you don't count the verbal blow-up. I do remember Vinnie, (as I'll call him from here on out) telling me once we all got back in the car after we ate, that I 'had the biggest set of balls of anyone he had EVER met; male or female'. To me, I took that as a compliment.

My mother told him, 'Shhh! Vinnie! Be quiet!' I just smiled all the way home. To me, I won that battle.

My school life was pretty boring; nothing that exciting to write about anyway. I had one boyfriend during High School. I remember his name but let's just say his name was Michael Green. I went to Middle School in Beverly Hills as well. My father lived near Mulholland Drive in Los Angeles, California for many years. He owned a movie studio in Hollywood, CA. He was very wealthy from that job alone, but he made most of his money in the illegal business' of the sex-trade, drug trade, white slavery and just about *everything* that is considered illegal. He is also the 'Head' or 'CEO', for lack of a better word, of the Luciferian Cult/Group, The Brotherhood or, better known to the World as The Illuminati. They have control and have HAD control over just about anything illegal for a very long time. Starting in the mid 50's to this day. The gambling business to the drug trade to white slavery and arms dealing are just a small part of what my father is in control of. What my father wants is what my father gets. He wanted me in his home, under his watchful eye, along with his huge, seemingly concrete, bodyguards. As soon as I was moved in and settled, I had one assigned to me by the name of Kevin. The rules were that if I was to go anywhere, I had to have him go with me. No matter what. My father did not have me get involved in his illegal enterprises until after three months of me living under his roof. As the three month time period came upon me, my father 'summoned' me into his in-house office to explain to me just exactly what I would be doing for *him* in The Brotherhood.

Chapter 5

I'd be lying if I didn't say that I was 'scared', 'nervous' or, at the very least, 'apprehensive'. I walked slowly down the two flights of stairs leading to his office on the 2nd floor and timidly turned my head around his office door. Somehow, as always, he *knew* I was there. After about five minutes of me sweating and waiting for him to acknowledge me, he looked in my direction and told me to sit down. Not asked, told. That was my father. He was very domineering, very intimidating and very demanding. His employees almost never said 'no' to him. And if they did, well.... I never saw them again. I walked to his impeccable sofa, which was directly across from his desk, and sat down. Now, before I go into the conversation we had, I think I should describe to you what my father looks like. He is, at this time, 62 years old, stands 6 foot 1 and has jet black hair with piercing brown eyes. Most of my girlfriends say he is 'the hottest father they have ever seen' and 'would sleep with him in a second'. That's exactly what I want to hear… *Not* so much. I am sitting on his sofa, waiting silently, until he addresses me again. He continues typing on his laptop for another five to six minutes until he looks up at me. 'Gia', he says. 'You know what this conversation is going to entail so I shall get straight to the point. Starting in two weeks, you shall fly to the Middle East and meet with an acquaintance of mine. He will then tell you the details of what your job shall be there. After you complete your job there to my satisfaction, you will then come home. Not until the job is finished and you are here at home, will you get paid. Most of that money shall go into a trust account that will be managed by my financial advisor. He will also be *your* financial advisor for a long, long time.' I continued to sit on the sofa, staring at him with, I am sure, big, bug, eyes. I knew this day was coming. I just didn't know that it was going to be this soon. I actually have to kill someone! And soon! Hell! I didn't even know if he was a bad person or even a good person. I knew that to 'The Brotherhood', he was a 'bad person'. And I also knew what they did to bad people or people they didn't like. Well, now I had a very good idea of what I was going to do for my father *and* The Brotherhood. But in the Middle East? As my first job? I looked at him as he was still staring at me. I replied, my voice practically a whisper, and asked if I was traveling with a bodyguard or anyone that I knew from his employ that I could trust. He replied, 'No. Not on your first job. You can go now and decide on what to pack.' He looked down at his laptop and continued typing like he had never stopped. I slowly stood up, said 'Thank You, daddy' and walked out of his office. Just like that. That was it. My mind was going 100 miles an hour. I had to re-think and remember all of the training that I received from my father, his associates, as well as his bodyguards and his security detail. His 'Detail' are guys that he had recruited, or they 'applied' through word-of-mouth, from Military bases around the Nation. They patrolled his property 24/7 and were armed to the teeth. Not to forget the 50 highly trained Rottweiler's. But they were not let out of their kennels until after dark. His main, number one bodyguard is called 'Steven'. He and I got along great. In fact, he and I had a brother/sister sort of relationship. I could pretty much tell him or ask him anything and he would tell me the God's honest truth. I did trust him. Out of all of my father's detail, he was the only one whom I did trust. After I got back to my room, I sat down on my bed and slowly laid down on it. Two weeks to prepare for something that I was trained to do but never actually thought I'd ever have to do. My total training began when I was six years old and still continues to this day. Even though now it is mostly just for practice. And to keep it fresh in my mind. My father told me, after I had asked him of course, what exactly I was going to be doing, he looked up at me and calmly told me, 'You're going to be the most highly trained, lethal, female assassin in the world.' I remember that day like it was some girl's wedding or some lady's divorce. Hell, I didn't know how or what to think about that! All I did know now, was that I needed to really think about what to pack, research what the weather was going to be like, as well as where the Hell I was going to stay, etc. The only plus that I did have, as far as Intel on this job, was Steven. As I have said above, we had always gotten along and I could tell he sometimes felt sorry for me. So, I took out my phone and texted him: 'Steven, could you please come up and talk to me whenever you have a chance? My dad cannot know'. Now, I knew this was risky because my father knew everything Steven did at all times, unless he was off the clock. Which was only when my father was sleeping. About 15 - 20 minutes later, I received a text back from him. He said that he would meet me in my room at around 10 pm. Perfect. At least I would have someone whom I could trust and who would know answers to my questions. A little background about Steven. Callahan is his last name. He was a former Marine who had served in the Military for 12 years and came back home with numerous medals, including, 'Most Lethal Sniper' as well as numerous others. I then decided what to do until then. I went to my trunk in my walk-in closet and pulled out *all* 15 notebook's that I had accumulated during my training and started reading them from cover to cover; each and every one of them. I had a very distinct feeling that I would need them; ALL of them. At exactly 10pm, I heard a soft knock on my door. I knew it was Steven so I said 'come in'. He walked in, all 6 feet 5 1/2 of him, and as wide as a Mack truck. He had received so much shit for his body type. But because of his particular body type, he has saved my father from getting killed, up to this point anyway, 11 times. By using his body to stop bullets – just like the Secret Service are trained to do. He walked in, sat on the edge of my bed and asked, 'What's up, Gia?' I looked at him and I couldn't help it. I started crying. And I am *not* a crier. He looked behind him and grabbed the box of Kleenex off of my bedside table and handed it to me. I told him everything. Including that I was scared, not sure that I could do 'All of this by myself'. I also told him that I was scared that I wouldn't be able to 'please my father', etc. He looked at me, not interrupting me once; never stopped looking in my eyes the entire time I was talking. I finished after about three hours. It was around 1 am. I am sure of that. After I was done, he got more comfortable on my bed and again, looked me straight in the eyes. 'Gia Mahari', he said, 'after all my years of being in the Military, being in enemy territory, and after meeting all of the people I have met working for your father, I have never met a person. Man or woman, who is as capable as you. You are a damn good shot. Lethal at every angle, agile as shit, smart as hell, and you know how to shoot a gun like no other person I have ever come across. And I mean that. You *know* that, Gia.' I sat back. I had taken in everything he had just said. I knew Steven. He never lied. Never. Not to anyone. Even if it meant death or a severe beating. I actually was in awe of what he had to say about my capabilities. Especially my shooting or accuracy. Especially compared to all of the people he had met in his life; in the Military or with my father. I felt a lot better. Even though I was still nervous as shit, I knew that Steven was telling the truth and if I truly used my full capabilities, I would be alright; or, should be alright. I thanked him (after I gave him a big hug) and he kissed me on the cheek, patted me on the shoulder and said, 'You'll do fine, GG. Goodnight.' After Steven left my room, I felt better. I don't know if it helped my anxiety or not, but it sure made me feel better about the whole trip/job. I got ready for bed, climbed between my 1,000 thread count sheets, and slept like a baby.

Chapter 6

Morning definitely came way too early. The light was shining through my westward facing window, open of course, and blowing my white curtains out about six feet from the wall. I opened one eye at a time and then I rolled over. I knew I had to get up for breakfast with my dad in the dining room or I would get it. I jumped out of bed, grabbed my robe, and raced downstairs. I glanced at my watch; 8:40 am, not bad I thought, and sat down. Three minutes later, my father walked down the stairs. In his slow, controlled, gait; as usual. I watched him out of the corner of my eye. I guess I did understand how ALL of my friends wanted to sleep with him. He was very handsome and obviously, very wealthy, too. But there was something about him that was different than all of the other Beverly Hills men/dads out there. He always held this air of mystery. It almost emanated from his entire body. Plus, he always smelled heavenly. I wish he was just a 'normal' dad; gave hugs of encouragement, kisses that were not expected, compliments now and then, etc., but no. It was just 'My uptight dad'. He was emotionally distant; cold almost. I think the last time I received a 'normal' kiss from him was when I shot someone, one bullet, from 500 yards, for the first time, when I was 10; using, of course, a Barrett™ sniper rifle. And that was a 'good job, Gia', with a quick kiss on the cheek. But, I guess, that's better than nothing. When my father sat down he put his pristine, white napkin on his lap, grabbed his paper and took a sip of his orange juice. He then looked up at me and said 'Good Morning, Gia.' I told him good morning and began to eat. Our maid of 10 years or so, Juanita, as usual, came out and asked us if everything was to our liking. And, AS usual, we both said, 'yes'. This woman was my savior, especially when I moved out of my father's house much later. She taught me everything from doing laundry to some cooking, (still *not* my strong suit) to how to fold laundry; even how to shop for food. Yes, there is a right and wrong way. Like, never go food shopping when you're hungry. You'll end up buying everything that looks good to you, which is pretty much everything in the store. After my father finished his plate, he put it aside and leaned back in his chair while putting his paper to the other side of the table. After years of eating with him, I knew what this meant. I pushed my plate aside and looked up at him and gave him one of my 'I love you daddy' smiles. I still don't know if he knows what that smile means to this day. He asked me if I had packed and if I had thought over my job overseas. I replied that I had but I still needed to pack. And that I had a couple of questions. He looked at me straight in the eye, as always, and said 'and those questions are?' 'Will I be traveling with any bodyguards?' 'No. This mission would cause too much attention if you did. You will be much safer if you travel alone.' I looked down, put some cream and sugar in my coffee, as did he. 'Oh. Well, I will be packing some today. What is the exact date that I have to leave?' 'In two weeks', he replied. ‘The weather should be perfect for you and HIS schedule is very much the same, every day; day in and day out. I expect that the job should take one day max. And then continue on with the plan as we had discussed last week. Yes?’ With that, he got up, told me he was late for the office, and left for work. I heard Steven pull the limo around and heard the driver get in, my father, then Steven. And that was our 'very informative' talk on my future job. I knew if I pulled this off without a hitch, I would be the first 12 year old female assassin/spy that actually flew into the U.A.E., by herself, and kill a top Middle Eastern resident, Al Bin

Talal Alsaud. So I had to pull this off and just get my mind in 'Mode'. Something Steven and my father had taught me how to do since I was four years old. Plus, I had plenty of experience getting my mind in 'Mode' from my childhood molestation days. As for the rest of my day, that was still up in the air. I decided to look for my suitcase; the special one that my dad bought for me, to be used only for jobs. I looked in my closet (one of my favorite places in the house) and it wasn't there. Then I remembered that Juanita had put it under my bed. I looked underneath the bed and there it was. I pulled it out and took a good look at it. Thinking what all I needed to take and put in there; without looking suspicious anyway. It wasn't that I didn't know how to pack guns in my suitcase(s) without them being found. I just needed enough room for my sniper rifle, my favorite, as well as two changes of clothes plus shoes. I decided that this particular suitcase was NOT going to do. It was just too small. I pushed my intercom and asked Juanita if she could call my father and patch him to my phone in my room. Ten minutes later, my pink, princess phone rang. 'Yes, Gia?' he answered. 'Dad, I need to go and buy a new suitcase for this job. And any other future jobs I will be doing. It is just not big enough.' There was about a three minute silence until my dad said, 'take two detail guys with you and call me when you get home'. I told him 'Thank you' and hung up. I pushed a button that went to the garage, which is where most of detail hung out during the day; washing my dad's collection of cars, cleaning and oiling their guns, etc. Sometimes, when my father was at work, they would play poker. I never told on them. As long as they were nice to me, I would cut them some slack. I knew that they didn't have the easiest job, by far, in the world. Some guy I didn't know answered the phone and I asked for Lane. Once he got on the phone/com, I told him I had to go out and buy a suitcase. He said he would drive me and I told him ‘Thank you’. After I showered, fixed my hair a little and just put some mascara on my eyelashes (the *only* makeup I was allowed to wear), got dressed in my best Chanel™, with Jimmy Choos™ (of *course*!), and grabbed my Balenciaga™ purse, I went downstairs and out the door. Lane was right below Steven in the Detail hierarchy and the two didn't have the 'best' relationship. I didn't give a damn. Besides, I think Lane had a crush on me that he knew better than to show. Or have for that matter. When I was outside the house I waited for Kevin to pull up with my favorite car. It was a Corvette™, beautiful and my favorite to ride in. A shiny, red, metallic, convertible, Corvette. I loved this car. And I never let anyone drive it neither, unless they were driving me, obviously. I hopped in and off we went. I was taught to drive defensively since I was 11 years old, slowly, of course. I wasn't allowed to actually drive, until I was 16, when I would be legal and reach the pedals. But my father and Steven started my driving training off with the mirrors; (always check them, in case I was being followed) when to stop and always use my blinkers when turning. And ended with, when driving on 'a job', never assume anything. Always assume and drive as if you *are* being followed.) I learned a lot from both of them about driving. And I still drive the same way. Sometimes, to this day. It has gotten me out of a lot of accidents as well as tickets. Go figure, right? Anyway, off we go, driving towards Rodeo Drive and I see the store I am looking for and tell Lane to Parallel Park. As we got out, Lane was bitching as I went in the store. He knew the drill. He found the closest couch and sat down where he could see me at all times; from all angles. I looked at all the luggage ALL over the store and finally found the perfect one for the job; a black Henk Travelfriend™, the perfect size and everything. It will fit my sniper and my changes of clothes and shoes. I grabbed a black one, walked up to the counter, paid for it and out we went. Since my father wanted updates about me whenever I went out 'alone', I called and told him we were on our way home. As I stared outside the car's passenger side window, I was thinking about my upcoming job in Saudi. Who was I supposed to kill? How long was I supposed to lie in wait until my target came across my crosshairs? I always thought these exact same thoughts before all of my jobs, especially as they were coming closer. I was never nervous anymore. I had gotten rid of that emotion a long time ago. Or my father brainwashed that feeling right out of my head. I don't know which. And to this day, I still do not know. We arrived home about 30 minutes later; traffic, as usual, was horrendous. I sat in the passenger seat staring out of the window. Damn, it was coming up close. Shit, Shit, Shit, I thought to myself as Lane pulled up to the huge wood and wrought iron gate. He put the car in park as he held down the button to talk and told him who he was and that he had me with him. He punched in the security key and the gate swung open slowly as the two guys that manned the gate at that time looked into the car. My dad was always prepared, especially for a breach of security. We drove up the long driveway; which, by the contractor's estimate was a half mile long. But it was beautiful. The trees on each side of the walls of the driveway grew to where they overhung on each side of the driveway. It looked exactly like driving up to a New Orleans mansion or plantation. It was pretty quiet and peaceful at night. Sometimes I would just take a walk down the driveway just to think and calm myself; to clear my head or just to come up with some song lyrics; (I wrote and recorded music with my dad, too.) We drove up the circular driveway and stopped at the front door. I thanked Lane, climbed out with my suitcase and walked into the house. My father was sitting in the main living room, on the couch watching the security tapes from last night. My dad's employees had planted security cameras; about 100 of them, all around the property. Anywhere a camera could be, there was one; for 'safety' of course. The main ones were at the front door, pointed right at the person or persons ringing the bell, at the front of the gate, right where you push in the code to get in and, the most important ones, pointing right at my bedroom windows, all six of them. I used to climb out at night, on the weekends, to go party with my friends. I usually was on restriction, hence *no* car usage. So I had to steal one of my father's cars. This went on for quite a few years. Sometimes my dad would find out and sometimes he didn't. But I had so much fun doing it that the punishment was worth the risk. I walked over to the stairs and began my ascent to my room. I heard my father instantly. 'Gia? Bring me your suitcase so I can take a look at it.' I rolled my eyes and went back down the stairs to the couch where he was sitting. He put the DVD on pause, looked me in the eye while holding out his hands. I pulled out my suitcase from of its bag and handed it to him. He looked it over with admiration in his eyes. I could *see it*! 'Way awesome', I thought. 'Dad approves'. He looked at the suitcase over for 15 minutes. The longer he looked at it, the more I knew he approved. 'Excellent choice, baby. Now go upstairs and get ready for supper. Juanita will call you when it is ready.' And with that, he gave me a kiss on the cheek, a pat on the ass and returned to his DVD of security footage. Now, I know you are still stuck on the 'he patted me on the ass part'. Hell, I would be too. My father considered me HIS property; and, HIS ONLY; which also included sex. The only difference between him and my step-father/monster was that my father 'seduced' me when I was 11 years old. Please don't wonder how a grown man could possibly seduce an 11 year old. I have been trying to think of that for years. With NO answer. I guess you would liken it to a male dog 'marking 'his territory'. When I first moved into his home, I was a wide-eyed, little girl; little in stature; huge on intellect. He showed me all around the house, (which took two hours at a fast pace) showed me my bedroom as well as his. After he showed me his bedroom (3,000 sq. feet) he also told me that I was welcome to crawl in his bed anytime if I had a bad dream, couldn't sleep, was scared, or anything else that was bothering me. I looked up at him, smiled politely and nodded. I knew what *that* meant. I just hoped to God that it would be much different than the step-father. I couldn't handle, physically or emotionally, *that* again. The best part of getting to know my new home was that he had two pools! One outside, which was a black-bottomed, rock formatted, pool. Gorgeous! The other pool was an Olympic size, heated pool. My father did his laps in here every morning before work and every morning on Saturday. Sundays were, he said, HIS day. Ok, whatever that meant. When the tour was over, I just kept saying to myself, I am the *Luckiest Girl In The World*!!!

Chapter 7

After my dad handed back to me my new purchase, I walked up the stairs again and into my room. I laid the case down, opened it, set up my personal password for the lock and opened up ALL of my dresser drawers, closets and my bathroom drawers. I went to my armoire and picked out my black Lycra cat suit. I have found that the black cat suit is the *best* outfit/disguise for *any* job. It fits your body like a glove and you can really move in it. And at five foot 2 and 99 pounds, I was pretty much invisible. I loved that. I folded it, put it in my suitcase, and continued to grab the bare necessities for my first top secret job. The very last items that had to go into my case I had to wait and put in the day of takeoff. Those would be my toiletries. Everything else was safely packed, secured and locked up in the suitcase. My two favorites? 1) My favorite Jimmy Choos, 2) My Barrett™ Sniper Rifle. A .50 caliber beauty. In my opinion, the best Sniper rifle in the business. People would also ask me, 'Why would you pack expensive, high-heel, uncomfortable shoes on a sniping job?' Here is your first lesson on being a Sniper. Or, Intel # 1 on Snipers: Women make the best Snipers in the world. Why? Because they can always go into places that men cannot, to 'get' their target. Case in point? The bedroom. See what I mean? It doesn't, by ANY means, mean that you always have to sleep with the person before you take them out. But you can sure get them drunk in order to get information out of them. Especially while in bed. Before long, they are out like a light. Right after they have told you everything you wanted to know. All recorded on a mini tape recorder stuffed inside your bra, lingerie, etc. After I put my packed suitcase on the floor by my bed, I went into my bathroom, grabbed a towel and took a shower. My dad insisted on everyone washing up before dinner. Not just more deodorant and run a brush through your hair, but an entire shower. Blah! At least I didn't have to wear makeup. That would suck major! In Luciferianism, women were not required to wear makeup at the dinner table. In fact, they were usually advised or told not to. That rule I didn't mind a bit. Unless it was a gala or a special dinner with guests. That was a whole different story. I walked down to the dinner table and saw that Steven had beaten me there already. Douche! Steven and I always, or at least since I can remember, had a silly competition on who could get to the dinner table first. He usually won because he was a man. They hardly have *anything* to do in the dang bathroom! They had to shower, get out, dry off and run a comb or whatever through their hair, and get dressed. Done! Not fair. And since Steven 'shaved his head' completely bald, he didn't even have to brush his hair.' He knew I was thinking something to that effect and flipped me off. I flipped him back. Of course my dad was not at the table. We would never get away with that shit if he was there. Not five minutes later, we heard my father walk down the stairs, in his quick rhythmic gait. I glanced up at him as he was walking down. And for that second, I could tell why all of my friends wanted to sleep with him. He was very handsome. Bluish/ Black salt and pepper hair, cut 'just so' according to his strict specifications. It very much complimented his six foot frame. He always dressed impeccably from whatever suit he chose for the day to the polished shoes on his feet. His cologne that he wore (since I can remember) smelled wonderful, and his voice had a lilting, deep, masculine accent. He walked to his seat at the head of the table and sat down. Looked at us, gave us a nod and a slight smile, flipped his napkin onto his lap and that was our cue to put our napkins in our lap. Not long after, in came Juanita with her daughters, carrying the appetizer of Caesar dinner salads and shrimp cocktail. Yummy! I didn't realize how damn hungry I was. I hadn't eaten since breakfast. After dinner we all went to our rooms and got ready for Ritual. I would tell you exactly how many there were in a year. But there are so many, I can't even remember right now. Let's just, suffice it to say, that there are *a lot*. I had already changed into my white 'sleeping' gown after my shower, so all I really had to do was rub body oil all over me. It was a 'special' type of oil that had been made especially by a High Priestess in the Brotherhood. A High Priestess is a witch for those who do not know. She is always a very revered witch in the Cult and almost always has her own Coven, or, group of witches. I had to wear that oil at every Ritual. And I had to wear it all over my body. It smelled pretty good but it was a pain in the ass to get off. After I was finished with the oil, I went to my armoire and got out my black cape. I went downstairs and waited for my father. About five minutes later, Steven walked in. He sat next to me on the chaise that was in the hallway. Not only did the lucky douche not have to wash his hair, he didn't have to participate in Ritual. Ever. He wasn't even a Luciferian. He was just my dad's bodyguard. Lucky Fucker. He looked at me and asked if I was alright. 'Yeah' I replied, 'just tired.' He looked at me and nodded his head. 'It shouldn't take too long tonight, Gia'; which was true. Tonight wasn't a 'High Holiday', thank God. High Holidays always took ALL night and the next day you almost feel like you were in a serious car accident. After Steven attached his cuff links, we sat and waited. My father's door closed upstairs and we heard his footsteps. He descended the stairs in his normal, controlled gait. Come to think of it, HE even looked tired. And that was pretty rare. He walked past us and Steven jumped up, opened the door for us and unlocked the Limo for us, with that tell-tale chirping sound. He opened the rear door for my father and then me. We rode in silence almost all the way there. I don't know what is worse. Riding in the car, in silence, with my dad or speaking to my dad while we were being driven. I guess, for this trip anyway, he decided to not say a word. Until we pulled up in front of the home where the Ritual was being held. The house was owned by my father's boss, Mr. Harris. My father *hated* his boss. I hated his boss. He always tortured me when he saw me. Verbally and sometimes, when my father wasn't around, physically. He also treated my father like complete shit. And no one ever does that. Ever. Well, at least no one that lives to tell about it. Mr. Harris's house was large but, in my opinion, was in no way as 'grand' as my father's. It was too damn gaudy and pretentious. Like he wanted to 'show' everyone that he was rich. And, the man had zero taste at all. Gaudy, Gaudy, Gaudy. There was not an empty space on the carpet or marble or tile or wood! Every space that you could find (and that IS the key word here) there was something standing or put there; almost as if he did not want any floor space showing at all. He was Very Fucking Strange, this man. We were greeted with a bow by his 'butler' and shown inside. I instantly started feeling the butterflies. I always did at his house. The smell inside his home, the Ritual music that he always had playing in the background, the incense, everything. I went into 'MODE' and made my 'rounds' with my father; Steven, silent, but close behind. Everyone knew who I was and they definitely knew who my father was. All of the women (the ones who were allowed too) took my father's outreached hand and kissed his ring (a black Opal; surrounded by sixteen, medium sized, pave diamonds with white gold). It was a beautiful ring, I agree, but it was a 'Ritual Ring'. He always wore this ring to Ritual and nowhere else. I stood to my father's left, nodding my head to everyone who kissed his ring and shook his hand. The men all nodded to me and the women all curtsied. I know it ALL sounds very lame, stupid and pathetic. And I don't blame you for thinking or feeling that at all. But this is ALL I knew. I grew up with all of this, and most of these evil people. Now, that I am completely out, people ask me, 'What do these types of people look like?' Or, 'How can I pick one out of a crowd or a mall or somewhere?' The answer is: You can't. They look like you and me, your mom and dad, grandma and grandpa, etc. They blend in with everyone. Just like child molesters, serial killers, bankers, accountants and doctors. Which, some of these people were, anyway. Hell. They were all child molesters. That was a no brainer. Once we made our way around the ballroom/Ritual Room, 'The Anointed Ones' sat on small foot-stools in a semi-circle while the other participant's sat, cross-legged, on the floor; one person between each person on a stool. We whispered amongst each other for about 5 minutes; my father and I only spoke to each other at these 'get-together's. Steven was standing against the far wall of the ballroom, along with the other bodyguards. Not too long after our 'chatter', the door to the room opened and in walked Mr. Harris. Well, the Asshole still looked the same as last time, I thought. He scanned the room and his eye's stopped at me for a second longer than everyone else, and my father, a good half a minute. Then he nodded to him. My dad nodded back. Sort of. A half nod if you will. He sat down in His, what I have always called, Throne. Like he was some sort of King. And, he thought he WAS. Shit, most of these people treated him as one, the Prick. Everyone fell silent and waited for him to speak. From this point on, we all spoke a foreign language. Mr. Harris was SO paranoid that he might be recorded or taped or God knows what, that he insisted on everyone speak in a different language. And that language was Turkish. Which was sort of a Middle Eastern tongue. When he spoke, it was in sharp, short quips. Almost as if he had something stuck in his throat (wish he had) so we were all used to it by now. And it wasn't hard to understand him. For me at least. I spoke Turkish. At first, I heard, that a lot of first timers couldn't understand him and made the mistake of asking him to repeat himself. That was the last time I ever saw THAT person again. My father hates repeating himself as well, but if it happened a lot; people constantly saying, 'What did you say?' or 'Could you please say that again?', my dad would get a fucking clue and go to his doctor or something. Not Mr. Harris. With him it was 'Deal with it, peon.' Mr. Harris clapped his hands twice, very quickly, which was a clue for my father to stand, in robe and all (with his hair covering on) and walk into the middle of the room where the Altar was. *The* Altar. The only one I have ever known all of my short life. On top of it were four 12 inch red candles, lit of course. Next to these candles were four 6 inch black candles. All of the red and black candles were pointing in the correct positions; North, West, East and South. My father stood in front of the Altar and said the opening incantation for this particular ritual. After he was done, 21 minutes later, we all stood up and everyone held hands. My father then held his left hand out in my direction. I loosened my hands from the other two 'guests' beside me and slowly walked towards him. His head was pointed up towards the sky. When I walked to him, I was not allowed to look at him. My head was to remain down. When my eyes saw the bottom of his robe is when I stopped. I knew the drill. I took his outreached hand and he guided me to him. He looked at me in the eyes. I looked up at him, took his left hand, put it up to my lips and kissed his ring. The Ring. I pulled my white gown up over my head to where I was standing in front of him. The entire congregation was looking at us with quiet anticipation. My father pulled me to him by the small of my waist and grabbed the back of my head. I closed my eyes and went into Mode. I knew what was next. I did ALL day. He pulled my head to his and he started kissing me. Hard. Then his tongue was in my mouth. It wasn't hurting me but it was Hard, that kiss. My breath was stuck in my throat. I couldn't breathe but I knew that I was kissing him back, also with my tongue; and just as hard. I felt 'him' against my waist/stomach. I knew he was ready. I did not know what the Hell to feel. He lowered me down on The Altar and took me. All the while kissing me. The entire 'Act' took about 20 minutes. But that was in MY time frame. I couldn't be sure. I kept my eyes closed the whole time. Then during the 'Act', he started making sounds. This was a first. I had never heard him make any 'sounds' before, during this 'Act'. After my dad was 'done', his boss walked over to check and see if, in fact, my father did 'finish' the deed. He did that by spreading my legs to look and feel inside of me. If there was any 'magic white liquid', as HE called it. There was, of course, and his boss stood up, yelled 'It Is Done'! Then all of the congregation bowed their heads in a Luciferian prayer and clapped when they were done. He then walked off of The Altar and disappeared. My father stepped closer to me; standing over me actually, held out his left, ringed hand and pulled me up, to my knees. I took his left hand in mine and kissed his ring, tears starting to run down my face. The congregation couldn't see if I was crying, but my father, obviously could. He secretly wiped my tears away with his fingers, kissed me on both cheeks and held my hand as we both walked down and off of The Altar. He took me to a Master bedroom where we were allowed to change and clean up. Well, HE was allowed to completely clean up. I was only allowed to wipe between my legs and put my white gown back on. He actually got to take a shower. I stood there in the bathroom with him until he was done with his shower, I handed him a towel for his hair. He wrapped his hair up in the towel and then stepped out. I took another towel, got on my knees and wiped him dry; from head to toe; literally. When he was done combing out his hair and then blowing it dry, we did not say one word. I wasn't allowed too. He then sat down on the chair or stool in front of the mirror and I got a brush and put oil onto his hair. When he was completely dressed, in his ceremonial robe, etc. we walked out of the bedroom and into the main ballroom; where The Ritual had been held, WHICH, I had found out later, was an 'impregnation' Ritual. The room was completely cleaned up. As if nothing had even happened in there. The only difference was when we DID walk out, there were five long serving tables in the room. Set up around the four walls of the room. On the tables were ALL kinds of different foods, refreshment, and everything you could possibly imagine. As I stood there amongst everyone, accepting their Congratulations, my father was taken by his Boss into another room. I looked after him as he walked away from me into Mr. Harris's office. 'I wonder what the Hell that Asshole was saying to my dad', I thought to myself. I just gave up thinking about that and again returned to the Congregation's words. After a while, I smelled the food from the tables and felt hungry. I excused myself and walked over to them. I got myself a plate and put some food on it. I looked around to see if there were any tables set up to sit at and I spotted one just outside the Ballroom. I took my plate and a glass of Cristal and walked over to the table where no one was sitting. 'Nice', I thought, 'Alone at last'. For about 13 minutes, I was alone eating. Then I felt the table move a bit and heard the chair, one over from me, scrape against the floor. I looked over at who the Hell dare walk up to *my* table without my permission and realized it was Steven. 'Hi, Stev-o'. That was a nickname I called him years ago. And still do to this day. He looked over at me and said 'Hello, Angel. How are you holding up?' I said that I was 'fine' and started eating again. Steven must have known I was lying because he kept staring at me for at least 3-4 minutes while I was eating. Gladly, he left the topic alone. I just couldn't talk about it to anyone right now; not even Steven. He started to sip his water and told me that we should be able to leave pretty soon. 'Thank God', I thought as I continued eating.

Soon after, my father came out of the room with Harris. Steven hated Harris as well, which was another thing that we both agreed upon. Hating that Asshole. I finished my 2am snack, looked at Steven, smiled and took my utensils, plate and glass to the folding table where there were other dirty dishes and started walking back to where Steven was. As I just sat down, I heard footsteps coming towards me. It happened to be my father, thank God. I looked up at him as he asked if I was ready to go. 'Yes Sir', I replied. I wanted to say, 'Like, yesterday!' But obviously, could not. 'Let us go, then.' We said goodnight to everyone that mattered. My father was saying 'goodnight' to the 'Douchebag'; me, not uttering a word to him. My father signaled to Steven and out the door we went. I stopped right as the big, oak door shut. I let in a deep breath and exhaled. 'Well, that was over for a few more weeks/months'. I didn't really know unless I looked at a calendar. Steven grabbed the keys from the valet and went to get the limo. My father put his arm around me and pulled me in close. I laid my head against him. Once the car was in front of us, Steven got out, opened the back door for my dad and then I got in. The valet said 'goodnight, Sir, Ma'am', Steven closed the door and off we went. As Steven drove us home, I sat and looked out the window. I was 15 and my father and I had just had sex. And not 'rough sex'. It was 'gentle' sex. I was totally confused. Normally, at any ritual where sex is involved, it was always rough or, at least, rougher. Why was it so gentle this time? It was almost as if my father was making love to me; like I was his girlfriend. I was feeling so confused. Plus, I had no one to talk to about it. I couldn't talk to Steven about *that* either. I would feel so embarrassed! How or who could I talk too about this? Juanita was out. Shit. She didn't even know we were all Luciferian. If she did, she would have probably run off a long time ago. Oh well, I had no one to talk too about it; except my father. That would be a very uncomfortable conversation, 'Oh, and by the way, dad. Could you tell me why you made love to me the other night at Ritual?' Nope. I couldn't do it. I will just have to accept it the way it was; or is; or whatever! Screw It! We drove in silence, as usual, coming home from Ritual. I sneaked a look at my father. He was also staring out of his window. He looked deep in thought as well. I wonder what he was thinking about. Maybe the same thing I was? Possibly, I would assume. It would have to be weird for him, too; knowing that he had made love to his daughter in front of fifty people or so. I looked away quickly before he caught me looking at him. Maybe I should ask him now. The partition window was closed so Steven wouldn't be able to hear anything. Better now than later, too. We were in a private place and 15 minutes from our house. I could feel the sweat starting to form on my upper brow and between my breasts. I slowly shifted my body away from the window and I crossed my legs. Damn! I was so sore between my legs too! How could I have *not* noticed that before now? Oh well, here goes. 'Dad?' I asked, as I looked over at him. 'Yes, Gia' he replied; his eyes still looking outside the window. 'I have a question I need to ask you'. He slowly turned his gaze to mine. I looked into his eyes. They were wet. Like he had been crying! I have never seen him cry! I decided to keep on with my question. 'I was just wondering something about this evening.' I said that sentence very slowly. And one decibel lower; almost a whisper. 'And that would be?' he replied. 'Why did you make love to me this evening when it is normally more…rough?' I said that sentence very fast, like I couldn't get it out of my mouth fast enough. 'We shall speak about that at a later date, Gia.' And that was all that was said as Steven punched in the code and we drove up the long driveway.

Chapter 8

Steven pulled the car around the circular driveway, around the statue, put the car in park and got out. He opened my father's door first, then walked around the car and opened my door. I gave Steven a quick kiss on the cheek and walked to the front door where my father was waiting for me. As I walked up the steps, he opened the front door. He walked in; me not far behind him. Juanita was standing in front of the centerpiece table. 'Can I get you anything at all Mr. F?' she asked. Juanita called my dad that all the time, except when we had guests over or something. 'No thank you, Juanita. You may go to bed now if you'd like'. He grabbed my hand and led me to the stairs. This was weird, I thought. He has never led me to the damn stairs before. 'Dad, I appreciate it, but I can make it from here.' I said with a half laugh. He looked at me, bent down a bit, (which was pretty much eye-level with me at 15) and said, 'I am going to take you to MY bed, Gia. For the night. And, I am going to show you how to please a man, as well as how a man should please you.' Oh God!' I was freaking o-u-t! This had never happened to me before. Not in our own house! With Steven and Juanita in close proximity? Damn! I knew Juanita would never hear nor know. She slept in a separate building on the back of the property. But Steven was just down the hall from my dad's bedroom! Between his and my room! What if he heard? What if anyone heard? Obviously I was freaking out and not thinking clearly. I mean, who would in this circumstance? Fuck! I knew I could not say no. But, I thought to myself, why not? Maybe this was some sick, perverted test that he was throwing at me. I had to risk it. I had to challenge him. At least to find out what the fuck was going on? He had never had sex with me outside of Ritual! And that wasn't even all Rituals. I took a deep breath as my father led me up the stairs to his bedroom. It was now or never. 'Dad?' He turned around once we reached the top. 'Yes, Gia?' 'I don't think this is such a great idea. I mean, I am not even sure this is right or what I'm supposed to do or say…' Before I could finish my words, he put his first two fingers over my lips and made the sound, 'Sssh.' Then continued speaking. 'I will run the bath water and then I will call on you when it is ready. Go and get anything you need for the night.' With that, he turned and walked down the hall and into his bedroom, door shutting behind him. I said, 'Yes Sir' to a closed door.

I quickly walked to my bedroom and went to shut my door behind me. I leaned against it and let out a long sigh. 'What in *Hell* is going on?' I thought. This is SO not like my father! He has never, ***ever*** done this to me before. He has never even brought a woman over to this house before. He kept his entire private life PRIVATE. I assume only Steven knew about that kind of stuff since he drove him everywhere. At night, mostly. I sure as fuck did NOT want to know what my dad did in his bedroom at night. Especially when it came to his sex life. Now I will have to find out exactly *what* he did. And why did he feel that HE had to 'show ME HOW to please a man'? When he had sex with me, did he think that I was going to do something 'wrong'? Well, EXCUSE ME, DAD! GIRLS DO NOT NORMALLY HAVE SEX FOR THE FIRST TIME WITH THEIR FATHER!!! Oh, God. What am I going to do? Have sex with him and stay in his room ALL night. THAT is what I am going to do; according to him. And Juanita always came into my room to wake me up at around eight or nine am for the day. What if she did and I wasn't there? What if she went and knocked on my father's door and saw me in *his* bed? I guess I could tell her that I had a really horrid dream or something like that. But I know she would never buy that excuse! I never get into my father's bed when I have a bad dream. I go downstairs to the kitchen, make myself some chocolate milk and then drink it in my room and go back to sleep. Oh my God! Oh well. Enough stressing about something I have no control over, I thought to myself. My father was waiting, after all. I pulled open my dresser drawer and pulled out a mini, mid-thigh nightgown; pink of course and silk. One my father bought for me in Dubai. I loved this nightgown and I never had a chance to wear it. Well, I might as well wear it for HIM. The fucking irony! I did look at it and wonder, 'should I wear this to his bed?' Well, shit. Again I had no clue. Would he take offence or think that I was mocking him? Crap. Why couldn't I just go to bed in my OWN bed? Like all of the other nights that I have lived under his roof? Screw it. The nightgown was nice, expensive, and classy. He bought the damn, gorgeous, thing. It should be perfect, (something a daughter should *never* have to think about. Let alone do). Forget it. This was happening. I walked into my closet, grabbed my Victoria's Secret™ sleep-over bag and went into my bathroom. I grabbed my toothbrush, my brush, hair elastic and put everything in my bag. I walked over to my Vanity and sprayed, lightly, my father's favorite body spray; patchouli, and sprayed it over my entire body. While I was 'getting ready', I just decided to put my mind in Mode during this entire 'lesson.' I had no idea what to call it so I decided to call it what he called it; 'A Lesson.' I heard a light knock on my bedroom door. I guess that was my 'clue' or 'signal' that he was ready for me. I took a deep breath, grabbed my bag and walked to my door. Opening it, I fully expected my father, or God forbid, Steven to be on the other side. But no one was there. Ok... I stepped out into the hallway and closed my door. As I was slowly walking towards my father's bedroom, I thought it odd that I always, at night anyway, dressed to please my father. Why did I DO that? I was so nervous! More nervous than I had been in a long time. Sure, before any Ritual, I was always nervous. But this was a different kind of nervous. When I was on the other side of his bedroom door, I heard the water being turned off. Oh shit. That's right. He said that 'he was going to run a bath for us.' Or was it just for me? I didn't remember. But, regardless, the sound was making me very nervous again. Not that I was never not nervous about this whole thing. I just had my mind 'turned off'. Or, in Mode, as I called it. My heart was thumping so hard in my chest I wouldn't be surprised that if someone was standing next to me they would be able to hear it. I reached for his door and lightly knocked. I heard his footsteps walking towards the door almost immediately. He opened the door, took my waist by his left hand, pulled me in and started kissing me. As hard as he did at Ritual. 'You were so damn beautiful tonight' he said as his tongue entered my lips. He started rubbing my back, up and down, with his left hand, as he kissed me. His tongue gently caressing every part of my mouth. At first, I was standing stalk still as he did this. Not exactly giving back what he was 'giving me' but not stopping him neither; like I could if I wanted too. It is very confusing to explain what I was feeling at that moment. He was kissing me as a boyfriend would. I never had a boyfriend before. I was just going by movies I had seen. But that, in itself, was making me feel excited and 'turned on'. But my mind could not get away from the fact that this man is my father. At that moment I decided that this, whatever 'this' was, was not going to stop. So, I either just give in to my physical feelings or I fight it and him and most likely get the beating of my life. I decided on the former. I started kissing him back with more intensity that he expected. Crap! More than I expected! I felt him grow against my leg instantly as he led me into the bathroom. He pulled his mouth away from mine and started undressing me. He lifted my nightgown over my head and put it on the chaise beside the bathtub, in the corner by the window. He reached out his hand, I took it and he led me to the bathtub. He stood me about four feet right in front of him as he looked me up and down with those eyes of his. At that time I had never felt so self-conscious! I looked down as he was still looking at me. I just couldn't look at him in the eyes anymore. He walked slowly up to me. He took his left hand and took his pointer finger, touched my chin and gently lifted it up too where I was looking him straight *in* the eyes. 'Do NOT be AFRAID of me, my sweet Gia. I shall never, ever hurt you, yes? Unless, of course, you disobey me. Got that? Do you trust me?' 'Yes Sir'. I replied too his question. 'Tonight, let's forget the 'Yes Sir's. Too formal for this evening. Don't you think?' 'I would think so if what's about to happen IS indeed going to happen, father.' I replied. 'Good.' He came towards me and with his right hand took the small of my waist and slowly pulled me towards him. He brushed my freshly brushed hair and ran his fingers through it. He did that for about ten minutes to where I was so relaxed that I wasn't really thinking about anything. I was just concentrating on his hand; rubbing back my hair from my face. After he stopped doing that he bent down and started kissing my neck, the top of my chest and then up to my lips. He paused only to take both of my hands and put them on the ties of his bathrobe. I untied them as I knew he wanted me too. At that moment, my mind went into instant Mode. It happened so naturally that sometimes; most times, I never knew I was doing it. I chose to remember this night though. Unlike other nights when my mind went into Mode. Like Ritual nights. After I untied his robe and threw it to the side, on the chaise by the bathtub, I started kissing him first. This came as quite a shock to him. At Ritual, he was the one who always started the kissing. I do not know why I did start it. Maybe it was because I knew that that was supposed to be the next act. Like the Ritual nights. Or, maybe to just get this over with. Once he got over his shock, he started instantly kissing me back with all of the intensity that he had. He picked me up; still kissing me and placed me in the warm tub, which felt like Heaven on my abdomen. He also got inside the bathtub with me. He was still kissing me as my left hand went under the water, with his hand guiding it, to grab 'him'. I was fully ready, in my mind to please him down there in the water. I did not think I could have actual sex tonight but I wasn't sore from sex earlier. I was sore from cramps. He came about eight minutes of me rubbing him. After that, he started putting his fingers in me, Cassienging me to orgasm. After all was 'said and done', he reached over me and grabbed the clean, warm, washcloth and rubbed soap on it. He rubbed my back, my legs, my arms, and my entire body. Even the 'sore' parts. He undid the plug for the tub and as the water was draining out, he reached for the towel that, I guess, was meant for me and told me to stand up. As I did so, he slowly wiped me down. From my neck to my toes. My hair had been pinned up. As I stepped out of the tub, he got out, handed me his towel and stood there as I realized that I was supposed to do the same to him. I took his towel and dried him off from HIS neck to his toes. His hair was still dry. I dried his entire body the best that I could. After he was completely dry, I reached for his blow dryer and blew out my own hair. I took out his special brush and brushed his hair as he was sitting at his bathroom sink. After we were done in the bathroom, we both heard the front door open and shut. We knew that Steven was home. I was thinking, 'perfect damn timing!' My father told me to crawl in bed and to Cassieng his hair brush with me. I replied and into his bed I went. My father went to his bedroom door and told me that he would be back in twenty to thirty minutes. I nodded my head and finished crawling into his covers. I thought about the evening so far and decided that even though I pleasured him in the bathtub, I was pretty damn sure that he would not try to have sex with me. He knew I was sore. Plus he knew I was on my ‘womanly thing’ as all the men, except Steven, called it. Men could be so ‘skittish’ about that sort of thing. But, I didn’t blame them. Hell, do men expect women to ‘accept’ and talk about ‘jock-itch?’ No! Women need to chill on that subject. Men did not need to *accept* the ‘womanly thing’. I think there were enough people or women to do that. Now, men who refused to buy tampons was another thing entirely. I knew women who bought their husband’s and women who bought their boyfriend’s jock-itch cream, condoms, etc. No big deal. But the other? Men do not have to talk about it in detail at all. I would expect my long-standing boyfriend and definitely my husband to go and buy me tampons though. If, by chance, I was an idiot and didn’t have a clue when it was coming and didn’t buy them myself. As I was pondering the difference between men and women, my father came back into the room and took off his robe yet again and crawled in the bed with me. He took the brush from my hands and brushed his hair. He did have great hair. Thick and salt with lots of pepper. Thick, too. He moved all the way against me, his right arm around my tiny waist. I took his hand and tucked it under my waist and drifted off to sleep.

Chapter 9

I woke up to the alarm going off. It was infiltrated into my dream so in my dream, I tried to turn it off. Only, in my dream, it was an annoying noise coming from my phone. Very strange. I reached to turn it off, realizing it was my REAL alarm going off. I reached my arm over to my right. All I felt was covers and part of a pillow. An empty pillow with no one sleeping on it. I opened my eyes slowly and realized where I was instantly. I remembered last night too. I slightly smiled to myself and slowly closed my eyes again. Then I remembered what day it actually was. Oh my God! I have to get going! This is the day! I practically jumped out of bed and walked fast/ran down to my room. I grabbed my new suitcase and lifted it onto my bed, opening it afterwards. I walked into my closet and went to my Fall/Winter clothes section. I walked up and down the aisles and grabbed my Juicy Couture™ sweat suit. Perfect outfit to wear when you are traveling a long distance. Especially in a plane. Very comfortable. Especially on a plane for so damn long. I took them off of their hangers and carried them to the bed. I hopped into the shower once I got the water temperature just right. I washed my entire body and hair, shaved and shut the water off. I grabbed my towel off of the hanger right beside the shower, near the nozzle outside the sliding doors. I toweled my hair and dried my body off. I wrapped my hair up in the towel and wrapped my silk robe around me. I sat at my vanity and put my make-up on. Light make-up; black eye-liner and nude eye-shadow with light rose blush, mascara and dark pink lipstick; my sweat suit was pink. I unwrapped my towel off of my hair and started combing my hair straight. I reached over and buzzed Juanita. 'Yes, Miss Gia?' she replied. 'Hi, Juanita. Good morning!' 'Good morning to you too, bambina. How was your sleep sweetie?' 'It was great, Juanita. Can I please have one pancake and a glass of Orange Juice this morning, please?' 'Si, bambina. When will you be downstairs and ready to eat?' 'About twenty minutes or less, Juanita. I am finishing my hair and getting my toiletries in my suitcase. Then I will be down. Is my father eating yet?' 'Not yet, Miss Mahari. He should be eating with you. That is what was said.' 'Ok then. See you in a few. And thank you, Juanita,' I turned off the intercom and started with my hair. I rubbed the mineral gel/oil that I had purchased from Dubai when I was with my father and then put mousse in my hair at the roots. I flipped my hair upside down, blew it dry halfway and then flipped it back over my head and finished blowing it dry. After that was done, I put my blow dryer away on its hook. I got up and walked to my bed. God! It had seemed like forever since I slept in my own bed! Hell. It probably had. Oh well. I got my pink sweat suit on and went to my dresser and pulled out some pink socks. I sat on the bed, put my socks and pink, Nike™ shoes on, grabbed my suitcase and put it on its side on the floor. I went back into the bathroom. I wondered what toiletries I needed. I doubted I would need any shampoo or conditioner. I grabbed my Dry Shampoo instead, just in case I needed a touch-up. I also grabbed a couple more colors of lip gloss as well. I took my favorite brush, 2 pony tail elastics and 3 scrunchies as well. I carried them all to my suitcase. I fit all of them in with no problem. Since I was first taking a private jet airplane to Chicago, I didn't have to worry about all of the B.S. rules that the F.A.A. had in place for *all* commercial flights. I would, once I had to fly commercial when I landed in Chicago though. Yay. Oh well, I'll just worry about that when I got there. I zipped up my case, stood it up, unhooked the handle and walked to my door, carrying my prized possessions behind me. I took one last look at my bedroom, blew it a kiss, said a little ‘prayer’ and walked out. Closing my bedroom door behind me. I reached into my purse to make sure my phone was in there as well as my ‘burner phone’. I also made sure my Gucci™ sunnies were in there too. Check on all of those important items! I walked down the stairs slowly, letting my case ‘bounce’ down each stair as carefully as possible. When Steven saw me, he hurried up the stairs, took my case from me and carried it for me the rest of the way to the front hallway and put it on the chaise by the front door. I thanked him as he came to the breakfast nook to sit down and eat his breakfast. ‘No problem, Gia.’ ‘Wow. How serious are we today, Steven!’ I said with a little laugh. ‘It’s a serious day today, isn’t it, Gia?’ ‘Yeah. I suppose it is.’ I forgot that Steven was probably just as scared for me as my father was. ‘I will be ok. Hopefully, Steven.’ ‘You will, Gia. No question about it.’ He looked at me, in the eye, with such a serious gaze that I rarely had seen before. Coming from him anyway. ‘Where is dad?’ ‘He should be down in a minute, babe.’ ‘Ok. Thanks.’ I replied while looking at him out of the corner of my eye. As Juanita was just finished filling up our plates, including my dad’s, we heard my father’s door upstairs open and shut. Then his footstep’s coming down the stairs. I glanced up and over to my left to see him walking down the stairs. He must be staying home from work today. At least for the morning; early afternoon. He was wearing jeans, a golf shirt and tennis shoes. Once he sat down and thanked Juanita, he glanced at me and then Steven. He put his napkin on his lap and started eating. Steven and I did as well. Damn, this was good. I was so used to eating just Fruity Pebbles™ in the morning, I forgot how good ‘real’ breakfast tasted. I’ll have to remember that when I get back, I thought to myself. I continued to eat and was on to my toast and coffee when Steven excused himself to go and prepare the car. As the door closed behind him, my father looked at me, put his napkin on the table and started on his coffee. ‘Are you all packed and ready for your first assassination job, Gia?’ ‘I gulped hard when I heard him say it out loud. Not because anyone could hear him but because I hadn't really thought of this job 'that way' before. Probably because no one talked about it. Out loud anyway. It was just assumed, that was what the job was. 'Yes, sir, I am. I have brought all of the things, I think, that I will need, as well as my rifle. I packed that on the bottom of my case, daddy.' 'Good girl, Gia.' He responded. Steven came back in through the front door and told us everything was ready to go. My father took one last sip from his coffee mug, set it down and stood up. 'Time to go, Gia' he said. I gulped down the rest of my coffee and stood up from the table, walked to the living room and grabbed the handle of my suitcase. Steven walked over and took it from me and said, 'I'll handle this, 'G'; why don't you go to the car with your father.' 'Oh. Ok. Thank you Steven.' I walked towards the front door, behind my dad. He opened the door and stepped aside for me to exit. That was a first, I thought to myself. Steven OR my father were always out the door first. Not today. They are all treating this very seriously. Damn, now I'm scared. I shook that feeling off and headed towards the limo. Steven opened the door for my father and myself. We got in; me behind my father. Steven, once we were in, put the suitcase on the seat across from us. He got in the back and sat next to my case. Steven rapped twice on the partition window and off we went. 'Well, my dad's driver is driving us today' I said to myself. 'Steven must be more worried than I thought.' We rode in silence the entire way to LAX. All three of us looking out our window. When we pulled off the 405 freeway, into the airport entryway toll lanes, my father looked at me and said, 'Now, Gia. I have one thing I want you to know. So, please listen carefully. Alright?' 'Yes, father.' 'When you meet with your driver once your Chicago flight lands, and you get to your hotel, please text, not call me. Tell me you are there safely. Alright? Then, after the job is done and you are safely back on your flight to Chicago, text me again and tell me that everything is ok. Got that? Then I don't want to hear from you until you are back on my jet on your way home. Yes?' I looked at him with all seriousness and answered, 'Yes Sir.' 'Ok baby. Be good. I know you will do an excellent job.' With that, he kissed me on the forehead and Steven did the same. The driver opened my side of the door, I grabbed my case and got out. I blew them a kiss and walked towards my terminal. 'Game time' I thought as I continued walking to the First Class line in the airport.

I stood in line and put my head down, which made my hair fall around my face. I dug in my handbag and found my sunglasses. I put them on without anyone noticing. When it was my turn to go up to the ticket window, I gave the lady my Passport and I.D. 'Going to the Middle East, huh?' She asked me. Duh, I thought. You have my damn ticket information right in front of you. 'Shit, Gia! She is just making conversation. Be nice.' 'Yes, Ma'am. I had never been, so I decided to go on a little sight-seeing tour on my own.' She smiled and told me 'that sounds nice.' After she handed me my ticket for the private plane area of the airport she told me to have a nice flight. I smiled and told her 'Thank You.' As I walked away from the counter with my case rolling behind me, I realized that I still had my sunglasses on. Oh well, screw it. Let people think I'm a celebrity or whatever. They made my eyes feel better. Especially from such a late night last night. Thank God I didn't have to do my 'job' until the day after tomorrow. Once I reached the entrance to the 'Private Plane Customer's' Entrance, I opened the door's and walked to the vending machines. I felt everyone's eyes on me. I still had my Gucci's™ on and I didn't give a damn if they stared at me. Personally, I thought it was rude. Looking or just glancing at me when I walked in was one thing but to keep staring is fucking rude. I got my Nutter Butter™ cookies and walked over to the attendant. He asked for my pass or ticket and I handed it to him. He looked at it and said, 'Good afternoon, Miss Mahari. How are you today?' 'I'll be great once I get on the plane. I've had a very tiring day.' 'Of course, Ma'am. I'll have someone escort you right to your father's plane.' 'Thank you.' I replied back to him. I stood there and let out a very loud sigh as well as started trapping my shoe. Of course I didn't have a 'tiring day.' I just wanted to sound important and stuck-up enough to have a father that would have a private jet. It must have worked because once all of those last words came out of my mouth, they all stopped looking at me. Even when I did my sigh and started tapping my feet. Four minutes later tops, the same man I had spoken to showed me the way to the stairway which would lead me down to the tarmac near my dad's plane. As I walked through the tunnel, pulling my suitcase behind me, I realized that even though I was doing a very important job for the Organization, I wasn't too stressed about it. Weird. You'd think I would be stressed and butterflies in my stomach. All of that. But I had none of that. To me, right now at least, I felt like this was just another plane trip. I guess that was a good thing. For my nerves at least. I reached the stairs that lead down to the tarmac and my father's jet. I looked up and saw that every single person that was sitting in the waiting area or lobby that I just left were looking at me walking towards the plane. 'WTF?' I thought. Haven't they seen a G4 (which was the current model at that time) before? Whatever. I started walking up the stairs and about half-way up the stewardess that was riding with me greeted me and took my case from me. I told her to please put it on the seat next to me; not underneath the plane. 'No problem, Miss Mahari.' I walked inside and turned right. I decided to sit on the couch-like seat in the back of the jet. Once the stewardess saw where I had decided to sit, she placed my case in the leather chair directly to my left. Right by one of the windows. Perfect, I thought. I sat and put my seatbelt on. I put my purse on my lap, took out my makeup bag and touched up my make-up. I waited for a few minutes, put my purse in the far corner of my 'couch' and then called for my stewardess. She came, walking quickly. 'She HAS to be new', I thought to myself. 'Could I please have a Screwdriver? Oh! And a Caesar salad too?' She looked at me funny and said, 'Um. Sure ma'am. Right away.' And walked off. She probably hesitated because I was 15 and looked it. If not thirteen or fourteen years old. I picked up a magazine from my purse and started reading it. 'Bitch. She'll get over it.' I thought. After about fifteen minutes she came back with what I had asked for and put it on the coffee table before me. 'Enjoy!' she said and off she went. 'Damn. Chipper with a bit of sarcasm too.' I am definitely going to talk about her to my dad when I return. *If* she hasn't improved when I get back on the jet for my ride home. After I finished my B.S. rag for the entertainment business, I put it in the trash. The reason I read some of them – EVERY once in a while, is to see if there is anything in there about any celeCassieties that my father represented. Any lies about them, actually. And if I do find anything written about them, I would tell my father. Then he would know how to go about it. First, he would call the celebrity in question, ask them a few questions about said 'issue' that I had read about and then decide whether a lawsuit was in order. He didn't have the time to do all that so I decided to take on that job whenever I had the chance too. And what better time to do so than flying? I do like flying…for vacation or some other pleasurable destination. But for a 'job', well, that is completely different. It Cassiengs about a lot of unwanted stress. Stress that I did not need. I ate my salad and drank my cocktail while I was thinking these thoughts. I reached into my bag and grabbed my Xanax™ bottle. I took two pills to chill me out and to help me sleep for the duration of the flight to Chicago. I would need it if something went wrong. Which it won't I hoped. This scumbag deserved to die. He did more heinous crimes than you could ever imagine. It is kept out of the press or Americans would go nuts regarding 'why aren't you doing anything about this pig?' So, I am very glad to 'help my fellow American people. Of course, I would be imprisoned and probably put on death row if caught. Especially since I wouldn't give up any names of my 'Group', The Brotherhood. And since I have been in it since birth THEY are my family. No one else. Especially my father and Steven. I loved them more than anyone on this Earth. And I have been taught/trained to survive any torture methods. Any.

So, if the Brotherhood trusts this, then so do I. And, I also was taught to go into Mode when I am being tortured. They would get nothing out of me. Anyhow, that is just how I was taught and raised. I felt my eyes getting heavy and my blink rate was getting quicker. I looked at my watch. I had about a little less than two hours to take a little nap. I thought I would take my body up on that idea. I got up and grabbed the nearest blanket that was laying on top of the big, comfy, reclining chair. Hell, I don't know what it is called. All I know is that it is one big-ass chair that sits upright and can also lean back too. Anyway, I had sat in it once and put it all the way back. It was as comfortable as Hell! Everyone should have one of these! Then I found out from Steven that since a private jet only has so much room, my father chose the Barca™ lounger to sit and relax in. Plus he has a full bedroom and bathroom on this thing. With a damn shower! Obviously NO expense was spared. Only the Best for Dad, I thought to myself as I laid down on the coach/sofa. I fell asleep instantly. Must have been the 'white noise' from the jet engines. Plus, my father's smell was all over that blanket. I woke up to someone gently shaking me awake. 'Miss Mahari. It's time to wake up, ma'am. I slowly opened both eyes and looked straight in front of me. I sat up instantly. I then focused on the stewardess. My eyes were finally fully adjusted to the light. 'Thank you.' I told her. 'How close are we to the airport?' 'We are circling it now, ma'am.' She told me as she reminded me to 'buckle up', blah, blah, blah. Like I wouldn't remember that. Whatever. I grabbed my seatbelt and snapped it around my waist, grabbed my purse and took out my hairbrush and make-up bag. I opened it and looked in the mirror. Damn! Thank God for make-up! I took my MAC™ powder out and fixed my face. Then I fixed my lipstick, put all of that back in my bag and zipped it shut and put it back in my bag. I grabbed my brush and fixed my hair and gave it a light cover of hairspray. I got all of my belongings in my carry-on bag and sat waiting until we landed at the private landing strip. I wasn't looking forward to flying commercial at all. First Class or not. It still sucked. People always made noise on commercial flights. Thank God I brought my eye mask and ear plugs with me. I also brought something my father bought me on one of his travels. A squishy type travel pillow. You wrap it around your neck and lean your neck back on the chair. It feels, almost, like you're laying down on a bed! I had never had one of these. I had seen people use them on commercial flights. But I didn't know if they worked or if they were comfortable or not. Plus, I thought, I was going to be flying private from now on so why buy something mainly for a commercial flight? Now, I was glad that my father bought it for me. And it was pink, too. Which made it extra special. Just kidding. But it did fit in with my love for all things pink. We were circling for about an hour and then I finally felt us descending upon the runway. It must be our turn, I guess I thought. And it must be hell-a-busy for the private runway to be busy at Chicago. THIS busy, anyway. I had never experienced that before. I finally felt the landing gear being released. I sat up in my chair and put my sunglasses on. We landed and taxied to a part of the tarmac where, apparently, my gate was for my next flight. At least close by it. The door to my dad's jet opened out and I got up, grabbed my suitcase and headed towards the front of the jet. I maneuvered the stairs like a pro. I wasn't thrilled that my case had to 'bump' down every stair though. And there was no one to take it for me, either. Douchbags. I guess everyone was just expected to know where to go and break every fucking breakable thing that was in their suitcase. Fuckers! As I got to the bottom of the stairs, I looked around for a door of some sort. I found one about 200 yards away. Not too far. I walked towards the door and opened it with my right hand. I had slipped my sunglasses on and intended to keep them on for the entire time I was in the airport. Personally, I didn't like O'Hare airport at all. It was too big and very confusing. Thank God I had been here before or I'd be screwed. I walked into the door and walked up a short flight of stairs. As I walked towards the ticket counter, I reached into my purse and grabbed my ticket information for my overseas flight and waited in the short line. Hopefully the flight won't be booked so I won't have anyone sitting next to me. I waited for about eight minutes until it was my turn. I walked up to the counter and handed the guy behind the counter all of my paperwork plus passport. 'Wow, Miss Mahari. Flying to the Middle East, huh? Have you been?' He asked with some surprise in his voice. 'No. This is my first time.' As he ran my passport and driver's license through some sort of National Database, he continued the conversation. 'Well then, have a good time sightseeing, ok? And be careful ma'am.' He handed back all of my paperwork, ID's and ticket. 'Thank you.' I replied. I took my carry-on and walked the long hallway to the Security Checkpoint. I sat my suitcase on the conveyor belt as well as my purse, and bag of water, trail mix, gum and magazines. Everything went through peachy keen. I walked through the metal detector and had no issues. I walked right through and waited for my case and other belongings to come through. I grabbed my case first, then purse and plastic bag. Once I was walking to my gate I felt relieved. Even though I knew how to pack a gun, knives, bombs, etc. too where they did not set off alarms or knew how to make them invisible to metal detectors, etc., I still got nervous that I would be caught somehow. I don't know why. I guess because I just had bad luck most of the time. Hopefully not on THIS trip though. PLEASE not on this trip. I saw the magazine stand/store on my right and walked in while putting my ticket inside my handbag. As I was perusing the magazines, I was, at the same time, looking at everyone that was passing me by out of the corners of my eyes. It was a habit. Especially if I was on 'a job'. A job like this especially. You never knew if anyone had received a phone call or an email regarding my upcoming job. Thinking about it more as I was in the store I started to question my ability and I started sweating. Not heavily but enough to make me feel uncomfortable. I took two deep breaths and reached into my bag to get another Xanax™. I walked over to the cold cases and grabbed myself a cold, bottled water. I opened it and took my pill. That ought to do it, I thought to myself. I went back to the magazines, picked up a few, and grabbed my favorite gum and some trail mix. I walked to the counter and paid for my purchases. Over the intercom, I heard that they were starting to board for my flight. 'Awesome', I thought. No waiting with the 'Unwashed Masse's' I thought to myself. After I finished in the magazine kiosk, I was thinking about my flight, my father's house, driving my own car, which car my father will buy me and when and life in general. I mainly thought about why we, as people, just couldn't say what we thought. I always found myself 'thinking to myself' because I knew that what I was thinking was 'Un-PC'. Un-PC to just about everyone around me or my dad or just people in general. I assumed that it was just the way I was raised. I arrived at my gate and walked right up to the First Class ticket line.

Chapter 10

I was second in line. Sweet. Please, let this one way flight be empty! I hoped. I handed my boarding pass to the stewardess and walked down the tunnel down to the 767. Too bad they never used double decker planes anymore, I thought to myself. That would be so awesome. I loved double decker planes. Oh well. Probably the economy shut that whole idea down. As I entered the plane, I handed my pass to the stewardess that was the 'meet & greet' one chosen for this flight. She took my ticket and showed me my seat. A window seat that was in the first row of the entire plane. Literally facing the stewardess' seats. Yuk. How… invasive! No privacy for hours! Oh well! I'll just have to deal. How? Earphones with no music playing, sleep as much as possible, read a lot and listen to some music while writing to my dad. Or Steven. Or no one. I'll think of something. I opened my overhead and lifted my suitcase and put the heavy bastard above me. I noticed that some 'over-weight' dude looked at me like I must be Superwoman to be able to lift that thing. I just gave him a 'look' like 'mind your own damn business and shut the door. I sat in my seat and instantly put my purse in my lap to get my iPod out. Once that was accomplished, I laid my purse back down on the seat next to me and put my headphones in. I had two empty seats next to me on my right. I wondered if it was going to stay that way. I sat and waited until I saw my stewardess. I wanted to ask her a question. I didn't have to wait long. She came walking down the walkway behind me. I heard her footsteps on the floor. Damn, this woman walks 'hard'. Weird. As she walked by my seat, I tapped her arm, said, 'ma'am? Could I ask you a question please?' She turned sideways and looked down at me, smiled and said, 'Why, of course. What can I do for you?' 'I was just curious if you knew if these two seats next to me were taken or not.' She smiled and answered, 'Let me go in back here and I'll see for you. Ok? Be right back, dear.' I smiled back, said 'thank you' and grabbed a magazine out of my paper bag from the magazine kiosk. It was 'Vogue™' magazine. Vogue™ had been one of my favorite magazines since I was four years old. While other kids were reading or coloring in their coloring books, I was carting that magazine around ALL the time. I memorized fashion designer's names, their clothes, models names, everything about fashion I memorized. I wished I would grow taller and taller every year so that I could be a model. My mother never knew that I wanted to be a model and my father would never had let me, even if I had grown taller. Needless to say, I grew up to be a whopping 5 foot 2 inches. I still laugh at that memory. 'But I bet I would be the hottest 'little person' model!' I smiled to myself as the stewardess came back to my seat and said, 'Ma'am? You seem to be in luck. No one has these seats reserved for this flight. It is pretty light on this flight tonight. So it should be pretty comfortable and quiet for you.' 'Thank you so much.' I replied. She smiled, said 'no problem' and walked back to where all the other stewardesses were. I continued to look at my magazine and looked out of my window. I realized that it was actually dark outside! Pitch black! Damn, time flies. I got my purse back in my lap and secretly texted my father (yes, I never turned it off). I told him that I made my commercial flight ok and had no problems at all. I made sure that my volume was off (thank God it was) and waited until he texted me back. It was about fifteen – twenty minutes before I did receive a text back from him. Must be busy at this time of night I thought. My dad wrote, 'Glad to hear it, Princess. Miss you, be careful and keep your eyes open. Love you, Dad.' I thought about the date and knew that it was not a 'Holiday'. Well, at least he sounded like he was in a good mood. Good for Steven, I thought. I sat back in my seat and heard the food cart being loaded with the food for Coach, so I knew our food in First Class was coming soon. I set my magazine down and pulled my tray down. I didn't wait long. My stewardess showed up about 10 minutes later and handed me my menu. I chose a Cobb Salad. It said 'Fresh' so we shall see, I thought. I waited for my dinner as I laid back in my seat. That was when I realized how tired I actually was. It had been a long day and I couldn't wait to take a nap. If not go to bed/bed. Like until the next morning. I knew that sleeping on a plane is never like sleeping in your own bed. Well, except on my dad's jet. He has a bed and a full bedroom with shower and all of those luxuries so that is actually as close to sleeping 'in your own bed' as possible. My salad was put on my table not too long after I was deep in thought. I looked at my drink for my dinner and I was glad I ordered milk. I only drank one alcoholic beverage on any flight. Regardless of how long it was. The salad was actually pretty damn good for plane food. It was very rare to find dinner or any other kind of 'meal' on a commercial flight that was edible. This was one of them. Many people are probably saying 'how could you screw up a salad?' Well, they can and have. This Cobb Salad was pretty damn good. The main reason for that was because the lettuce was fresh. Obviously that makes a big difference. After I finished my dinner and swallowed the last of my milk I was sleepy as hell. I took my plate and stood up, gave it to the stewardess and took a trip to the restroom. I grabbed my brush out of my travel bag as soon as I was in the restroom. I closed the door, locked it and did my business. I did not want to be woken up just because I had to pee. That would suck. After I flushed (a *horrible* noise), I took out my elastic/pony holder, and brushed out my hair. I did the best as I could washing my face, too. Damn I was tired. I wished for a second that I would magically morph back home and walk out of the bathroom into my bedroom at home. I shook that thought out of my head. 'Get your mind off of 'home' and into 'job' I said out loud to myself. I shook my head as I washed my hands, dried them and opened the door to the walkway of the plane. As I walked to my seat up front, I casually glanced at every single person on my flight. My father had taught me to do that as well. If you are going to let yourself fall asleep on a commercial flight, always make an excuse to stroll along the walkway of the plane to check out your fellow passengers. When you sleep, especially on a cross country trip, you leave yourself completely vulnerable. And only eat the food that you see the stewardess hand you. Since my father checked out the flight that I was going to be on, I knew what that meant. He checked everything and everyone. And Steven did as well. If they needed Buzz's help, they used him too. They checked out every stewardess' background, home life, as well as how long they have been working at their job. They also checked out their families, kids, husbands, past and present. You name it, they checked it. And everyone from the ticket taker to the plane staff. Yes, including the pilot. The reason my father, and sometimes Steven, did this was because we hardly ever took commercial so it was worth all of the trouble; and time. I reached my seat and sat down. I reached over and closed the pull-down visor too. The stewardess would wake me when we reached our destination. Usually when we were circling the airport. Or, if that particular airport was not busy, they woke up the sleeping passenger's when we were about 30 minutes from the airport. It all depended. I grabbed my blanket and pillow the stewardess gave me about an hour earlier and looked up for a second to see if any of the other passengers were looking at me for no reason. They were not, thank God. All most of them were doing were doing was the exact same thing that I was doing. Getting ready to go to sleep. And since First Class had extra room in front of you AND behind you, I had the luck to be able to push my seat ALL the way back. Almost as far back as the lounger on my father's plane. Sweet! I reached into my carry-on bag and took out my 'night time pills' and swallowed them with my left over milk from dinner. I removed my carry-on bag from the chair next to me and put it on the floor underneath my chair. I positioned the pillow and blanket and took off my Juicy tennis shoes. I put them on the chair next to me; all the way back towards the aisle seat armrest. I took out the current book that I was reading and started reading. Dammit! The fucking ceiling lights! I leaned on my left arm and lifted half of my body up and turned them all off. I had my own little book reading light so I didn't have to worry about leaving the lights on the whole time I was sleeping for the night. I grabbed my cellphone secretly from my handbag and texted my father a ‘goodnight text’ and turned off my phone and plugged it in to charge. I read for, I am guessing, an hour until my pills kicked in. I remember the softly fading voices of the other passenger’s. I woke up all by myself. No one had to wake me up. That was weird I thought. Usually, someone always had to wake me up when I was dead asleep. Especially after I take my ‘night time’ pills. I sat up, pulled the blanket off of my face and looked around. People around me in First Class were also slowly waking up, getting up from their chair to go to the bathroom or coming back from the restroom. I saw the stewardess walk by me. I said ‘excuse me, ma’am?’ She turned around and said, ‘Oh good! You woke up! I was just about to wake you. Breakfast will be served in a bit and we should be arriving at our destination in about thirty minutes.’ ‘Oh. Ok. Thank you’, I replied. My stomach was already growling. I sat up, folded the blanket in a square and put it in the seat next to the isle. I grabbed my handbag and put it in my lap. I dug around for my make-up bag and got up to go to the restroom. As I walked down the short isle, I turned to look to see if anyone was new on the plane in First Class since last night. No one was. Good. That was that then. No one knew why I was going to Saudi or what I was planning on doing there. At least on the plane anyway. I reached the short line to the restroom. As I was standing there waiting to pee and do my hair (I would do my damn make-up in my seat) I grabbed a menu someone had left on their seat. I marked what I wanted for breakfast as well as what seat I was in. I quickly turned around to hand it to the stewardess that was Cassieskly walking past me. ‘Thank you’ I said as I turned back around. Finally someone came out of the bathroom. ‘Damn! What were they doing in there? I hope I do *not* have to go into that restroom I thought. Yuk.’ I thought, as one door down at the end opened up. I quickly walked into that door, shut and locked it. I looked into the mirror. ‘Not too bad’ I thought. ‘It could be a lot worse’, I said out loud. I quickly opened my bag as I was on the toilet peeing like there was no tomorrow. I took out my brush, brushed my hair into a pony-tail and twisted it around the elastic. I tucked the ends into the elastic. I got up, did my business and flushed. I looked in the mirror again and put three bobby pins into my bun that was centered in the middle of my head. I fixed my make-up and re-applied my lipstick. I put my contacts back in and my sunglasses. As I opened the door to the restroom, the line for them must have grown tenfold. 'Shit! They'll never finish their breakfast in time to get to the airport. Let alone get off of the plane close to the front at all. Maybe they didn't care, I thought. Hell, I do' I was thinking when I was walking quickly to my seat. I was going to do my make-up in my seat but being in the bathroom made it almost a habit. Make-up was always done in the restroom. At least that was how I was raised. I reached my seat and sat down. I saw that people were starting to receive their breakfast already. I forgot that these meals were pre-made. I just won't think about that little bit of information, I said in my head. As I put my bag back into my purse, I looked for my shoes. I finally found them half-way underneath my seat. Well, at least no one stole them. That would be lovely! I slipped my shoes back on and actually felt pretty decent. At least decent for sleeping all night in an airplane seat or seats. My breakfast had arrived. She put my plate and glass of orange juice on my table. 'Did you think of anything else that you might like, ma'am?' she asked. 'Just one thing. What time will we be arriving at the airport?' 'Oh, I would say in about 10 minutes we should be circling. I can check with the pilot if you would like.' 'Oh, no bother. Thank you.' She nodded, smiled and walked away. I started in on my food since I was an extremely slow eater and I decided that it wasn't that bad. The scrambled eggs were not runny, and the cheese was melted. Not bad for 'plane food.' Or maybe I just haven't been on a commercial flight in so long I had actually forgotten how bad it actually was. I was taking the last bite of my bacon strip when I felt the plane banking off to the right. I looked out of my window as I chewed my last bite. I put my fork down and I wiped my hands off with the napkin. I reached into my bag and grabbed my make-up bag again and opened it. I pushed my plate to the side and put my bag on my table to take out my mirror and lipstick. I re-applied and zipped it back up. As I put my make-up back into my purse, I grabbed my phone and turned it on. It vibrated three times. Shit. It's probably my father. I looked at my watch. It was 2pm Saudi Arabia time. 10am my time. Lovely. 'Thank God for pills' I thought. I leaned my head against the window and closed my eyes for a bit. I thought of home, my bed, my father and Steven. I realized that I was homesick. I 'shook myself' out of it and paid attention to the task at hand; why I was here. Once my job was done, I would be going home. And I will do it right. I wanted my father to be very proud of me. Especially since this was the first 'job' I was going to do without my father present. Sure. I had killed people before, but that was during ritual and didn't count. To me, at least. But traveling to the Middle East and doing a job as a 'favor' too one of 'They' at The Table; that was a different story. I wanted this job to be perfect. It had to be. We were circling the airport now. Close enough for me to see the cars and airport itself. I also saw the runway we would probably be landing on, as well. I was getting excited now. I was completely ready for this job. I was going over in my head my instructions for the job that my father had given me. I had them memorized since he *had* given them too me. Not hard at all. 'Just go with my instincts' he had told me. And that was what I did in my 'actual' life. My life. Well, except this 'relationship with my father' thing not counting. That I had *no* idea what to do with. Or where to put it. Until another time, I thought to myself. Right now it was my job at hand. As we started to descend, I buckled up and just laid my head against my headrest. I just wanted to get this job done with and get home. Back to reality; school even. And, yes, my father. Not because of any romantic reasons. But because he made me feel safe. And, I was safe when he was with me. 'Listen to me', I thought as I realized we had landed and people were standing up to get their things. I shook myself out of that frame of mind and got into Mode. I got up, grabbed my handbag and put it in the seat I was just sitting in. I reached up above me and unlatched the overhead where my suitcase was. I reached in and grabbed the handle to pull it out. Some guy that was sitting in the seat in front of me asked if I needed any help and I replied, 'No thank you. I've got it.' He smiled at me in a flirtatious way. 'Yuk.' I thought. I pulled my bag up and out and set it on the ground in front of me. Sort of as a barrier between me and the man in front of me. As soon as I heard the door to the plane open, I was ready to get the hell off of this plane. I felt claustrophobic all of a sudden. Finally the line started moving. Thank God we sat in front of the damn plane and not in the back by the restrooms. As I reached the front door of the plane, I felt the air of the Middle East. Dry and slightly windy. As it usually was in their 'springtime'. I took a deep breath and walked out of the plane. I instantly put my 'Mode Face' on. Which was basically my 'character's face'. My character was a visitor from the U.S. who was in the Middle East just for a couple of days on business. I walked through the airport with my head held high but not too high as if too cause any unwanted attention. Women were treated *very* differently here. I walked out of the airport front doors and opened the back door to the first cab I saw that was in front of the cab line. I did not want to wait anymore. I wanted to get to my hotel and rest, prepare and get comfortable with my job at hand. Which was tomorrow. As I sat inside of the cab, I told the driver my address to where I was going. I sighed and leaned back in my seat. When we got to the hotel, I opened my door, paid my driver (thank God my dad gave me ريال or Saudi Riyal's, before I left) and got out of the cab with my case. 'Damn, will I be glad when I reach my room and set this thing down! I am exhausted. Mentally anyway.' I just thought that I was talking to myself a lot lately. I wondered if that was normal during trips like 'this'. I'll have to ask Steven or my dad when I call him. This time, I said that out loud. God forbid that anyone remembered a 'woman talking to herself in the hotel lobby.' I reached the front desk and told the man behind the counter my 'name' and handed him my credit card. He smiled and spoke to me in Arabic. I spoke to him in Berber. A lesser but common language in Saudi as well. If you spoke your native tongue, especially English, you really stand out. Especially in a country like this one. Hell! Especially after 9/11 happened *and* you were American. Even if you *looked* American. He handed me a key card and off I went. I actually got to ride to the top floor in the elevator by myself. Thank God! Alone! I want to be alone! Once I reached my floor and my room, I slid the card key through the door and walked in. I sighed involuntarily. I put my suitcase on the folding contraption that was in the open closet. I opened it, put all of my toiletries as well as my wigs into the restroom. I remembered to put the 'Do Not Disturb' sign on the outside of my door. After I did that important little extra, I got my pajamas on the bed. I grabbed my purse and walked to the bed with it. The rest of today was a no plan day; a do nothing day. I grabbed my cellphone and plugged in the charger and hooked my phone to it. I stared at my phone and decided to call my dad instead of texting him. Especially with my burner phone. I pulled out the phone from my purse and made the call. Steven answered and I quickly looked at my watch. Which, on purpose, I kept on California time. Shit! Of course my dad won't answer. It was around 3am there. Steven sounded like the dead had awoken. He answered unintelligibly. 'Ello?' "Hey Steven. S'up?' I said just to annoy him a little. And I said it a bit loud, too. 'Gia. Hey. Are you alright?' He sounded a lot more awake now. 'Yes. I'm fine Steven. I am at the hotel now, in my room. I wanted to talk to my dad but I just now looked at my watch and realized what time it is over there. So, I guess I'll have to wait until the morning. Your time.' 'Gia, he didn't want to go to sleep until he heard from you. Let me hand the phone to him.' 'Wow.' I thought. He didn't even go to sleep until he heard from me. Coolness. He loves me. I smiled a bit. Of course I knew he loved me. I just loved hearing it. Especially from Steven, who was one of the few who were close to him… If only they knew, I thought. I waited for about four minutes until I heard some whispered words and then the handing over of the phone. 'Gia. What a damn pleasant surprise. How are you?' I smiled. 'I am good, daddy. I just got in my hotel room and put my toiletries in the bathroom and just folded my cat suit and put it on the chair next to my bed. So I'm good until tomorrow morning.' 'Good girl, baby. Just do what *needs* to be done and then head out. Got it?' 'Yes sir, Father. I cannot wait to get home. I miss you.' 'As do I.' He said. His voice a little higher than normal. That meant that he had emotion in his voice. For some reason, I felt bad. And that made me feel more homesick. 'I'll be fine, daddy. I promise. I have had, as you know, the best teacher's in the world.' 'Ok then. Get in bed. It should be, what? Two or three in the afternoon there?' 'It's three twenty five in the afternoon here, dad.' I replied. I'll take a shower here in a minute, order dinner and then get in bed and read for a while. Once I get drowsy, I'll take my nighttime pills and go sleepy.' 'Alright, Princess. You do that and be careful tomorrow. I'll be ready to see you at the airport at the appropriate time then baby.' 'Ok. I love you and sleep well dad. Ok? Promise?' 'I promise, Gia.' We hung up the phone and I stared at it for a while. Damn. He sounds so close yet he's miles away, I thought. I sighed, got up from the bed, and grabbed my pajamas and toiletries all the while wondering why I was starting to feel 'more feelings' about my father than normal. Was it because he slept with me? Because I ALWAYS figured that if you *slept* with someone you would get 'emotional' feelings for that person. More so than if you did *not* sleep with them. As I entered the bathroom, I grabbed a towel and laid it over the hanger by the shower, put the bathmat at the foot of the bathtub and grabbed my shampoo, conditioner and razor. I put it all inside the shower and turned the water on. I walked back inside the room, to my suitcase, and took my hairdryer. I plugged in the special plug, that pretty much only worked in the U.A.E., onto my dryer and plugged it into the wall in the bathroom. I got undressed and got in the shower. It felt good to rinse off all of the 'travel-grime' off of my body. Yuk. Once I was done with all of my shower duties; a half hour job if I hurried, I stepped out onto the bathmat. I reached over and turned on the fan so that my mirror didn't get all fogged up. Once I dried off my entire body and towel dried my hair I combed it straight back. I rubbed my special StriVectin™ cream on my face and my under-eye cream; I also applied some under my eyes and on the outside corners of my eyes. Once that was all done, I grabbed my hair serum and rubbed that all through my entire hair. It was a strengthening cream for colored hair. Once my towel-dried hair was taken care of, I grabbed the hairdryer and blow-dried my hair to my preferred style when 'undercover'. A style I would never wear at home. Hair straight, my longish bangs swept over to the right (instead of the left) side of my face and both sides of my hair covering half of my cheekbones. I put my dryer back inside my suitcase as well as my hair products, except my hair spray in case I needed it tomorrow for putting on my wig. I hated wearing wigs but they came in so damn handy when trying to look like someone other than who you really are. But I was so used to wearing them that I hardly even thought about wearing them anymore. Which was a good thing. Especially for my 'line of work'. At least for this part of my life. I walked back to my case and put the rest of my toiletries in it. I left my toothbrush and paste, my brush, and folded cat suit in the bathroom. The cat suit underneath the sink in the bathroom. I didn't want the maid to see my wig or the cat suit either. Just in case she happened to come in here before I headed out for the trip home. I kept my rifle in my case, hidden, until I needed it tomorrow. I went to the bed, put on my P.J.'s, climbed into bed and picked up the phone and ordered some early dinner. Some people would argue that that, in itself, would cause a red light to go on but in actuality, I was a new arrival and 'getting into the swing of things', as far as the time difference goes. I ordered something light, as usual. A medium Cobb Salad, milk, and a small bowl of baby, spring peas, in butter. Yummy. Normally, if I was traveling for pleasure I would have ordered a cocktail. But not on a job. I made a rule for myself. Not to drink when I *was* on a job. Never. I wanted to always think clearly, and not possibly have a headache in the late night or morning. And since I was a lightweight when it came to drinking, it didn't take much. I grabbed my book and started reading, waiting for room service to deliver my food. After about an hour, I heard a soft knock at my door. I jumped a little. I guess I was really into my book. Damn! Jumpy much? I got out of bed, put on my robe and opened my door. In came room service. He rolled my food cart to the middle of the room and smiled and spoke in his native tongue. I smiled and replied back in his native tongue. He looked up at me and gave me the biggest smile. He asked me if I was Middle Eastern and I said, 'No, but that I knew the language very well. I was just passing through his beautiful country.' That seemed to satisfy him. I handed him a very generous tip but not SO generous as to stand out. He looked down, smiled huge again and thanked me. He walked out the door, me smiling back and holding the door as well for him. When he was gone, I went to my cart, moved it close to the bed, sat down and began to eat while reading. I was not interested in watching TV in a foreign country. I rarely did. Even when I traveled for pleasure with my father and Steven. This was damn good food. No wonder this hotel was rated five stars. Only the best for daddy's girl, I thought. After I finished my glass of milk, I sat the glass back down on the cart, rolled it outside of my room and made sure my 'Do Not Disturb' sign was still hanging on my door correctly. I closed my door and locked every possible lock that they had. I went back to the warmth of my hotel bed (which was actually wonderfully soft, yet firm at the same time) and got into my book again. I stopped for a minute, set my traveling alarm for 4:30 AM and settled in for the night. Me, my book and a job that I had to do perfectly for the Organization and for the very first time. E-v-e-r. After reading for about two or three hours, I felt my eyes getting really heavy and realized that I was reading the same damn sentence repeatedly. I folded my page, closed my book and got up from my warm bed. Damn. I forgot how cold it gets here when I turn the thermostat way down. I liked my room cold as shit as I slept in a warm bed. Weird, I know. But, I *am* weird. Plus, I got *that* from my father. He always slept like that when traveling. I never knew why because I never asked him. I was just used to it after a while so I never felt the need to ask him. I put my book inside my suitcase, which was on its stand by the window to the left of my bed. I grabbed my purse, my valuable jewelry and opened the closet safe. I took out all of my night time meds and then put everything else inside. I closed the safe and used the password I used for everything. I took my pills into the restroom with me, took them with the nice, ice-cold tap water and used the toilet. I knew I was going to sleep wonderfully tonight. And I always woke up to my travel alarm. I was, by nature, a light sleeper, when away from home. Especially, I would assume, on 'a job'. *Especially* without my father with me. I crawled into bed and turned out the light. Before I let myself be 'out' for the night, I grabbed the piece of paper from my purse with my orders/directions from my dad. I wanted to read them before I turned in for the night. It strictly read that when I was too shoot him, too *not* hit him in the head. My father did not want his head too splatter all over the place. He wanted it to be a clean hit. But, that the shot was to be a Kill Shot. Ok. No problem. I knew how to do that since I was 9 years old. My father, as did Steven, had been training me with guns since I was very little. How to kill, where on the body that will kill with one shot and where on the body to maim and not kill with one shot. I had all of that piece of paper memorized and put it in my purse, in a zippered, secret place inside my handbag. Under the flap of the opening. No one would ever find it, let alone know that there was a zippered pocket there. I just had to remember to destroy that piece of paper before I got on my commercial flight to Chicago. I laid my head on my pillow, reached over to my bedside table, turned on my alarm and grabbed my eye-mask. I put it on my head and slipped it down over my eyes. I slowly fell asleep. And, as far as I know, had good, calming dreams.

Chapter 11

The driver stopped his cab right where I was supposed to be dropped off. Perfect. I handed him the fare plus a nice tip. Not too substantial but nice enough. He smiled, and nodded his head a bit too me and said 'Thank You' in his best American and I responded with 'You're Welcome' in Arabic. He seemed too really like that. When he did speak his 'Thank You' in Arabic, his head was completely down. Not looking at me. In the Middle East, men don't act too 'nice' too women. They do not know if they are married or not. It was a huge no-no to talk to a woman if she is married to another man. That was considered a 'crime' of sorts and, if the woman took offence at that man, she can tell her husband who would, in turn, either kill the man (which was legal) or, most recently, be brought to court and all of that. But since most Middle Easterner's didn't have any money, they couldn't afford an entire court proceeding. So, they would just beat the living Hell out of them or kill them. Mostly the latter.

He got out of his car, opened the passenger side door and took out my suitcase. I watched the expression of his face to see if he had a weird or confused look on it. Like, 'Why is she being dropped off here instead of airport?' type of look. I didn't see one weird or confused look. I think he was still excited to get American money and that I 'respected' him by answering him in his own native tongue. I got out, thanked him again in Arabic and walked away. I looked out of the corner of my eyes and saw that he didn't hesitate to get back in his cab and drive off. Probably back to the hotel, no doubt. I walked about two blocks to where I was supposed to 'do my job'. On top of a small Cassiedge. I could see the building where my target was supposed to be giving his speech to the local news as well as some American news companies. Probably CNN, I thought. I kneeled down, turned my case on its side and unzipped it. I took out my gun, loaded it, screwed the silencer onto the tip of my muzzle and checked the sight. It was perfectly aligned. I just had to hope that it was adjusted correctly. I couldn't very well check it by putting it over the Cassiedge railing and check it. I might as well just turn myself in to the Military Police. They were crawling all over the place. Trying to look inconspicuous, of course. To me, they stood out like sore thumbs. But that was all because of my training. Anyone else, especially the Middle Eastern citizens, wouldn't be able to tell at all that they were there. Only the ones that walked out with my target. I looked at my watch. Three more minutes and the job would be done. Hopefully without a hitch. I stooped down again, after looking one more time to see if anyone else was on my walkway on my Cassiedge, (no one was), and text my father's burner phone and told him where I was and too turn on CNN or the news. I heard a commotion and that, I knew, was my cue to stand up and aim. I looked at my watch, waited another 15 seconds (enough time for him to get into position and comfortable) As well as too start addressing the media. I stood up, my heart speeding up just a little and took aim; looking down and through the sight of my rifle. Perfection. I couldn't have asked for anything more precise. He was perfectly aligned inside my scope. Especially the area of his body where I wanted to hit him. I took careful aim and waited about 20 seconds. As he rose his right hand to make his point, (I assumed), I took my shot. Down he went and commotion ensued. I instantly stooped down, unscrewed my silencer, put that in the bottom of my case, my main rifle between my jeans, tennis shoes and toiletries. I zipped up my suitcase, stood up, arranged my Burka and started walking down the Cassiedge stairway. Towards where my cab driver let me out in the first place. I got to a pay phone and put my 'panic face' on. I picked up the handle of the payphone and dialed the military police's Hotline for emergencies. I spoke my 'panicked Arabic' and told the man on the other end of the phone 'that the person who had been shot' was shot by someone that wanted him dead for highly personal reasons! All bullshit of course but the authorities wouldn't think so. I told them to come and come fast!' It was hard for me not to laugh at the tone in my voice. The man on the other end of the line told me to not worry about it and to go about your household chores. (Swear on my life) I thanked him but hung up right as he was about to ask me something. I continued walking towards the block where the cab had dropped me off. I called the same cab company that I had memorized when I got in the cab at the hotel, and asked for a pick up at the location where I was. I made sure my voice sounded a little panicked as well. Just to make sure that call didn't come back to bite me in the ass later on. I waited for four minutes or so until my cab arrived. As I was waiting, I saw tons of police race by me. Not one of them looking at me. Just in case though, I kept my panicked face on and looked down. As women out and about were supposed to. Once my taxi pulled up to me, I grabbed my case and tried to look as 'meek' as I could. My cab driver sure looked stricken and in shock. As we both were in the car, my suitcase safely on the seat next to me, I asked, in Arabic of course, if he, please, knew what had happened. He looked quickly behind himself and told me that the only thing he has heard on the news was that somewhere a shot rang out and in seconds, the 'person I shot' went down, his bodyguards landing on top of him. I said, in reply, 'Oh Allah!' and sort of shoved what I could, onto the cab's floor and bowed down in the submissive pose as if I was on my Praying Mat, or a specially woven Persian Praying rug.

Most families that did have money had them woven specially for each member of their family. Since most everyone in the Middle East was Muslim, I thought that would make myself more believable. I even saw my driver look in his rear view mirror and see me do that. Good, I thought. He asked me 'Where to' and I told him that I had a flight to catch, unfortunately, to America. For business. He told me 'That was very unfortunate. Especially losing someone so important in our Country and for our people. Those American's deserve everything that they get.' I agreed of course. 'If only he knew' I thought. He turned on the news and I listened, raptly, too everything the newscaster/ reporter was saying. They, so far, didn't know a damn thing. Thank God. I so wanted to text my father that but I didn't dare. Besides, I had thrown out all of my burner phones away. But not before I took them all completely apart first. I could not text him until I was safely on his jet in Chicago. It was at that moment, in that cab, was when all of the adrenaline left my body. All at once. I was instantly exhausted. I couldn't wait to get onto the plane to take me back to Chicago. Commercial or not. I didn't care. I wanted food and sleep. I decided that this ride to the airport was going to be completely silent. I was too busy pretending to be concerned as well as listening to the radio. Obviously for very different reasons why, than the driver was. As the driver pulled up into the 'Departure Lane' in front of the airport, I handed my driver his money plus tip; still with my 'concerned look on my face. I thanked him again, bowed a little and walked, with suitcase in hand and handbag on my shoulder, to the front desk of the commercial flight that I was supposed to take all the way to Chicago. I handed the lady behind the counter my ticket plus passport and ID. She looked up at me and noticed my 'stunned and concerned look' on my face. Since she had the same look on her face, we did not say one word to each other at all. She slowly handed me my boarding pass. I took it and continued toward my gate. As usual, I stopped at the Starbucks™ right outside the airport bookstore. After I purchased my usual, I continued into the bookstore. I perused the magazines and noticed, on the front cover of the just released newspaper, evening edition, the story was already out. A picture of him being hit was on the cover. The look on his face was of total and complete surprise. Not to mention pain and agony. 'Good, you son-of-a-bitch', I thought to myself. I also hoped that he would think of that very pain the next time he tortured innocent American reporters when they came to this country, the prick. I picked up the newspaper, put my 'concerned face' back on and continued picking up my usual magazines for airplane flights. I also picked up an XL t-shirt for Steve that said 'Moscow' on it. Steve always asking me to pick him up some t-shirts on my travels. Since this was my first one, I wasn't about to forget. Especially since because of his and my father's training, I did such a perfect job. In my eyes anyway. I SO hoped my dad was satisfied with the job. As well as the gift I had picked out for him when I landed in this country yesterday. Was it really yesterday? Damn! Time does fly. And I could not wait to get home! I realized that I really missed my dad and Steven. Especially my own fucking bed.

Chapter 12

When they called my flight and for First Class to start boarding, I grabbed my handle and my purse and took out my boarding pass. As I was in the short line for First Class, I was thinking, when I was looking at the people seated that it must be a very empty flight. Great news to me. No loud noise, screaming babies, no bullshit. Loved it already. When it was my turn, I walked up to the stewardess and she took my boarding pass. She looked at me and then looked down at my boarding pass. Then she looked up at me again with an expression that even I couldn't read. 'Uh-Oh' I thought. What the fuck is wrong? I was going, through my head, what the hell COULD be wrong. Nothing came to mind. 'Is there something wrong, Miss?' I asked her. She just put her head down and whispered that she thought that I was 'Paris Hilton'. My racing heart slowed down about, it seemed, one thousand beats. 'I get that a lot.' I replied as I took back my boarding pass. I sort of laughed with her. 'Oh! Really? Well I am so glad you are not offended, ma'am.' I laughed at that. 'Well, looks wise? No. Plus? I actually like Ms. Hilton. She is very, very sweet. Now, if you said that you thought I was someone that was 'famous' for no reason at all and did nothing but marry someone who was famous for actually *doing* something in Los Angeles, no names spoken here, of course? Then I would be offended.' I told her, smiled and continued on down 'the tube' as I called it, too the plane. When I reached my seat in the front of the plane, I put my suitcase above me in the bin, sat back down and buckled in. God! I could not wait until I could take my wig off and all of these damn bobby-pins! My head was beginning to itch. Suddenly I had an idea. I grabbed a small bag from my carry on and went to the restroom. Hopefully I had time before we started to take off. I took off my wig, along with the bobby-pins and placed it inside of the bag. I covered up the wig, since the bag was see-through, with a scarf I was wearing around my neck. I took another scarf that I had folded and put in the zipper pocket of my handbag and after I brushed out my hair and put it into a high ponytail, I tied the scarf around the ponytail holder and fixed it into a bow. Perfect for now, I thought. I needed to eat, have a cocktail, and sleep. I walked back to my seat and as soon as I sat down I took out two Xanax™ from my prescription bottle in my purse and put them on my food tray. As I was ready for my late lunch/dinner tray, I waited for the stewardess and thinking about getting home at the same time. Damn, I missed everybody! I had no idea *how* much I would miss my father, Steven, Juanita... Hell, everybody! As I was thinking my thoughts of home, my dinner tray was set in front of me. I looked down and everything looked just as I had ordered it. 'Good', I thought. 'No unnecessary drama.' I straightened my tray and started eating. Not bad. Especially for commercial airline food. Or the crap they usually serve in coach anyway. With how expensive even Coach Tickets were, they should serve First Class food to the Coach patron's as well. Oh well. Like that will ever happen. After I finished my meal, I pushed the tray away from me and put my napkin, folded, on top of my tray as well. To me, that makes it pretty damn obvious that I am done with my meal. We shall see how well my stewardess can 'catch signals.' Not long after I finished with my tray test, low and behold, my stewardess came walking by and took my tray with my napkin and my cocktail. Wow. Pretty good. All of the other First Class stewardesses never caught on for *at least* 20 minutes. I'll have to make sure to leave her a tip when I disembark. After my pull-down tray was empty before me, I pulled it back up, snapped it securely to the seat in front of me, looked at my watch and decided to take my night-time sleep. By the time I wake up, with my pills inside of me, it should be time to descend at Chicago's O'Hare airport. I picked up my random crap off of the empty seats next to me and arranged the pull-down arms in their upward stance. I stood up, opened up the over-head above me, unzipped my Louis Vuitton™ carry-on, took out my sleepy blanket and zipped it back up, closed the hatch and got back into my seat. As I sat down, I looked around me and noticed the people around me. They seemed to have the same idea as me. It was 'dinner' that they had just eaten and they wanted to sleep until they landed as well. Perfect. That meant that there would be no noise as I was sleeping. Not much anyway. Just whispers, probably. After I asked my stewardess for a glass of water, I stretched my legs out in front of me and reached down to take off my shoes. I set them underneath my seat that I was sitting in for the entire trip. I put my handbag up on the seat behind my back, the handle wrapped around my waist. Zipped up of course. I received my glass of water and that is when I gave her the tip for being a 'perfect' stewardess, in my opinion. She was quite taken aback, actually. I guess they don't tip much anymore on airlines. 'Douche-bag's', I thought. I took my pills, gulped them down with the water and put the empty glass on the tray by my feet, at the end of my row, by the aisle. I laid down, put my eye-mask on my face and pulled my blanket on top of me. Practically covering my entire body up with it. With the plane's engines running, the hum of the few passengers that I could hear as well as the slight noise coming from the 'kitchen' behind me, I was asleep in no time. Very comfortable too, surprisingly. I dreamt of weird things when I was sleeping. Obviously, I cannot remember all of them now. But I do remember one dream; or part of a dream that I had on that flight on the way home. I was standing on the top of a grass hill. A very steep hill. I couldn't see anyone or anything around me for quite some time. I stood there for a very long time it seemed. Then, I saw my father, on my horse, ‘King Abu’, at the bottom of this grassy hill. I knew it was him because of his posture in the saddle. But I was still squinting to make sure that it was indeed him. Then, I wasn't so sure. Gone was the clear horizon behind him. What I did see then was a man, still on a horse; but not King. It was a tall Bay instead of Abu's Dapple-Gray color. The man was sitting tall on that horse, very short hair, and brown in color. A dark brown. He was holding the reins with one hand and in his other, was something that he was holding out to me. I couldn't see what it was. Maybe a black box? It was small enough to fit in his hand. I couldn't, for the life of me see what it was though. I was too far away. I slowly started to walk down the hill. When this man saw that I was walking down the hill, he guided his horse up the hill towards me. As we got closer, I could make out some of the features of his face. I saw that he was handsome in a rugged sort of way. Wearing jeans and cowboy boots as well. Cowboy boots? What the Hell? I remember thinking that very clearly. Once we were almost eight feet away, I saw that he was indeed holding a black, velvet, ring box. Then, instead of reins in his other hand, he was holding copies of paper or documents. Weird. He then said to me, 'Please make me two copies of each, babe? If you're not busy?' I pondered that for a while in my dream. Copies? In the middle of fucking nowhere? Then he, or something, was shaking me. I tried to open both of my eyes. I only managed one eye at a time. It was my stewardess. Telling me that 'we were circling O'Hare airport and to 'get up sleepy-head and put my seat in the upright position, please.' I looked at her for a while, realized where the hell I was and then smiled. I sat up. Rubbing my eyes at the same time. As I was trying to wake up, I folded my blanket up and put it in my lap. I slowly stood up, reached up to open the overhead and unzipped my bag. I put the blanket inside and zipped my bag back up, closing the overhead again. As I sat back down in my seat, I slowly put my shoes back on and reached for my handbag. I lifted it up out from behind my back, took out my make-up bag and unzipped it, still thinking about my weird dream, and took out my compact. I opened it up too look in the mirror. Damn! Thank God I didn't have to go to the restroom to fix my hair. It hadn't moved since I laid down. I must have been exhausted. I didn't move an inch it seemed. It even looked like I didn't. Well, that's good. I re-applied my lip-gloss and powdered my face a bit. And that was it. A first, I promise you. I usually look like I went through a tornado when I wake up from a plane sleep or a car sleep, etc. I was all ready for Chicago and my dad's jet back to California. As we were circling O'Hare airport, I looked out of the window to my right and saw the familiar runways, the terminals, etc. I could not wait to get inside my father's plane and just 'be.' As the plane started descending, I saw the whitish/grayish runway below us. Thank God I knew this airport and knew how to get to the private jet terminal. It is a beating for people who have never been too O'Hare airport. It is quite big and confusing. Especially for a first-timer. As the landing gear came down, the plane touched down without a hitch, 'thank God.' I thought to myself. I was not afraid of flying. Hell, I was flying since I was in diapers. But whenever we started to land, I always began to get very antsy. I don't know why. But once we were actually on the runway, I was completely fine. I still feel that way. As our plane was taxing towards our terminal, I got up, along with everyone else in First Class, and unlocked my overhead. I took out my carry-on and set it on the seat next to mine. I closed the door and sat back down until we came to a stop. I put my handbag on the crook of my arm. 'Only one more damn plane flight and then home', I said to myself. As the plane stopped and the door was opened to let all the passengers out, I was already up and standing. I was the first one in line to get out of the plane. As I walked down the stairs and into the tunnel leading inside the terminal, I looked straight ahead and reached inside my handbag to get my sunglasses. They were always on top of all the crap that was inside my purse for easy access. I put them on just as I started seeing people in front of me; looking for their loved ones, friends, whatever. I walked right by them and, again, was thankful that I did not have to go to baggage claim. That was always a nightmare. I walked down the long hallway towards the Private Plane Terminal/building. I secretly hoped that my father had been on the plane recently so that I could at least smell him when I walked in. The blanket I took with me had lost his smell when I left the hotel in the Middle East. I opened the double doors to the smallish building and walked up to the counter. This time there was a guy about twenty something behind it. I handed him my ID and passport. He took it and pulled up my information on his computer. As he was reading the information on his screen, I told him that I needed to use the restroom. He looked up and replied, 'No problem, Miss Mahari. It's just too the right. Behind that big potted plant. He pointed in the direction as I said 'Thank You.' I left my carry on at the desk with him, knowing that it would be safe. Especially since he knew my last name. Everyone seemed to know that last name. And once they did? I was always treated completely different. Not that I was complaining. I just didn't know how or why they did know my last name and why they did treat me differently when they did. When I was done in the restroom, I had too pee bad, I walked back to the desk. My carry-on was right where I left it. Like I knew it would be. 'Miss Mahari? You can go and board whenever you are ready, Ma'am.' The young guy said to me as I came into view. 'Thank you very much'. I lifted my bag and walked out the back doors; excited just too even see my dad's jet. And there it was. Waiting for me. Engines humming. That guy must have called the pilot and told him I had arrived, I assumed. As I walked towards the steps up to the plane, my heart started beating faster. I didn't know why either. As I walked a little faster, I looked down at my feet and took a deep breath. I thought to myself that it was only a two and a half hour flight to Los Angeles. I will only read and snack on my trail mix. And in no time at all, I'll be at LAX, go home and be with my dad. I smiled at that thought as I lifted my head. I looked at the steps. All of a sudden I slowed down a bit. Until I came to a complete stop. A dead stop. 'It couldn't be.' I thought out loud. Standing at the very top of the steps, a glass in hand, was my father. I must have looked hilarious. I knew my mouth was wide open, looking up and just staring. For once I knew I wasn't hallucinating, I started running. As I got closer to the jet and HIM, I saw that he was smiling. And smiling very big. I hadn't seen him smile that big since he saw his last bank statement. And he had his arms outstretched like he wanted to catch me. That was impossible with everything I was carrying. But I didn't care. I only ran faster. I secretly wished, deep inside my mind, that it was a regular Dad/Daughter reunion. I felt and knew it was much more than that. But at that moment, I did NOT care. I ran up those steps as fast as I could and into his arms. Before he completely hugged me, he practically ripped my bag and purse out of my arms and pretty much threw them at the waiting stewardess. I was finally in his arms. I smelled his safe smell, felt his thick hair, his suit that I was probably getting make-up on, everything that I had missed but just did not allow myself to think about. He pulled me away, just a little bit and kissed me. A normal father/daughter kiss, on my cheek. The stewardess was right behind him and to the left of him, after all. He took my hand and led me to the living room area and as we were both just over the threshold of the Living Area, he shut the door that separated the cabin and the very room we were in. That was when he took me in his arms and kissed me as a husband/boyfriend would. What I was used to from him, unfortunately. I kissed him back just as I always did. Saying, at the same time how much I missed him, his body, his mouth, everything. As I was speaking those words, he was speaking as well. Only in Arabic too me. And saying basically the same things. But he was also making groaning noises as well. Not like an animal or something that 'The

Monster' would do; but my father's kind of noises. The ones that I had grown to know. Good noises. Next thing I knew, we were laying down on the couch, making out. Those are the only words that I can even say to describe it. All of our clothes were on of course. We were not alone after all. This was just an 'I Missed the Fuck Out of You' kiss. And I enjoyed it; needed it. Especially as I was 'home'. On American soil. After about forty-five minutes of kissing and rubbing each other all over, my dad pulled me slightly away from him so that he could look at me in the eyes. 'Thank God you are home, my baby. I missed you so much, Gia.' I looked at him and told him that I thought of him every second of every day that I was gone. Missing him so much. He smiled. We sat up and he stood up, took a deep breath, 'collected himself''. He looked down to see if THAT worked. Satisfied, he walked to the door that he had shut and spoke to the stewardess. He turned back to me, leaving the door open halfway. As he sat down, I thanked him for taking the day off to meet me here. That I was secretly hoping some surprise was waiting for me in this plane. I never imagined, in a million years, that it would be he, himself! He chuckled at that. 'I was thinking of something that I wanted to do for you when you touched down at O'Hare. I couldn't think of anything special enough. It was actually Steven's idea, G.G.' 'Really?' I said. 'I'll have to thank him when I see him at the house. Or is he on the plane, daddy? You never fly without him.' He looked at me after he took a sip of Brandy and set it down on the glass table in front of the couch. He is here. Just sleeping in the bedroom, love. We had a very busy evening last night. He was pretty damn exhausted when I woke him up this morning. So that is why he is catching up on his sleep while we are in the air. I assume that he didn't even wake up when we landed. He should be up in a bit.' 'That's fine, Daddy.' He got himself comfortable on the couch; took off his coat jacket, loosened his tie a bit and leaned back on the cushions. 'I heard and saw all that went down overseas. I am extremely proud of you, Gia. You did an extremely perfect job. I couldn't have asked for better.' I looked up at him and smiled my biggest, honest smile. That's what I have wanted to hear from him forever. That I did a 'perfect job'! 'Thank you, father. That means a lot to me. You have no idea how much, daddy.' I smiled as I said that to him. When I was done speaking, my stomach made this huge grumbling noise. My father's eyebrows arched up a bit. I said, 'Excuse me, father. I must be hungrier than I thought I was.' He laughed a bit. 'Well, we can fix that, Gia.' He pushed the intercom to the cabin and told the stewardess to Cassieng out some appetizers for us to munch on. 'Munch' being my word. She replied with a 'Yes, Sir.' He asked me about my trip and I told him everything. From the moment I landed, to the rude stewardess on his jet, (not the one that we had right now), to the job itself and the entire trip home. He told me that the stewardess would be 'dealt with'. I had hoped that only meant 'fired.' As he sat there listening to my story, his gaze never left my face. He heard every word. 'Well, Gia, I will say you handled your first professional job very, very, well. The Brotherhood is very pleased. Very. They have decided that you will be at the top of their list if they *do* decide to use a female. Great job, my love. I am very proud. I heard from them an hour after the deed was done. Per the telephone. Pretty personal, I will say. Coming from them that is. He then smiled at me. As we started just small talk, the door opened and in came the appetizers. They smelled so good. Real food in almost four days. I dug in immediately. But, still waited for my father to start eating first, as well as putting his napkin in his lap. As we were eating, I heard some noise in the back room. Behind the couch we were sitting on. 'It walks' my father commented. I looked up and saw Steven standing at the opening to the bedroom and the Living Room. He looked presentable, but half-assed. I got up and gave him a hug. He hugged me back and then said, 'Great job, Gia. I'm very proud of you. According to what your father and I saw on CNN and other sources, you did everything you were taught to do. As well as everything your father told you to do. Great job, babe. He kissed me on the cheek and sat down in the chair across from us. He picked at the appetizers as well. The stewardess walked in and set a glass of ice-water in front of him. 'Thank you' he said without looking at her. As I sat there, all three of us talking about what I had 'missed' when I was gone, not much, apparently, I realized how much I had missed these very two people when I was gone. They were the only two people in my life that only meant a shit to me, at this point. At that moment I did feel like a very special, young girl. As well as loved too. That meant the world to me. I also knew that now that I was back, my father and I were supposed to deal with 'Our Relationship.' He had told me sometime during my last few days before leaving that we could not carry on as lovers and I had inquired about therapy. I wondered if he had done any research as far as therapists that were in The Organization that he would trust with such information. This 'therapist' would have to be a part of The Organization. If any other therapist heard of 'Our relationship', they would lock my father up for 'child molestation' or, God forbid, 'Rape against a Minor.' Not that he would 'get convicted', but it would be literal hell for The Organization as well as me and my father. I had no earthly idea how this was supposed to go down. I just decided to wait until my father brought it up again. As we all sat there talking, the intercom from the cabin said that we were circling LAX and to buckle in and get ready for a 'Kick-Ass Landing.' That was my father's pilot. He was pretty damn funny. Sometimes. He must be in a good mood as well. When my father heard that, he sort of smiled his half-grin, smile. He put down his empty glass, put his seat belt on and continued speaking. 'Also, Gia?' I turned to look at him. 'Yes, Tata?' 'You will also be getting your payment, a bank transfer, in a day or so. Most definitely by tomorrow evening I would think.' As we landed and were taxing to our limo that was parked in its usual place, Steven got up and went into the bedroom to get his suit jacket. As he walked out, he already had it buttoned up and his shoes were on. His shoulder holster on as well, I assumed. 'Don't worry about your bag, Gia. The driver will walk on and retrieve it.' 'Ok, daddy.' I replied. 'Oh! I sort of 'borrowed' your blanket' that you use for naps on the plane. I hope you didn't mind. Or, rather, don't mind.' I watched his reaction. He didn't have one. He just smiled like he 'knew' WHY I took it. 'That's fine Gia. Just put it back on my chair. Yes?' 'Absolutely, daddy.' I unzipped my carry-on and took it out. I kissed it while looking at him and stood up to put it on his favorite chair. We came to a complete stop and the door was opened by Steven. My dad stood up, as did I. I walked to the door of the jet and waited for my father who was texting someone. Probably his driver waiting for us in the limo outside. After he was done he placed his phone in his suit jacket inside pocket, walked towards me, put his arm around my waist, and waited for Steven's signal to exit the plane. Steven must have gave him the signal because the next thing I knew, we were walking down the stairs to the pavement. In good old Los Angeles. I took a deep breath in. No damn smog! That is a *rarity*! I started walking as my father had stopped to wait for Steven to walk right in front of him. As Steven got into place, we walked to the limo. Steven in front; just a bit. Me behind him, too his left and my father to his right. Steven's gun, un-holstered and at the ready, at his right side. My father's driver got out of the car, opened my father's door first, as always, and then mine. As we were getting in, Steve got in the front with Mohammed. 'Ahhh. Alone at last' I thought. As Mohammed started the engine and turned the car around, facing the exit of the airport, my father softly patted the leather closer to him. Since I was touching the door on my side of the car, I scooted right next to him and leaned my head against his shoulder. Actually, my head hit the middle of his bicep. 'It is so good to be home, Tata.' 'The feeling is mutual, my darling. Did you sleep well while you were there, love?' 'Yes and no, I guess. Some nights were ok and some were Out-Like-A-Light nights. What about you, father?' 'I slept some and mostly did not sleep all through the night. Steve and I had A LOT of shit to clean up here while you were gone. I thought of you every night though, baby. Regardless if my head was on a pillow or not.' I looked up at him, inches away from his face. 'You must be exhausted, then.' I asked him. 'No. Not really, love. Not that you are home now. But, I shall go to bed early this evening and catch up. Don't you worry about me, Gia. You also need to catch up on your sleep tonight too, yes?' 'Yes, Sir. I will. I am *so* glad I will be sleeping in my bed tonight. Or my home, rather. Wherever I end up sleeping.' After that statement, I glanced at his face to see if I could read his expression. All I saw was a smile. Not a full-blown smile. But a half-smile. I deep down knew that since this was my first night back from being out of the country and me doing a 'Perfect Job', according to him as well as the Organization, I knew that I would probably be sleeping in his bed tonight. I knew that was wrong. In *so* many ways. But I almost wanted too. I left the topic alone and just put my head down again on his arm and closed my eyes. 'Father?' I asked, looking up at him. 'Yes, love?' 'Since, obviously, I have never done this before, how much does the Organization pay for things like this? Or, rather, jobs like this?' 'Well, baby girl. They will probably pay you between $100,000 to $300,000 dollars. Take a look at your bank account and look tomorrow evening. Before bedtime, yes?' 'Yes, Sir, I will.' I fell asleep then. For who knows how long. Next thing I knew, the car had stopped; or the rhythm had stopped. I opened my eyes and saw that we were outside the gatehouse. I slowly sat up and glanced in my father's direction. He was still seated as he had been when I must have fallen asleep. Eyes wide open, staring straight ahead at the gate as it swung open. Once I was upright, he looked over at me and smiled. 'Have a nice nap, Princess? My arm is asleep.' 'Yes, I sort of did and I'm sorry Tata.' He laughed a bit. 'I expected you to sleep, hon. I was going to move, but when I glanced down at you, you looked so peaceful that I didn't want to wake you.' I smiled at that and looked straight ahead. 'Now, how in the hell can I stop, or whatever, this type of relationship when we both so enjoyed it so much? He could be so nice and caring. But, at the same time, he could be the most evil, uncaring, human being on the planet. Not counting Mr. Harris. He was the *worst*. As the car drove us toward the house, I wondered what I was going to do today. Probably un-pack and read. Or take it easy. Maybe take a swim in the lap pool and then get in bed or ON the bed and read. I did not want to fall asleep right now. I would be so screwed with my internal time clock, plus jet-lag if I did that. As Mohammed pulled the limo around and parked it in front of our house, in front of the steps leading to the front door, Steve got out, thanked Mohammed and opened my father's door once he heard from his walkie-talkie that the gate was closed and all was clear. As my father got out, he walked around and opened my door. I grabbed my handbag and got out. Steven leaned in on my side, grabbed my bag and up the stairs we went. As my father opened the front door with his keys, we walked in. I involuntarily took a deep breath inward. Ah, the smell of home I thought. It was so missed. And smelled so good. I saw Juanita, standing in front of the stone, circular, centerpiece and even noticed that the flowers had been changed since I had been home last. The things you notice when you've been gone, I thought to myself. Even for only five full days. Weird. I turned around and reached out my hand to take my bag from Steven. He handed it to me, I took it and walked over to Juanita to give her a kiss on the cheek. 'Hola, Bambina!' she said with a big grin on her face. 'Hola, Juanita! I replied. 'I missed you!' I said to her. 'Mucho, Bueno!' she replied. After that, she asked my father, as he was heading upstairs, if he needed anything. 'No thank you, Juanita.' and continued up the stairs. As I followed him up the stairs to my room I turned my head and said, 'Thank you, Steve-O.' He smiled. 'No problem.' And then mouthed the word, 'bitch'. I almost laughed. I turned my head back to my father's back and realized that I had missed home more than I thought I did. As I reached my bedroom door, I looked over in my father's direction. He had already opened his bedroom door and closed it. Him being on the other side, of course. Hmm. That is strange. I would have thought he would have given me some kind of signal to come inside his room when I was done. Or now. Whichever he desired. Maybe he was going to take a quick nap. Who knew? I closed my door behind me and set my bag on my bed. I noticed that Juanita had made my bed, which meant that she had changed my sheets as well. I glanced over to my laundry hamper and it was empty as well. So at least all my clothes were washed as well. And put away, of course. Awesome. I unzipped my carry-on and started the boring process of un-packing. Most, if not all, of my clothes were dirty so I threw them all in the hamper. I picked up my Jimmy Choos™, walked into my shoe closet and put them in their specified place. As I reached my bag again, I took out my rifle and put that beauty, after making sure it was completely empty of shells and clean, under my bed, way in back towards the head of the bed. I also covered it with an old beach towel used just for covering it up under there. After all of my toiletries were put away, I took my bag and walked into my handbag portion of my closet and set it on the floor while I went and got my step-stool. As I positioned it right underneath the shelf where it went, I picked up my travel bag and set it way up on the highest shelf. If anyone (well, except maybe Steven) walked in here, no one would be able to see it. Not that it mattered. It just looked better up there. In fact, ALL of my big items/bags went up on the top shelf. Including my Louis Vuitton™ Carry All. Again, one of my all-time favorite bags, ever. I stepped down off of the step-stool and put it away, grabbed my swimsuit out of, you guessed it, my bathing suit drawer and put it on. As I was putting a beach towel around my waist, I walked over to one of my vanity drawers and took out a hair clip to put up my hair. I picked it all up with my hands and twisted it into a semi-messy knot and clipped it on top of my head. There. Done. Finally! I needed to relax! Damn! As I was starting my trek downstairs to the ground floor, I saw a few detail guys sitting on the couch watching T.V. Since it was the start of football season, they were probably watching a game. Normally, if my father was at work, I would be sitting with them, next to Steven, watching it with them as well. But I needed to relax. And a heated pool sounded like just the medicine I needed right now. I reached the door to the basement and down I went; closing the door behind me. I thought about how much money I had just made for such a simple job. Damn! It will have to be a shopping day and soon, too. I will go alone. I would never let Mariah know how much money I got to spend. Let alone, how I made it. Not in a million years, obviously. Once I reached the pool, I tossed my beach towel on one of the lounge-chairs and got in the pool by the steps. I normally just dove in, but since my hair was up and I didn't feel like getting it wet, I chose the 'pussy's' way in (according to Steven) and took the steps. As I started my laps, I thought about my trip for a while. After that, my mind wandered to my father and our relationship. Again. I knew it was wrong. That was obvious. Stopping it completely was something else entirely. I was attracted to him in a way that I shouldn’t be. And I *knew* that. He knew that but wasn't quite so verbal about it. Why? Was he even serious about stopping it? I didn't know. But I did know that I wouldn't be allowed to even see a therapist unless he set it up. And with one that he could trust. Which meant an Organization therapist. If there even was such a person. I had never heard of one either. But they had Organization doctors, and dentists, etc. so why not a therapist? Oh well, I'll just have to see. I will Cassieng it up tonight with my dad I said to myself. As I was on my last lap, I heard a door open and shut. As I finished my laps and was sitting on the middle step, I turned around and saw my father. He was in his swim trunks and also threw his towel onto mine. I wondered if he had planned this. But how could he when he had no idea that I was even coming down here? He was looking at me the entire time he was in this room. Even as he also walked down the pool steps. He always dived in but this time he didn't. Strange. As he stood on the top step he looked down at me. I sat on the middle step, still looking at him with a half-smile but also with a curious expression as well. 'Hi Tata. Are you going to do your laps, too?' I asked. He shook his head 'No'. 'Oh. I just came in here to relax. But I just finished my laps. It felt... good.' As I finished my sentence, he was walking down to where I was and sat right next to me. 'Come here, Gia.' He said. His tone was firm; not 'mean' nor 'strict' but, well, firm. Like, do it or....or what? When I least expected it, he grabbed me by my left arm and pulled me too him. Once he had me where he wanted me, he took my head with both hands, managed to sit on the edge of the pool; up a 'step', so to speak, and pushed my head towards his lap. I instantly 'knew' what he wanted me to do. He ripped off his swim trunks and got 'himself" out. He was as hard as a rock. 'Oh God', I thought. 'I hate this part.' I took him in my mouth, hoping above all hopes that I wouldn't have to finish. As I was pleasuring him, he arched his back, speaking in Farsi, and rubbing my back as well as the back of my head. 'God, that feels so damn good, baby. Don't stop.' I had an idea to stop and ask him a question, but thought the better of it. I'll just ask him later. I was thinking, as he came in my mouth. With such *force* that I choked and gagged at the same time. I wasn't prepared like I usually was. As I raised my head, he pushed it back down and told me to 'finish all of it.' Now *THAT* pissed me off. I raised my head and as fast as I could swam in the opposite direction of him in the pool. Towards the deep end. But, as usual, he was much faster. He caught me, took both of my arms in his hands and slapped me across the face. 'Don't you *ever stop* when I am not finished Gia!' He practically yelled at me. Two inches from my face. I put my hand up to my cheek, feeling it burning red already. I instinctively dunked under water too cool my cheek. He yanked me up again. 'Listen to me' he yelled. I knew no one would hear. This room was completely sound proof. 'Daddy!' I yelled back. 'You know I hate doing that! Why do you insist on making me do it? 'Do all of your other whores not *like* doing it either? Huh?' I knew I shouldn't have said that even as it was coming out of my mouth. After 'it' was said, I winced a little and was about to say 'sorry' when he beat me too it. *'WHAT DID YOU SAY?'* I looked at him and he was so angry that his entire face was as red as hot coals. And his arms were shaking too. 'Uh oh.' I was screwed I said to myself. He whipped me around. So that I was two inches from his face and looking straight at him. 'How fucking *dare* you say that to me, Gia. I have not called any of my 'so-called whores'. Ever. I do not sleep or have Sexual Relations *with whores*. And, even if I did? It would be none of your business.' He turned his entire body away from me and just stood there. His head down a bit. I stood there looking at his back and decided that I did take it a tad too far. I did not have to Cassieng up who he *did* sleep with at all, for that matter. That was out of pure meanness. Hell. I don't even know why I said it. Out of jealousy, no doubt. I slowly walked up to him and very gently put my arms around his waist. Telling him that I was so sorry. That I shouldn't have said what I did. That I loved him and no one else in the world....' Shit. There it was. The 'elephant in the room' so to speak. He slowly turned around. His head was still, sort of, down. Once he was facing me again, he raised his head and I saw tears running down his face. 'I love you too, my dear Gia. And I cannot, no matter how hard I try, cannot stop.' I looked at him. In awe. He said 'it' too. Thank God he felt the same way. That explained so much. The back and forth moods, his unpredictable behavior, etc. All of it. Not that he wasn't 'unpredictable'. But how he treated me, most of the time. Instead of just one way. Like he treated Steven. 'Tata, when we go to therapy, we can find a way to love each other in a healthy way. Like we are supposed to. Ok?' He looked up at me, after wiping away his tears and dunking his entire head underwater. 'I guess, kitten. Do you want 'it' to stop?' I thought about that for a while. I guess too long. He then said, 'Ok. We shall talk about this, obviously, in private, at a later date. No hitting, fighting, or yelling, yes?' 'Ok, daddy.' 'I am truly sorry I struck you, G.G. baby. I have been so frustrated lately, babe. No sex, no cuddling at night, no...You.' Even though his words, and his complete honesty (a rarity), was making me so, confused? In love with him more? Hell. I did not know. 'Tata? Come here.' I said. He looked at me with slight suspicion as he slowly walked towards me. As he was basically so close that he was touching me with his upper body, I took his head in my hands and started kissing him. Out of my *love* for *him*. Not lust or urgency nor even ‘desperate’ because I haven’t had sex in so long. Just pure love for him. This was a first. Not in my plan after what had just happened but it almost had to happen after all that had just happened. Or whatever. I was so fucking confused and sick of being so! He, obviously, returned my kisses, a little hesitantly at first but then with equal intensity and then we were both full on making out in the middle of the pool. As he was untying my bikini and I was untying his swim trunks, he picked me up, laid me down on the pool tiles and grabbed his towel for the back of my head. As he entered me, it was with such gentleness and caring that I almost forgot who I was having sex with. More like 'making love' with. I had never 'made-love' before. Except the time when 'it' was during Ritual and I had asked my father about it. But this time there was no comparison. Right now was the most gentle he had ever been with me. At least in regards to sex. Or anything for that matter. *Now*, this felt heavenly. No pain in the beginning, no pain during, or after. And it lasted long enough for me to 'enjoy it' or 'finish' if you get my meaning. And I had never had that happen before. Never! By a man, at least. No wonder women raved about sex! This was awesome! Then my mind almost forced me to remember who

I was with. I pushed that out of my head. 'No! Not now!' I said to myself as we kept on making love right next to the pool.

As Juanita put the last bowl of calamari on the table, she asked Steven, who had joined detail on the couch, where Mr. F was and Miss Gia was. 'I'll take a look. If they didn't answer their Com's, they are probably down at the pool. I'll get them.' As Steve walked down the stairs towards the pool area, he heard noises on the other side of the door. As he got closer, they were not the 'normal' noises of swimming neither. 'Oh shit.' He noticed that the door wasn't locked or completely closed. He slowly cracked it open a bit. Enough to see in at least. What he saw blew his mind. He knew it was happening at Ritual. Hell, he had been there. But *not* at Ritual? Hell, Dominick! That is your daughter! He watched as my father kept going at 'it' with me, kissing me and rubbing my smooth, tanned thigh. He instantly took his head out of the door, slowly closed it too where it was when he got there and quietly walked back up the steps to the kitchen. As he reached the door to the kitchen, he paused. Trying to collect himself. What the fuck was he doing? Damn! She wasn't protesting either. How long had this been going on? So many damn questions, man! Steven opened the door, walked into the kitchen and told Juanita they'd be up in a bit. That they were just doing their laps in the pool. As he sat down, back on the couch, he couldn't simply watch the game anymore. He stood up, grabbed the remote and asked if the game was being recorded. One dude said, 'Yeah, man.' So Steven promptly turned it off. Too many 'Oh Man's!' and 'What the Fuck's?' was said. 'Get washed up for dinner and get your ass' downstairs. Now!!' All of the guys on the couch and in the chairs took off. He sat down to take in what he had just seen. My God Dominick, Steve thought to himself. That is your daughter! I guess I 'get it' if it is some Ritual religious crap that you and the rest of them practice. But outside of your religion thing? Inside your home and by the damn lap pool?

That I do not understand. And to make your daughter think that's alright? Hell, I don't even think I can 'get there' and I sure as HELL know I cannot Cassieng it up to him. Shit. Well, I'll maybe talk too Gia about it later on, I guess. He stood up to wash for dinner and shut the restroom door as he did so. After we had finished and my father got off of me, the Com from the pool went off and told 'us', or anyone whom was down here, 'that dinner was about ready. Fifteen minutes away.' We looked at each other and smiled a little. He got up first, reached his hand out to me and I grabbed it. He pulled me gently to him and looked at my cheek. Where he slapped me. 'I am sorry, my love. I got… angry over something asinine. I do apologize. Yes?' 'Yes, daddy. Sorry that I just swam away from you when you wanted to beat me?' He looked at me sort of funny and then gauged the way I said it. To see if I was being a smart ass to him or if I was 'joking' with him. I would never be a smart ass to him. Not now anyway when he had the advantage. I actually *did* mean it as a bitchy thing to say. But I just pretended that I was being funny/sarcastic about the whole thing. He actually started laughing after watching me for a bit. Which, in turn made me laugh. After he put his trunks back on, he tossed me my bikini bottoms and I slipped them on, he took my hand and we walked up the stairs to the main house. Once we opened the door to the kitchen, the TV was already off and Juanita was alone pouring dinner into serving bowls. I walked behind her and wrapped my arms around her and told her I was going upstairs just for a bit to get semi-presentable. 'That's ok, bambina. It will take me at least ten to fifteen minutes before dinner is served, my baby.' As I walked up the steps, Steven passed me only going the other way. Without saying a word. Weird, I thought. I walked into my room and into my closet. I slipped some Juicy Couture™ sweats on and sat at my vanity. As I fixed my hair to make it more presentable for dinner, I also put my 'Miracle Cream' on my face too as well as sprayed some leave in conditioner in my hair. Since my father made my damn hair wet anyway, the fucker. I knew then that somehow this ‘thing’ had to stop. It was just a matter of when. As I left my room, I shut my door and saw that my father was standing outside HIS door as well. 'Perfect timing, daddy' I said as I started walking down the stairs. 'Yes it is, love.' he replied. He started walking right behind me on the stairs to the dining room. I felt him looking at my ass. Maybe I was 'dreaming' or 'thinking' he was. But I was pretty sure THAT he was. That made me smile, somewhat as I smelled the yummy food coming up the stairway. 'Tata, dinner smells wonderful, doesn't it?' 'Yes it does, my love. Yes it does. As usual. But I am especially hungry this evening. Aren't you?' I looked back at him, smirked and replied, 'Oh yes. VERY much so.' As we came into view of Steven at the main dinner table as well as Juanita walking back and forth, serving, we both sat down. 'Hey Beavis. How are you?' 'Quite tired, G.' As I'm sure you must be.' I looked at him sort of funny. 'And why would that be? I asked. 'Oh...from all of that traveling and extracurricular activities you did when you got home. I would imagine you would be extra tired.' 'Oh. Well, I guess I am a little. But not...that...much. As I said those last three words, I remembered what my father and I did and where Steven was when we did it. Could he have seen any of it? He should have been watching the game with the rest of Detail. The ones allowed in the main house, anyway. My father, on the other hand, heard the weird answer and thought that it was just as strange as I did. What do you mean by those answers, Steve? He asked him. Steve looked up at my dad. I glanced at him, in surprise. Complete surprise, actually, and quickly shook my head 'No!' He saw me do this out of the corner of his eye but continued on with his conversation with my father. 'I just thought that for all that she has done since she has gotten home, she must be exhausted, is all, Mr. F. 'I see.' my father answered. 'And what 'all did she do?' I am not quite caught up, I guess, Steven.' I have never seen Steve look so uncomfortable. And since he wasn't used to feeling that way, my father could read it like an open book. Hell, I could. Shit! Did he see us? No! Steven kept chewing his food, swallowed and then answered my father. 'Sir, would you like me to have this conversation now? Or in private?' Steve, looking at my father as he spoke, of course. 'Well, there is no time like the present, is there, STEV-O?' I had never heard my dad call Steven by my nick-name for him. Ever. This was a first. 'Well, if you insist, Mr. F.' Steve set down his cutlery and turned his chair just a little to his right so that he could look my father straight in the eye. I wanted to be anywhere but here. God, please take me *away* from here! I whispered to myself. 'Well, Steven, I'm All *Ears*.' Now, my father did say that with sarcastic malice. And I also saw very clearly that Steven noticed it too. I saw a slight. Just a slight hesitation in his expression. Almost like, 'Should I really go on with this?' My father, having finished his dinner, pushed his plate away and tossed his cutlery onto the plate. Which he had never done before, either. Or at least since I had known or been living with him. Steven looked at my father and started his story. 'I told Juanita that I would go and find you and Gia for dinner. She asked me if I knew where you two were. I figured that you, Sir, were finishing up your laps like you said you were going to do when you got back from the airport. Plus I also figured that if Gia wasn't in her bedroom she may be in the pool or Jacuzzi OR in the room with you. Catching up or whatever.' As he spoke, there was no quivering in his voice and zero fear. 'So, I walked downstairs towards the pool room. I heard voices so I knew I was right. Both of you, or you, to be exact, were in the pool. Or at least in that room. I only heard your voice, Sir. Not Gia's. I saw that the door was not locked and it was also a little ajar. Oh fuck! I thought. 'I then heard different sounds coming from you, sir. Not your normal conversing voice. And Gia's voice was not so much a speaking voice. More of a moan or a talk-moan. I had never really heard a sound like that before. Especially coming from her. I then decided that she was either having sex with a guy down there and that guy sounded awfully like you, Sir. So, I just decided to look and then decide what I would do from there. Being that she is *only* 15. I opened the door a bit and I see you, sir. You having sex with your 15 year old daughter. And that is about it.' Steve started to pick up his fork and eat the rest of his food. Not even looking at my father after he was done 'telling his story.' My father listened to every word Steven had to say. I was completely dumbfounded that he had seen us have sex by the pool inside! My God! Why didn't I even think about dinner time? Shit! My dad finally turned away from Steven, finished what was left on his plate, and pushed it aside. Along with his napkin. Steven glanced quickly at my father, then went back to eating. My dad got up, told Steven to go to the ballroom 'NOW.' He yelled *that* word. At that moment I was really scared and freaking out. I stayed where I was and watched as my father got up out of his chair, walked out of the dining room and headed towards the ballroom. He opened the door and stood there, toe tapping; waiting for Steven to follow suit. When Steve heard that, he got out of his chair, gave me a quick look of 'I deserve whatever is coming to me' and walked towards my dad. I watched both of them as they entered the room and the door closed. I sat there, alone, looking around me. I don't think I had been alone at this table in years. Eating, anyway. I looked down at my plate and the little food that was left on it. I had completely lost my appetite. I took my napkin off of my lap and put it on my plate, pushed it away and got up. I stood there for a minute. Thinking what was I supposed to do. I walked, slowly, over to the ballroom door and put my ear too it. I heard yelling from both parties. My father's voice being the loudest. Steven's being the most complacent. But he was still telling my father how wrong it was to have sex with his daughter. Let alone his 15 YEAR OLD DAUGHTER. I couldn't listen anymore. Just as I was about to pull away from the door, I heard a loud 'smack/punch' sound from the other side. I knew that someone punched the other. And, chances are, it was my father doing the punching. I couldn't be here. I ran from the ballroom door and up to my room. I closed the door and lay down on my bed. Almost crying. But I started thinking instead. Deciding that I probably needed a bath, I got up and went to my bathroom. I turned on the water to the correct temperature and walked back to my room to get my nightgown. As I picked the one I wanted, I put it on my chaise beside the tub and grabbed one of my towels. I tossed that on the chaise as well. Just as I was getting undressed to get in the water, there was a knock on my door. I froze for a second. Honestly, I didn't know if I would rather it be my father or Steven. I quickly kicked off my shorts and threw my top off towards the hamper and slipped on my bathrobe; yelling, 'Hold on a second!' As I opened the door, there stood my dad. I looked him in the eyes and he still looked like he was coming down from some sort of 'Anger High' or something. 'Yes, Tata?' I asked him. 'What are you doing, Gia?' He asked me. 'I was about to take a bath, Sir.' 'I see. When you are finished, come to my room. Yes?' 'Of course.' I said. 'See you then.' He turned around and walked to his room. I slowly closed the door, standing on my tip-toes to see if I could see Steve on any part of the stairs. No can do. 'Oh well' I thought. I shut the door closed and walked back into my bathroom and slid into the tub, tossing my robe onto my chaise as well.

Chapter 13

As I laid in the tub for almost an hour, I got out, dried off, undid the clip in my hair and brushed it out. 'Just as my father liked it'. Fuck. Everything was as 'My Father Liked It. Geez!' Yes, I loved him. But what could I do? I was completely stuck *and* fucked. As my robe was on, my hair was 'just so' and I smelled 'just right', I headed towards my father's bedroom. I heard a slight noise a flight down from me. A flight of stairs. I looked down and saw Steve. His face was battered. Black and blue; bleeding in some places as well. He, apparently, was about to walk up to his bedroom as well. I felt horrible. But I kept on walking, came up to my father's door and knocked softly. I heard my father's footsteps, he opened the door and told me too 'sit on the bed'. Verbatim. No certain emotion that I could hear in his voice. I walked in slowly and closed his door behind me. I walked over to his bed and sat down on my side. Waiting for him. Then the main telephone to the house rang. As I heard him brushing his teeth and then brushing out his hair, I fiddled with *my* nails and hair. I sat there for about fifteen minutes. As my dad walked into the bedroom from his bathroom, he actually looked much better. As far as his 'emotional well-being' went. I hoped anyway. But he did look better to me. God, I hoped I was right. For my sake at least. For ALL of our sake's, actually. 'Gia, I assume you know that I would like, or rather, *want* you to spend the night in my bed this evening. Do you have *any* problem with that? And be honest with me, Gia.' I looked at him. In his eyes of course, as always, and replied, 'Of course, daddy.

And no, I have no problem with it. I never have. I have questioned it quite a lot as I've gotten older, but I love you, father. Whatever Steven said at the table, I believe, was inappropriate. Maybe not the question, per say. But the timing was wrong. I believe that IF he had a 'problem' with it, he should have took you aside privately. I personally believe that it is also none of anyone's business. I truly believe that, daddy. And if we decide to go to therapy for 'this issue', we will. But that would have to be both of our decisions. As I am sure you already know.' I continued looking at him, waiting for HIS reply. He stood there, looking straight at me, just as he had when he was speaking to me. 'Good, then. I figured that IF you did have a problem with sleeping in my bed, with me, you would have said something to that effect. As far as therapy is concerned? I have checked to see if there are any therapists in the Organization and there are none. I figured as much. But I checked just to make sure.' I let what he said to me sink in and I asked him, 'what if I ever wanted to get married daddy? Or you wanted to get married? What would we do?' He still looked at me with those steely greenish/grey eyes of his. Thinking that one over. Finally he responded. 'You think that one day you will want to get married, Gia?' 'Yes, I believe one day I will want too. As well as give you a grandchild. Hopefully a son.' I looked at him carefully at the response I gave him. I saw him actually thinking about that. 'A grandchild. Well, I will say that is the FIRST time I have ever heard you voice that. To anyone, actually. When did this longing begin?' 'It's not so much a 'longing' as a 'want to' type of thing. Unless that word means the same thing?' My dad actually chuckled at that response and told me, 'Yes, that word does mean the same thing, Gia.' 'Oh. Sorry. English is so damn hard sometimes, father.' He continued looking at me as he walked closer to his side of the bed. 'Let's quit talking about 'wants' and 'likes' for the moment, alright? It has been a hell of a fucking day and I need some release.

And, of course, pleasure from my favorite young woman in the Universe. How does that sound too you, my love?' 'Sounds fine, father.' As he got undressed he never took his eyes off of me. I decided that tonight I would not go into 'Mode' and just be completely, 100%, 'there'. In the moment, so to speak. As he was completely naked, he opened up the covers, got on top of the bed and slid between them. He laid on his back, closed his eyes for a while and stretched. He continued staring at the ceiling. Once he opened his eyes again, it looked like he wanted to talk some more. Turns out, I was right. 'Gia. As far as what Steven said at the table this evening, do not repeat it to anyone. Alright?' 'Of course not, daddy. I wouldn't dream of it.' 'I didn't think you would, Princess. Also. One more thing before we…enjoy the rest of the evening, yes?' 'Ok', I replied to him. 'The phone call you heard a bit ago; in the house? That was The Organization. They requested you for another job, baby. And this one is twice as important. Alright? Up to it? It also pays triple of what the other one paid. How does that sound to you, kitten?' I looked at him and thought about the money I had made from my first job two days ago. Just about two days ago, actually. 'I would be honored, father. Why don't you tell me about it tomorrow morning, ok?' 'Sounds acceptable, my love. Now, come here, my baby.' I looked over at him. He had moved over onto his right side, head resting on his hand. I scooted over to him and started rubbing his hair. From his forehead to the back of his head. He closed his eyes and moaned a sigh of pleasure. 'That feels so good, baby.' 'I know.' I replied. He slowly opened his eyes and looked at me after I said that statement. I smiled back at him. To make sure he knew it wasn't supposed to be sarcastic in any way. He then, slowly, took my hand and put it on the side of his face. He started kissing my hand and licking my fingers. I leaned into him and started licking his neck and at the same time, rubbing my pelvis against his. It only took two minutes, if that, for him to get 'ready'. I stopped licking his neck for a second and asked him, 'Daddy? I hate to Cassieng this up right now, but...' 'Then don't... after. Please.' was his reply. I, of course, complied. Because I wanted a 'Yes' answer. I continued doing what I was doing and he rolled me over onto my stomach and got behind me. As he was kissing me, he lifted me up onto my knees by my waist/hips. In a nut-shell, his 'love-making' was rougher than usual but, at least it was in my favorite position.

The next morning, I felt something rubbing my arms and breast's. I made a noise and rolled over to my left side. Which was facing my dad, of course. Not that I was consciously aware of that at that moment. I then felt, in my dream, of which I do not remember, lips, or something that felt like lips, touching mine. And then a tongue. I slowly opened my eyes and saw my father staring right at me. Smiling. I smiled a very lazy smile back at him and asked him if he slept well. 'VERY well, my love. After what you did to me last night, I think anyone would have, Gia.' I sort of half laughed at that and rolled into his arms. I rested my head against his chest. Why couldn't I be older? And why couldn't he not be my father?' I thought to myself. 'Daddy? I love you so damn much. I just wish above all else that I can find someone just like you. I cannot stand younger 'boys' or 'men', if they want to call themselves that. They are so immature!' He laughed at that. 'One thing to always remember, Gia, is that all men, in their own way, are immature. You just have to decide if the one you fall in love with is worth putting up with his little immaturities.' I thought about that for a bit. I then asked him, 'Will you accept the man I choose to be my husband, father?' He looked at me for quite a while. 'I think you shall choose well, Gia. We shall go from there. How is that?' 'Sounds fine, daddy. Oh! I forgot to ask you last night, father. Can my friends and I go too Las Vegas sometime soon? And stay in your suite at your favorite hotel? Please???' He looked at me from down his nose. 'At the Mirage™, Gia? In my suite?' 'Yes, daddy.' 'Let me think about that one. Give me until tomorrow after work, alright?' 'Sure, father. And thank you.' 'You're very welcome, G.G. Now for a shower. I will see you downstairs for breakfast, yes? Try not to take too long.' 'Yes, Sir.' I said. I watched him get out of bed, head towards his bathroom and shut the door. I laid there, in his bed for a bit until I felt like moving. I then slowly got up, pulled the covers half-assed up towards the pillows and walked out of his room. As I shut my bedroom door behind me, I decided that since I had nothing planned for today, I wasn't going to take a shower. I sort of wanted to smell my father on me all day. I know that sounds gross or weird, but I did. I loved his smell. I loved having sex with him. And I still didn't know why. Especially since it was 'so wrong'. And, I also knew that it wasn't my fault. HE started that whole 'deal'. I also made up my mind never too think about it again. Unless, of course, we went to therapy. I sat down at my vanity and proceeded to make myself presentable for today. I took out my clothes and shoes for the day. And since I had nothing exciting planned, meaning zero plans, I decided to wear my super-comfy 'boyfriend jean's'. 'Boyfriend Jeans are semi-baggy, button-fly jeans that are fit for a woman's body but low-slung in front. My boyfriend jeans are super low cut in front and were a bit baggy all over. Very comfortable. I also wore one of my father's old belts that once wrapped twice around my waist, I looped over the end of the belt inside the other side of the belt; or, rather, on the other side of my waist. I know it sounds confusing, but it is really not. I just needed to keep the damn things from falling off of me. Plus, they looked sexy on me, I thought and that was all that mattered. After I put minor make-up on, just eyebrows and a little mascara plus lip-gloss, and was dressed, I went downstairs to have breakfast with my dad. I also remembered, as I was walking down the stairs to the breakfast table, that I would be seeing Steven for the first time since he got, 'reprimanded?' last night. Damn, he was gutsy for saying what he did too my father. Regardless of what he thought personally. Well, that was one of the things that I did look up to him for. Being gutsy. As I hit the bottom step of the staircase, I turned right towards the dining room table. I DID see Steve sitting there, but the side of his face that was, 'fucked-up', as he called it, was not facing me. Well, I'm sure it wasn't too bad? I was hoping anyway. Not that Steve couldn't take it. It just made me feel bad whenever my father and Steve fought. Especially like that. And that hasn't happened in years. Physically fight, that is. I walked towards my chair and that is when I heard my father's door close. I heard someone coming down the stairs as well. I sat down and put my napkin on my lap. I was famished! I started putting scrambled eggs on my plate, bacon and toast. I also poured myself a glass of O.J. as well. 'Good morning Stev-o.' I greeted him. He looked up at me and didn't even give me a smile. He just shook his head. WTF? Now I felt like total trash. Or a slut or something. That was not cool. Did he not know that I really had no control over sex with my father? He couldn't possibly think that it was my idea all along to have sex with him. I had to settle this with him. And soon, too. I did not want him to think I was some sort of sicko or something. I had to tell him about this 'sick?' religion that I was born with and what they required. Not what I wanted for fuck's sake. Shit. Now, I was mad at him. Hell! He didn't even ask me. I was pretty pissed off, to say the least. I said not a damn thing as my father sat down at the table. I waited until my dad put his napkin on his lap and then I started eating. Looking down at my plate the whole entire time and not saying a fucking word. My dad, obviously knew something was up. He looked up as he was chewing his first bite, swallowed and said, 'Alright. Will someone tell me what the hell is wrong here?' I looked up at him, smiled and told him that I thought Steve was mad at me for some reason. Because he hadn't said a word to me since I sat down. I even greeted him as usual. My father looked at me as I said what was on my mind. He took a sip of his coffee and looked at Steven. 'What's going on, Steve? Do you have a problem with Gia or something?' Steven put his fork down. Looked up at my father and that's when I saw his face. 'Oh my God'. I thought to myself. He *did* get the living shit beat out of him. And good! Damn! 'Well, Mr. F., I do have some questions that I would like to ask your daughter. But I do not know if now is the correct time or place, Sir.' He looked at my dad for a few seconds after he finished, and then continued eating his breakfast. 'Well, Gia, when would you like to speak or answer Steven's questions?' My father looked at me as he asked me this. 'Well, now is fine, I guess.' I looked at Steven after I answered my father. Steve looked up at me, chewing, and said, 'Alright. If I may speak freely, Dominick, I would like to ask her a few questions now. If you do not mind of course.' My dad looked at him with a very strange look on his face and said, 'I have already *told you* that you may. SHOOT.' Steven looked at me and said, very casually, 'So, Gia. Do you enjoy having sex with your father? Meaning, outside of your sick religion?' That question completely caught me off guard. I was not expecting that at all! 'Umm, excuse me.?' I asked him. 'Sick religion? Why do you call it that, Steve? When you know nothing about it?' Steve, again, set down his fork and replied, 'ANY fucking religion that requires your biological father to have sex with his daughter, is a sick religion. At least, too me. Disgusting, in fact. And, I *do* have a problem with that, Gia.' He looked at me a little while longer after he was finished speaking and then picked up his fork again and continued eating. I looked, dumbfounded at him and then slowly turned my head too my father. Who looked so angry, I was surprised he hadn't already jumped out of his seat and beat Steve all to shit again. Damn. Why now? Steve had to know that speaking that way about my religion *and* my father's and employer's religion, in that way, was a huge no-no. Plus, his face looked like it had been hit by a Mack Truck anyway. Did he truly want a repeat? My father, knowing now that Steve was done speaking, asked him 'So, Steven, are you finished? With all of your bullshit, now?' Steven, while I was looking at him (it was like watching a fucking tennis match between these two) nodded his head and said to my father, 'By all means.... Dominick.' 'Let me ask you something; you piece of shit, mother-fucker. If I may, of course.' 'By all means... asshole.' 'Oh NO.' I thought. Here we go. My father's eyes got as big as saucers. He had never heard Steven speak to him in that way. Ever! At least to my knowledge. He got up from his chair and threw his napkin at Steve. It hit him square in the face too. Oh God! I so did not want to be here! 'Please take me away!' I said out loud, only in a whisper and with my eyes closed. I slowly re-opened them and saw my father standing directly above Steve's chair. Steven was still chewing, it looked like, his last piece of food on his plate. Steve looked directly up at him and, copying my father, replied, 'Shoot, Dominick. What IS your excuse, by the way? For fucking your 15 year old daughter?' 'Get in my office right now, Goddammit. Now!!!!' Steven took his time; putting his napkin on his plate, taking a sip from his water and then slowly got up. Then, as he was standing, looked down on my father, pushed him with his hand and walked towards the stairs to my father's office. My father, after collecting himself from that push, looked at me angrily. 'If I were you, Gia, I would go into my bedroom or yours, if you'd like, and wait until I SAY it is alright too come out. If you need to bathe or what-have-you, go ahead. This may take a while.' He turned on his heel, as he normally does when he is pissed off or angry, and off he went towards the stairway, following Steven. I slowly, very slowly, finished my breakfast not knowing what to think. I did know that Steven was going to lose in some way in this 'argument/fight. If he was going to allow himself to get his ass kicked, that was a totally different story. But, my father has never, in his life, let anyone kick his ass. In fact, I don't think anyone has. Except his boss. And my father never fought back. With his boss, that is. When I was done with my breakfast, I walked up the stairs and into my bedroom. I picked up my phone and dialed Mariah's number. I talked to her about Vegas, that it was 'still on the table' with my father, but he would probably say 'yes'. I also told her I'd call her tonight and for her to call Cassie for me with that news too. I had to go to the store with my dad. A complete lie but it kept me from having to call Cassie who would, no doubt, try to keep me on the phone forever. And I was completely not in the mood for that. Not now, with all of the bullshit going on at my house today. Mariah said no problem, after she let out a groan and we hung up. I sat on my bed thinking about what was happening in my father's office. At least it was his office and not the ballroom where a complete fight would be expected. Hopefully, my father asked Steve too sit in the chair in front of his desk and they were talking it out. Not punching it out. That would be my ideal. I sat in my room, listening to my iPod hooked up to my stand alone speakers. After about ten minutes of this, I heard the main phone line ring. Since I knew Juanita was too damn busy too answer it, I picked it up from my room. Something that I hardly ever did. Of course it was for my father. I asked who was calling, after I told him that 'he was away from his desk for a bit' and asked if I could take a message for him. The guy on the other end replied, 'No problem, Ms. Mahari?' I answered, 'Yes, this is Ms. Mahari. Dominick's daughter. He said, 'Oh. Ok then. Could you please tell your father to call James Shoemaker? Was this guy serious? Then he gave me his number and what city he was calling from. I didn't know whether it was his home or office, but I knew instantly, from the tone of this man's voice that it was business related. And I also did not recognize his voice from Ritual either. So, I then asked what this is regarding. 'What is this? The third degree?' I paused; not saying a word. He sort of laughed and said, 'I'm sorry, Miss Mahari. That was a joke.' He then laughed a completely normal laugh; quite an infectious laugh, actually, and gave me the reason why he was calling. Something about a Doheny doctor's office building that my father was considering purchasing. I answered him with a little bit of amusement in my voice as well. 'Ok, Mr. 'Shoemaker'. I'll give it to him right away' and hung up. After I had written down the message, I heard my father's office door being shut and someone walking away from it. I quickly got off of the bed and went to my door and opened it just a crack. I saw Steve walking very slow down to his room. I actually got to see his face. Not a mark on it, thank God. I walked out of my room and went down one flight of stairs to my dad's office. Since it was an all glass office (four walls of glass) he saw me almost instantly. 'Come in, Gia.' he said. And loud enough for me to hear it too. I walked in, standing directly inside the door and about six feet from his desk. 'Sit down.' I did as I was told and waited until he asked me to 'speak'. When he finished typing, he looked up at me, closed his laptop and addressed me. 'What's going on, baby girl?' I looked down at my lap and said, 'I called Mariah and told her to call Cassie for me. Everything is a 'go' for Vegas, daddy. I just need the 'ok' from you and all of the arrangements, etc. Also, a Mr. Shoemaker called you when you were busy with Steven.' He looked at me, as usual, when I was speaking to him. 'When did Mr. Shoemaker call, Gia?' 'He called when you were, um, punishing Steven in the other room? Remember?' My dad looked at me. 'Of course I remember, love. I'll call him back as soon as we're done here.' 'Ok. I assume you have his number where he is, then? And both of my friends can still go, right?' 'Yes, I have his number and yes, your friends can go, Gia. I shall call my pilot and tell him that he shall be flying too Vegas in a few days. How is that time frame, my Princess? Say... four days?

That is the soonest my Jet will be ready for use. It is getting a make-over. Just a full engine clean and all of that. Nothing 'serious' or anything you would have to worry about.' I looked at him, my hands now squeezing each other incredibly tight. 'Four day's is perfect, daddy! Thank you so much! What bodyguards will have to go with us? Or, rather, me?' I saw my father, after I asked that question, thinking about it for a bit. He had the tip of his pen in the side of his mouth. Well, Steve will not be able to go with you, as you probably guessed. He has to stay with me. I cannot stay at home alone and be without him as my bodyguard, Gia.' 'Oh, I knew that daddy. I was just wondering who would be going, is all.' Secretly, I was hoping that Lane was not going to go. Even though I knew he had a crush on me, I wasn't about to tell my father about that feeling. Just in case I was way off. He looked at me, took the pen out of his mouth and opened up his laptop. 'Probably a few of my top guys as well as Lane.' Inside, I felt bummed. I did not want him to be there! Oh well. Better than not going at all. 'Ok daddy. I'll go upstairs and call Mariah. I'll have her call Cassie. But I'll also be sure to tell Mariah to tell Cassie to 'act appropriately'. I decided that this trip will be her final test for me to decide if she is going to continue to be my friend or not.' He raised his head up after that little statement and smiled one of his 'devious/mischievous' smile's and said 'Good idea, Gia. Very good idea. I'm sure I'll find out when you return how that turned out.' 'Yes, you will, Tata.' I stood up and told him I better get to calling Mariah and start writing down what I need to pack. 'After Ritual tomorrow night, I will tell you what I have decided about your 'Rules' regarding when you and your friends are in Vegas, Alright?' 'Yes, Sir.' I said. 'There is a Ritual tomorrow night, daddy?' I said with hesitancy and a bit of fear in my voice. 'Yes, there is, Gia. And it is a pretty big one, love. It is the Spring Solstice. The Sacrifice has been prepped for a few weeks as well. Don't worry, Gia. I will do my damndest not to have him touch you, as I have said before. I also have told him the same thing in person. Yes?' 'Um, ok, daddy. What did he say once you did tell him that?' My father looked up at me again and told me that Mr. Harris told him to 'fuck off.' 'But we'll see if he truly means that. If he *will* actually act on his sick, perverted actions in regard to you. Yes? I did all I could do to protect you, Gia. We will just have to see if he abides by that or not.' I swallowed quite loud just thinking about that sick, creep's very presence; let alone his face, body, etc. 'Ok, father. I trust you. And if he doesn't abide by your 'wishes/commands, then I will just leave it to you, Tata.' 'Good girl. Now let me get back to work. I also have to make a phone call to The Mirage and arrange the Suite for you three.' He smiled after he said that as I smiled back. I walked up to his chair and gave him a kiss on the cheek. 'Thank you, daddy.' 'Of course, my Princess. Now, go.' I smiled and walked out of his office while closing the door at the same time.

Chapter 14

As I got to my bedroom, I called and told Mariah everything that my father had told me. So, everything was a go! We were so excited that we didn't even care that Cassie had to go. Well, it wasn't that she had to go. We just knew that if she didn't go, we would hear about it, in a whiny, bitchy voice for months afterwards. And she was sooo pathetic! I couldn't even tell you why I had her as a friend. Maybe because she had the best cocaine you could get. And then, when I could get THE BEST out there on the street, she was no longer 'needed' in my life. I know. It sounds totally mean and completely selfish. Maybe that's why I kept her around and was as nice to her as I possibly could be. Without being too obvious, that is. After I took care of the Cassie issue with Mariah and told Mariah that Lane had to go, plus other bodyguards, I hung up the phone and walked into my closet. As I was perusing my clothes and deciding what to take to Vegas, I was also thinking WHAT we were going to do. I decided that I would write down a semi-itinerary list, whether or not we 'followed' it or not. I also wondered if Cassie would visit her boyfriend before we left. He lived in a shack (literally) off of Mulholland Drive. I had been in it once. And only once. He was a dirt-bag loser, in my opinion. But Cassie said she loved him. But ONLY when she was drunk. And I do believe she was an alcoholic as well. Oh well. At least, in Vegas, we could only take cabs around. As I picked out some clothes to wear, I walked back into my room and put them on the bed. Laid out so that I could see them, in full, so that I could choose. I walked back to my jean's shelves, I took out four of my ultimate favorites and put them on my bed, folded up, as well. One last trip to my shoe closet, restroom, and then I would be done. At least with my clothes. As I was looking at my shoes, I was thinking about Ritual tonight. I knew I took a late shower this morning, after breakfast... or did I? Shit. I didn't remember. Oh well. My father would know if I did not, once I was at Ritual, so I better take a quick bath after this. I picked out my shoes that I knew I would be wanting to wear. At clubs, etc. and put them on the floor, below my clothes I had put on my bed. After that I walked to my bathtub and turned on the water, made sure the temperature was just right and walked back to my bed. I slid out my travelling suitcase and started packing. Once I had pretty much finished, I went to my lingerie drawer and took out the necessary panties and garters I would need. I pretty much knew that I wouldn't need many of those but I packed two more extras than I knew I needed and put them in my suitcase as well. I left the top open just in case I thought of something last minute and slid it over in the corner of my bedroom. Next to the head of my bed but in a place I knew would not be in the way. I realized, once I was in my bathroom that my water was at the perfect height and turned off the faucets. I sat on the chaise in the restroom and buzzed my dad. He answered from his office and I asked when or IF dinner was going to be served or if we were going to be eating after Ritual. He answered that there would be no dinner for us. Only Steven and Detail. I thanked him and hung up. As I sank into my hot bath, I could almost feel the tension leaving my body. Hell. I need a bath after Ritual more than I needed it before Ritual, I thought to myself. As I washed my body and hair, shaved my arms and legs, I unplugged the tub and stood up. I grabbed my towels and wrapped my hair and started drying off my body. As I was bent over at the knees, drying my legs, I heard a knock on my bedroom door. I knew it had to be my father so I said come in Tata. I heard the door open and then close with 'his' footstep's walking towards my bed. 'I'll wait, Gia. Take your time.' As I was done drying off, I stepped out of the tub, wrapped up my hair and un-plugged the tub. I sat down at my vanity and un-wrapped my hair towel. With my towel that was wrapped around my body firmly in place, I took out my big-toothed hair comb, unwrapped my hair towel and brushed out my damp hair. As I was looking for my hair vitamin serum, I saw my father's shoes out of my peripheral vision. I grabbed my hair product and sat back up. I looked at my father. 'Hi daddy.' 'Hello, Princess.' As I squirted some serum into the palm of my hand, I put the bottle on my counter and rubbed the lotion-type substance into my hair. I looked at my father as I was doing this from my mirror and smiled at him. He smiled back at me. A side-ways grin basically. That was his normal 'grin' anyway. 'Is there something wrong, Tata?' I asked him. 'No, love. Just enjoy watching you getting ready is all, kitten. Is that a problem for you? Tell me the truth now. Most people get self-conscious.' 'Tata, first, as you know, I am not 'The Norm'. And second? I enjoy having you watch me. What time are the guests arriving?' 'They're not. We have to go to Harris's place. Unfortunately.' 'Oh, joy.' I told him, continuing to get ready. My attitude had completely changed since I was told that bit of information. 'When was that decided, daddy?' 'He called me late this afternoon. Not too long ago. Asking, of course, if he could have it over at his place. AGAIN. I agreed. No harm. He will not be touching you. I can PROMISE you that my love.' 'But what if he wants too, daddy? He ALWAYS does what HE wants to do. The asshole.' My father gave me a look that pretty much said it all. He agreed with my statement but he wasn't thrilled that I called his boss an asshole. 'Let me put it this way, Gia. IF he decides to touch you. Without asking me or 'telling' me, there WOULD be a problem. And, quite an embarrassing one for him, too say the least. So, Gia. I seriously DOUBT he shall touch you.' 'Ok, daddy. You're the boss.' As I continued finishing up with my facial lotion as well as putting the patchouli oil on my body, I was thinking to myself 'what would I do IF he decided to take the 'wrath' from my father and 'have his way with me?' What would I do?' I just thought that my dad would take care of it. With Steve possibly. Who knew? I just had to hope and pray to GOD that he would not take that risk. And, to be perfectly honest, it wouldn't be a 'great' risk to take. To put it mildly. Especially in having to deal with my Tata afterwards. I can't even 'go there' in my mind how mad my father would be. 'Mad' wouldn't, or doesn't, even cover what he would be feeling. After I was finished getting ready for Ritual, my father was still sitting on my chaise in the bathroom. As I walked out of my closet, I walked over to my dresser drawers to get out my white dressing gown/nightgown. 'Father? What is this Ritual for? I always forget. So, I am sorry I keep asking. Or it seems that I always ask. I don't even remember that.' I looked at him and he smiled a bit. 'It is not a High Holiday, kitten. But it is an Initiation Ceremony for a member. The young man that has the longish, brown hair? I believe his name is Lane. He has been with The Brotherhood for around six years to the date, love. So, an initiation ceremony is in order.' I thought about it for a while. Trying to remember who this 'Lane' is and then I remembered who he indeed was. This guy had been flirting with me for months. At least I thought he was. Maybe he was just 'overdoing' it because he wanted a 'good report' from Steven. I wondered, as I brushed my hair and secured it into a bun. I just decided to wait and see how he acted tonight when he saw me. With my father by my side. I was required to give ALL of the Initiation Incantations. So we shall see how he acts this evening, I thought to myself. As I presented myself to my father, he smiled, leaned down to me and took my hand to lead me to my door to go outside to the car. I knew Steve was waiting for us. Instead, on a whim, I suppose (I do not remember), I took his outreached hand and pulled him backwards a little. Alongside me. I let go of his hand and stepped in front of him. I stood on my tip-toes and started kissing him. For some reason, smelling him since he had walked into my room while I was in the bath, I had the incredible urge to kiss him. I did not know why, either. I seriously did not. I continued kissing him. Deeper and more passionately. He was completely taken off guard. I could feel it in his reaction and his expression; though Cassieef. I took both of my hands and put them on both sides of his face, drawing him to me. He paused at first and then started returning the kiss. Once I was kissing him with my tongue, which I only did when we were in bed, he started, after a few minutes, making groaning noises. More like moaning noises. He put his right hand around my waist and took his left down towards my white, ritual gown. He lifted it up a bit with his hand and realized that I wasn't wearing anything underneath. He looked at me, quite surprised. After pulling himself away from me for a bit, he then continued probing inside of me as well as kissing me at the same time. After twenty minutes of this or so, he pulled himself away from me pretty roughly. 'Sorry, kitten.' He said between breaths. We do have to leave now. If we did not have to go anywhere, believe you me, we wouldn’t be going anywhere. Except bed. Yes?' 'I understand, father. I don't know what came over me. I'm sorry.' 'No need for an apology, love. I am not complaining. Let me put it that way. Let's go, shall we?' As we walked down the stairs, I saw Steve sitting on the chaise by the front door. He looked up carefully. His face was pretty messed up. Dang! I forgot that my father pretty much kicked his ass the other night. I didn't know how bad because I hadn't seen him really since it happened. Except a Cassieef, half-way, side glance of him walking down the stairs. He stood up and waited for us to get to the bottom of the stairway. Once we were walking towards him, he opened the door, pushed a button on his keychain to open the locks on the limo doors. He waited for my father to walk through the door and then me. After that he locked up the front door and opened our doors. He then climbed in the driver's seat. I assumed HE was driving because he did not want to face me or my father. Especially with the way he looked. I made a mental note to ask, or if need be, tell him that I wanted to talk to him when we got home this evening. As we made our way down the driveway to the gate, he closed the partition between our section of the backseat and his section. That was weird, I thought. He has never done that before. I knew it wasn't a sort of temper tantrum. Steve never has those. He is WAY too mature to have one of those reactions. My father and I sat in silence. Thinking our own thoughts of what tonight will be, no doubt, as we drove to my favorite douchebag's house. As we sat thinking, I slowly reached over and grabbed his hand and held it for some sort of comfort. He squeezed my hand in return. I barely felt it. As I looked out my window, I knew all that I had to do is get through tonight and then the day after tomorrow, Las Vegas! I couldn't wait! No dad, no Steve, only a few bodyguards. That was IT! Damn, you have *no* idea how special this was for me. I had not been anywhere alone; let alone out of state, without my father and Steven, tons of bodyguards, sometimes switching cars if it was a long trip, as well. This was as close to freedom as I was ever going to get. At least for a long time. And I was going to take advantage of it as much as possible. THAT was for SURE! Without getting in trouble, that is. Before we got to Harris's place, I looked at my father and asked him what job The Organization wanted me to do for them. And when. He looked at me, waiting for my voice to come to a finish. He looked at me and said, 'We will have a complete conversation about your job as soon as we get inside my bedroom, my kitten. Alright my love?' 'Yes, Sir. And thank you.' As we came to a stop, I realized that we had actually reached Harris's place. I let out a deep sigh which my father heard. He looked over at me with a 'curious' look on his face. 'What is wrong, kitten?' 'Nothing out of the ordinary, father. I just HATE coming here, hate him, and hate pretty much everything that he does AND says too you, daddy. I want him so gone out of our lives, Tata!' My father sighed as well, still looking at me and replied, 'Well, unfortunately, that is not going to happen anytime soon, kitten. You know that. I just cannot pull out my piece and blast his head off... even though the thought HAS crossed my mind a few times. I just cannot do it right now, baby. But what I did say last night stays true. He shall not touch you sexually in any way. Understand me, love? Not anymore he won't.' I nodded my head as Steve opened my father's door. He got out and waited for me to get out as well. As I stood by his side in front of Harris's front door, my father knocked and we waited. In seconds, his butler answered and my father didn't even wait for him to speak. He just walked in, bumping him as he did so. I followed since I had no choice. I was holding his arm. The crook of his arm. As if on a 'date.' As we walked towards his 'Ritual Area' of the house, we passed some people that I recognized. They curtsied and bowed, according to their gender, obviously. My father ignored them, as did I. We kept walking to 'The Room'. Once we reached the semi-large Ritual area, we saw that everyone was, for the most part, all there. We, or rather, my father, always liked to arrive later than everyone else. I guess he felt entitled too. I spotted Mr. Harris instantly. He frowned a little. Probably because we arrived late. But I also knew that he wouldn't say a word too my father about it. Everyone became quiet rather suddenly and then Harris clapped his hands and everyone in the room stood up instantly. He decided to open up this evening with a little speech, apparently. 'Well, well, everyone. My regarded, important, flock of followers. That ALL know how important you all are too me.' I rolled my eyes. Hoping that he saw that. I figured he did not, but it felt good to do it anyway. He, of course, continued. 'My second-hand man,

Mr. Dominick Mahari, and his revered, beautiful daughter, Gia, decided to join us this evening. But fifteen minutes late? That is quite rude, don't you think?' He looked around the entire room as if expecting an answer. I looked at my father who was looking directly at Harris. With the most hate I had seen in him, REGARDING Harris, in a long time. No one said a word to that question hanging in the air. All of them looking at each other with complete...what? Fear? Bafflement? Confusion? I knew they had never been asked such a question before by him. Especially regarding the second High Priest in The Brotherhood. AND, with that very person standing in the room WITH them. I felt sweat starting to develop at the roots of my hair. My father let go of my hand, walked forward a bit. Right in front of Harris. They stood about ten feet away. 'I am *SO* sorry, Harris. I was running late at home. Why, you will ask? Because I was and I can. As for my daughter? Maybe I wanted to fuck her first before we came over this evening. You certainly love to do that. Just dive right in and take advantage of her; a High Priest's daughter, who is also a High Priestess, as you well know, Harris. So, my advice to you is, do the damn Ritual and get it over with. Before all of us get food poisoning or something horrid from your shit food!!' Mr. Harris looked as though he was about to have a heart attack. Or a seizure. Or, hopefully, both. Harris kept looking at my father as if he had been punched squarely in the face. In front of his entire 'flock', as he called them. I figured that he was both embarrassed, humiliated, as well as pissed as *all* Hell. He almost did not know what to do. He then turned his gaze away from my father and addressed 'his flock'. 'I guess Mr. Fahari, as well as his pig of a daughter do not know, after all of these years, how to be polite. Of all things! Can you imagine? He must have had a very hard day today. Maybe we should just give him a rest while we take care of the 'Ritual', as he calls it. And we, in turn, can pray to our Great Lucifer for him to get well'. As well as give our Great Lord and Master, the service and devotion he deserves. Am I right, ladies and gentleman?' He received a smattering of applause here and there. They were all still in shock, I assumed. 'And by hearing your clapping to my words, I assume you are all uneasy. Well, I completely understand, my loved and revered ones.' God, what a Douchebag, Fucking Liar!' I said to myself. And, I sure as Hell wanted to say that out loud too him. Especially after what he said about my father and myself! Prick! Mr. Harris walked down off of his platform and walked over to the Altar and stood right in front of it, gave the sign for everyone to take their seat. They all walked over to their 'spot' on the concrete and slowly sat down. I just followed my father. Who walked, albeit slowly, to where he usually sat and sat next to him and his chair. His eyes never leaving Harris as he did so. I noticed that Harris noticed that as well. I also noticed that Harris had, once he noticed that my father was choosing to sit where he normally did (right in front of him), put two big, muscular, 30'ish looking guys, right next to himself. As if that would protect him if my father chose to attack him. Damn, he was an idiot and so in over his head. I sort of laughed softly at that. Out loud. Harris heard my laugh and looked in my direction. Somehow, I managed to gather enough strength, and chose to look right back at him. Challenging him with my eyes. He didn't say a word in regards to me. Thank God, I thought. Harris continued on with his Ritual. 'Now, let us bow our heads in prayer. To the Great Lucifer and thank Him for everything he has done for us and our Congregation! We all did as told. After prayer was over, we all got in position to cast a spell on a deserter (a huge no no) and then Mr. Harris gave us an update on said deserter. As he stood in front of the Altar, he explained, in detail, where the deserter actually was. 'Well, my loved ones. I bet all of you remember our past member, Mr. Smith. And how he so quickly left. And not even saying goodbye!! Can you imagine that? Well, I'm sure you have. Given the two years that he has 'been gone.' Well, my friends. I have some great news for you today.' I watched as Harris lifted his head to the sky and said a silent prayer. As he took his head down to be able to view all of us seated before him, he said, in a much loader voice, 'The man that deserted us. Without so much as a 'good-bye, is here with us now. And we shall deal with his deceit tonight! Now, all of the Priests and Priestesses may go and change for this sacrifice. Mr. and Ms. Mahari, you may get ready *a-l-s-o.*' Yes, he spelled that word out. Just for my father and me. What a complete and total asshole. Plus, I had no idea that we were doing a sacrifice this evening! Normally the person actually doing the sacrifice is called the day before from Harris's home to tell them what they were supposed to do the next night. As everyone separated, I followed my father, taking his arm as he extended it towards me. We walked, through a man-made path that the congregation made for us. Once our door was closed to the 'bedroom' for High Priests and Priestesses, my father walked quickly to the armoire and took out the two black, cowled, Ceremonial robes that we were too be wearing during this sacrifice. 'Father, who is going to be doing the sacrifice? Do you know?' He looked at me as he walked back to me and handed me my robe. 'No, kitten, I do not. I guess whomever Mr. Asshole, Fuck-Face deems 'special' or 'Anointed'. Who the hell knows, my love. If it *is* you, just do it as I have taught you, yes, Gia?' 'Yes, Sir.' I answered. I wasn't afraid of doing the sacrifice. I never was. But I always felt 'sorry' for the poor person that I had to do it too. I shouldn't have to be the 'One Who Decides Who Lives or Dies.' Wasn't that God's decision? I took my robe from my father and started putting it on over my clothes. Just as I was about to put it over my head, I changed my mind and took off my white ceremonial gown first. If I was close, which, chances were, I would be to the 'victim', I did not want to be too messy. As that was completed, I put on the robe. I walked over to the mirror and looked at my hair to make sure it looked presentable. As I sat on the bed and watched my father change, I let my mind wander. I will definitely have to go into Mode when this person was sacrificed. I had seen plenty and done enough for a lifetime. At least in my opinion. In Luciferianism, it was considered an honor to sacrifice someone. Me? I thought; and always considered it, as a punishment. When we were both done with getting dressed, we both walked out of the bedroom door, arm in arm and walked over to the room where this 'deserter' was being kept. As we were walking along the crowded room, I noticed that every single person that was not allowed inside the Sacrificial Room were standing, (more like hovering), around the door to it. Sick, sick, people they are, I thought. But what does that make me? I pondered that for a while until I found myself standing in front of the 'victim'. 'Oh My God', I whispered, 'I'm the one that is supposed to sacrifice this person.' I looked over at my father and he was looking at me. He nodded his head and looked down. I looked before me and saw that this man was strung up by his wrists. His hands had long turned purplish/blue. His eyes were taped open. He couldn't even blink for fuck's sake. I looked as closely as I could to see if he was even conscious. I saw his eyes moving slowly, in horror no doubt, from left to right. He knowing what was going to happen to him. I picked up the Sacrificial Knife that was laying on top of the rectangular table before me; covered in deep purple velvet of course. The color of 'Royalty'. As if we were royal or some shit. At that moment, knife in hand, I knew that everyone in the room was waiting on me. I quickly bowed my head, took a deep breath in and lifted my head high. Upwards towards the ceiling. I let my breath slowly out of my lungs and started reciting the incantation before a sacrifice is supposed to be made. After that was done, I took the sterling silver Chalice, that was also on the table before me, towards the victim. I lifted his left arm to where I could see his wrist and made a slight cut, vertically, and let the blood drain into the cup. As I waited until the Chalice was half full, I looked around me. With my head still down, of course, and saw that everyone in the room had their heads down as well. As the Chalice was filling up, I started to watch it carefully. I quickly looked up at the victim to see if he had even noticed me down in front of him. Or if he even knew what I had just done too him. He was looking right down at me. One tear falling slowly down his cheek. 'Oh. My. God. I couldn't handle this anymore', I thought. I didn't even remember, at that point what he had 'done' to get to this position. Nor did I care. Not anymore. Wait, I thought. 'Was this the man who so-called, 'deserted' The Brotherhood?' I thought, yet again, too myself. I looked down at the cup again and saw that it was filled just above the half-way point. I reached quickly behind me to grab a scarf, took his wrist and wrapped the scarf around the deep cut. I put the chalice down on the table which was now behind me. After tying off the scarf, I walked back to the table, wiped off the knife with a purple towel and set it down in its box. I picked up the Chalice and walked around to pass the cup to every person in the room. To me, this was the gross part. The first person I came too was my father. I handed him the Chalice, he took a sip of the man's blood and started handing down the Chalice towards his right. I walked back to the small table and picked up the knife. I walked towards the man, while chanting an incantation, and finally it seemed, I stood before him. I said the last part of my 'prayer' in a much louder voice as I shoved the long knife deep inside his belly. I twisted the knife, all the while looking into the man's eyes. He closed them just as the knife went into him. Somehow, he pulled the last amount of strength that he had to raise his head to the sky; eyes still shut. After I had twisted the blade inside of him I pulled it upwards. Towards the top of his ribcage. He finally bled out as his head flopped downwards; chin resting on his sternum. After the deed was done, I walked carefully, hoping not to slip on the buckets, it seemed, of blood all around me back to the table. I took the Chalice, which was to my right, picked it up, took a sip and set it down. I turned my head, knowing that everyone's head was still bowed in prayer and spit the blood into the purple towel. I had always done that when I had to sacrifice someone and take a sip of their blood. GROSS! I would never, in a million years, drink anyone's blood. Period. As usual, no one saw me. I said my closing incantation and as I was finished, cleaned and put the dagger away as well as cleaned out the chalice. As I was finished, I walked to the left of my father and took his hand. We all prayed together and then left the room, one by one, and shut the door. When my father, Steven and myself got home for the evening, my dad and I instantly started walking upstairs to go and shower or bathe off the blood from our 'lovely' evening. As we both reached the top of the stairs, my dad grabbed my arm and said, 'Shower with me, Gia.' I decided that regardless of what happened inside his bathroom, I needed to be with someone. Especially after tonight. And since he was the only one whom I trusted, I obliged by the nodding of my head. I followed him into his room and then walked into his restroom. I stood there while taking off my clothes. My dad walked in a minute or so behind me. As I was getting undressed, my dad opened the all glass shower and turned on the water. As he started to get undressed as well, I dropped my Ritual gown on the floor. As I was completely naked, I bent down to pick it up to inspect it for any blood. I hoped that I didn't find any. I loved that 'nightgown'. As I slowly turned it over in my hands, I noticed that my dad was standing there, in front of the running water of the shower, waiting for me. I hadn't, so far, noticed a drop of blood on my sleeping/Ritual gown so I dropped it on the floor again and looked at him. I saw in his eyes a look that, I think said, 'I believe my 'baby' is a bit traumatized.' I walked slowly towards him and waited to see who he wanted to get in the shower first. I stopped just beside him and he raised his left arm up as if to say, 'After you.' I stepped in and let the warm water run all over my hair, body, everything. I heard, as well as felt, my father step into the shower along side of me. Since it was a double-headed shower. Meaning a double-nozzle shower, he walked to the other side of the shower and began to wash his body as well. I took my shampoo and started washing my hair and then rinsed it out. As my conditioner was setting in my hair for five minutes (I knew it was time for me to deep condition it), I glanced over at my father and saw that he was looking into his shower-mirror and shaving. I let my eyes travel downwards. Damn, his body was perfect. I didn't know how he did it! The man had the body of someone half his age. Which, now that I was thinking about it, Steve really pushed him hard when they did their workouts. I looked at the clock that was hanging above the mirror and saw that it was time to rinse out my conditioner. I stepped underneath my shower-head and rinsed my hair out. When it was all rinsed and clean, I squeezed all of the excess water out and twirled my hair into one long rope-type strand and tucked it underneath the rest of my hair on the crown of my head. As I took my razor out of its holder, I took my bar of soap and lathered under my arms and started shaving. When I was done with my arms and my legs, I finally felt tired. I guess all of the night's activities wore me out. Plus the anxiety I felt and what I ‘had to do' this evening took a lot out of me, I guess. I turned off my nozzle and grabbed my towels that were hanging over the side of my end of the shower and wrapped up my hair. I took the other one and started too dry off my body. Just as I started to do that, I felt my father's body pressed up against mine. He was massaging my shoulders. It felt so damn good that I just stopped what I was doing and let my towel fall to the floor of the shower and closed my eyes. As he started rubbing out all of the tension out of my upper back, I let out a moan of pleasure and my head went back; eyes still closed. I felt my dad walk directly in front of me and then started to kiss me. I instantly started kissing him back. It was A lot better than remembering what happened tonight. That was for fucking sure. As we stood in the shower, kissing and rubbing each other's bodies, there was a slight knock on my father's bedroom door. 'Fuck!' He said. And quite loud, too. 'What is it?' he asked out loud. It was Steve. 'Sorry, sir. Just wanted to know if you had seen Gia. But, I guess you HAVE. Never mind. Have a wonderful night, *SIR*.' 'Oh damn.' I said to myself. 'Not now, Steve!' I thought that this 'whole issue' regarding that had been resolved. Apparently not. My father was looking at his bedroom door as if wondering if he should go out there and 'handle it'. He decided against it, thank God. I did not want Steven to get his ass beat again over this. I will have to talk to him tomorrow about it. Face to face. My father opened his shower doors and we walked out. As we stood there, I realized that I had nothing to wear to bed. As I was pondering that, my father picked me up and carried me too his bed. 'What were you 'pondering' just now, my kitten?' I grinned and replied, 'what I was going to wear too bed, Tata.' 'He laughed and said, 'and why would you need something to wear to bed, hmm?' 'Well, now that I think about it, nothing, I suppose.' He smiled and laid me down, my head on the pillow. As he laid beside me, I wondered what this ensuing conversation was going to be about this time? 'I wanted to ask you a couple of questions regarding this evening, Gia. Just a few. Alright?' 'Like I had any choice in the matter', I thought to myself. 'That's fine, daddy.' He glued his eyes too mine and began. 'How did you feel, this evening, when you made your first 'Official' sacrifice to Our Lord Lucifer? In front of the entire congregation, that is.' I laid there, on my side facing him, and replied, 'Honestly, father? I felt so many emotions. One being, well, scared.' That word, 'scared' actually surprised him. He looked at me with complete surprise on his face. 'Scared? Why on earth would *you* feel scared, Gia? You have been prepped and primed for this. For years. And it hasn't been the first time that you have culled before, my love.' 'I wasn't necessarily scared because I actually had to 'kill' someone, father. I felt scared because I wondered...what God would think of me.' As I said that bit of news, my head was down. I just couldn't look into his eyes when I said that to him. Now he really looked surprised. His eyes were as wide as saucers as well as disbelief. 'Because of what God would think? Of you, Gia? That is absurd, my love. God has killed many, many people. Believe you me. And, as you know, you do not pray to God.' (If only HE knew) 'God, since you were a little girl, is not your Lord and Master. Lucifer is.' This time, I was looking at him square in the eyes. 'Yes, father, but that choice was made for me. To pray too Lucifer and to be a Luciferian. I did not make that choice myself. And I am afraid that He will send me too Hell, Tata. And I do not want to go to Hell! I am scared of it. I truly am, daddy! And didn't your father choose for you as well, Tata?' He was looking at me with multiple expressions. Almost, it seemed, all at once. I had never, in my entire, young, life, seen this look on his face before. 'Let me tell you something, Princess. You have nothing to be scared about. I'm here. Plus, when I am gone, you shall be well taken care of. And be a lot older so you will make the correct decisions as time passes, I am sure.' 'Ok, Tata. I believe you. I always believe you.' I decided to end that conversation as soon as it started so I did not have to lie to him anymore about that subject. The subject of my religion, now. As he got more comfortable, he realized that he was 'hot' or 'warm'. I don't remember the exact word he used. He got out of bed, opened his Westward facing window wider, and climbed back into bed, facing me again. When he was back, comfortable, in his position, again, I brought up the question of what was my job for The Organization. He looked at me and thought, probably, how he was going to tell me. 'Ok Gia. Well, you will be flying closer; a lot closer, actually, than last time. You will be flying to New York. A certain Congressman is staying there. For business and, later, for pleasure. Unfortunately, he won't make the 'Pleasure' part. You only have to pack one pair of shoes, socks, panties, and just wear one of your track suits. The same one to and from New York. As well, obviously, as pack your sniper. Yes? Anymore questions for me, baby?' 'No, Sir. I think that about covers it, Tata.' As he slowly pulled only the sheet over our bodies, he started kissing me, pulling back, kissing me again and pulling back again. This was odd. And very frustrating to me. He would start kissing me hard and deep. His normal, 'I'm going to have sex with you now' type of kissing but then he would pull back and lay back on his back. Was this a test? Did he want me to start this? It would be a rarity, but as he was kissing me for a bit and stopping, it made me extremely frustrated and excited as well. I rolled onto my left side and looked at him. He was now 'checking out his nail's? What the Hell? I tapped him on the shoulder, thinking, 'he started this. He is going to finish it.' He looked at me in a very nonchalant way and asked, 'what's wrong, Gia?' 'Seriously Dad? *Seriously*?' He laughed a semi-laugh. But for him, that was a laugh. He rolled me onto my back and did what he was supposed to do. And, very well, I might add.

Chapter 15

As we finished, I was drenched in sweat and I know my dad had to be. Which, for some reason, brought up another topic in my head. Therapy. I looked over at my father who was just about to get out of bed and clean up in his bathroom. 'Daddy?' I asked hesitantly. 'Yes, Gia?' he replied, absentmindedly. 'Can we please talk about something important when you get back to bed?' He turned on the faucet in the restroom. 'Yes, Gia. What about? I'm exhausted.' I looked down at my hands as I answered. 'It won't or doesn't have too last that long, father. Not tonight, anyway.' 'Then, I have zero problem, Gia, with talking with you about 'your' something.' He looked at me through his bathroom mirror and grinned. 'I also have to tell you about something that 'We' need you to do, yes?' I looked straight at him. 'Of course, father. Whatever you want.' Oh God! What now? And it is probably for Harris. Definitely for The Brotherhood, no doubt.' I thought. As he climbed in bed with me after he was finished, he turned on his side to look at me. I sat up, legs to my side so that I could look at him, too. 'Shoot, kitten.' I took a silent, deep, breath and began. 'Father, I really think we... or I, should see a therapist. Regarding... you know what.' He looked at me with an expression that said, 'Oh God. Now? Really?' But, I couldn't be sure. Hell. For all I knew, he felt the same way too. He HAD to. Didn't he? 'Gia. I told you, there are no therapists, Psychologists, or Psychiatrists in The Brotherhood or Organization. I doubt there ever will be, actually.' I nodded, though slowly. 'Besides, love. Can you imagine what they would say when they heard all that we do? Not just the Organization But us? As father and daughter, so to speak?' 'But dad! That is the whole point! We shouldn't be doing half of what we do, anyway. You know that. Don't you feel just a little bit guilty for what we do? Together?' I looked at him intently as I asked or said my entire 'speech' too him. He looked at me, in the eyes, as normal and was thinking. About what, I do not know. And never will know, I guess. 'Gia. I completely enjoy what we do together. Yes, I do know that it is 'wrong'. By society's standards, anyway. But no one tells me how to live my life. Nor should they tell you how you should live your life. Ever…until you reach the age of eighteen, that is. Do you understand what I am saying, love?' 'Yes, I completely understand what you are saying, daddy. Absolutely. But, like I had mentioned before, what if I wanted to get married some day? What if I meet the man that I do want to marry? What do we do then?' My father looked at me as if that scenario was the worst scenario he could *ever* imagine. 'Then we shall talk and deal with that when and if we come to it. How does that sound?' I thought about what he had said and decided that 'IT' was never going to change. At least for now. I felt that I would cross that Cassiedge when I came to it. When I was older, working 'out in the field' and out of my father's home, in one of his offices or whatever. Now was not the time. It wasn't going to happen anytime soon. He made that abundantly clear. 'Ok, father.' I replied. I tried to sound as positive and normal as I could. Vegas was in two days so at least I had that to look forward to. Not that 'THIS' was 'horrible' for me. I just knew it was wrong and the sooner I stopped it, the sooner I would get used to it, healed and normal. At least in the sense that I wasn't sleeping/having sex with my father. 'Ok, then. Now, my Princess. This is what I need from you. Remember every year that I go 'on a trip to Northern California? In the summer, in July?' 'Yes, daddy.' 'Well, I'd like you to go with me this year. When you return from Vegas after your birthday. How would you like that?' 'What or where, actually, are we going? And why?' I asked him. Some hesitancy in my voice. My father looked carefully down at his hands and quickly looked to his left. Bad sign. He was lying to me and he knew, I knew it. 'Well, Gia. It is not my choice. I would rather you did not go, actually.' 'Why?' I asked with trepidation. 'Gia, baby. It is Harris's fucking idea that you go, alright? I cannot lie to you. And, you know that. Yes?' 'I know, daddy.' 'Alright then. This is what you're supposed to do there. And believe me, Gia. If I could stop it, I would. You do know this, right?' I looked at him. This time with fear in me. In every part of me. For my father to be acting and talking like THIS; with fear or doubt/regret in his voice? I was very fucking scared. 'Well, I don't know exactly what it is that he wants me to do. But, knowing that asshole, it is not going to be pleasant. What is it?' My dad looked at me with complete disgust. 'Oh Shit', I thought. 'All of the men that belong in the Organization go to this place. Every year. It is called The Bohemian Grove. It is in Sonoma County. 'Obviously you know that is in Northern California. It sits on around 3-5 thousand acres. No one, who is not a member, knows for sure. Anyhow, security is very, very tight because of the people that do go there, as *you* know. Harris told me that you were going this year to 'service' all of the member's that go to this place. But, there is one saving grace for you. Some of these 'men', that are in the Organization like little boys; the sick fucker's. So, obviously, they will not be asking for you. The worst part is, that according to Harris, 'You are to do *anything* that they ask you to do. And, yes, my love. That is verbatim. Coming from his mouth.' It took me quite a while to even process this information. F-u-c-k. Vegas, and then Hell? Oh, Lucky me! And even my father couldn't do anything about this, either. Shit. Mode 24/7 it will have to be. 'Father. I know, obviously, that you cannot do anything about this. So, all I can say is, 'Ok.' He looked at me as he was caressing my face. As he was doing this, one tear started falling from his left eye. Then he pulled me towards him and held me, rubbing my back at the same time. He buried his head into my shoulder and started really crying. This was 100% the first time, in my entire life that my father had ever cried this hard in front of me. Let alone in my arms. I, this time, rubbed *his* back as I told him it would be 'ok', that I would 'get through it' and 'I would be ok'. 'That *I* was always ok.' 'Shit, Gia. If there was anything I could do! For fuck's sake! I cannot do anything about it! Fuck!' He shouted that. I kept rubbing his back and that seemed too make him cry harder. 'God, if anything happened to you, I would die, Gia.' 'Daddy, nothing will happen to me. I promise, ok? I promise. I will just go into Mode. Ok?' He lifted up his head, face entirely wet, reached over and grabbed tissues from a box on his bedside table. After he cleaned up his face, blew his nose, etc. as well as tried to collect himself, he said, 'Gia, it's really not the other Organization members that I am worried about. It is Harris, my dear. He will try and hurt you physically and mentally in *every* way possible. If it comes to that, I will get involved. You understand that, baby?' 'Yes, I do, father. Of course I do. You always have and I love you for that. Very much, lover.' That word completely caught him off guard. As it did me also. Hell, lover? Shit. Oh well. I did mean it. I mean, he was my current lover, right? I exited those thoughts and turned my complete attention to him again. As he had cleaned up his tears and face, he got up off of the bed and walked into his restroom again. He turned on his faucet, grabbed a washcloth and washed his face. As he dried himself off he threw the towel into his hamper and walked towards the bed again. As he got himself comfortable he rolled onto his right side and settled onto his pillow. Getting ready for 'sleep' mode. I scooted down deep into the covers and scooted back towards him where he could put his protective arm around my waist.

As the bedside alarm went off, I got out of bed, in an extra good mood than normal. I knew that this was my last day of school before my Las Vegas trip. I was semi-packed; knowing that when I got back from school I would finish packing and finish any homework that was going to be due when I got back to school on Monday. Then I was supposed to leave on Friday afternoon, and go to the Bohemian Grove for a weekend of Hell. Nice. A wonderful little trade-off. Harris probably knew that I was going to be going to Vegas for my birthday to have complete fun. So that's why he made sure that I was going to be going to The Grove to please these sick, perverted men. Afterwards. I just decided not to think about it as I was washing my hair and body in the shower. As I was finished and wrapped up in my towels, I sat down and toweled my hair dry and then combed my hair out straight down my back. I reached underneath my chair and into my drawers, grabbed my hair serum and rubbed it through my damp hair. I then proceeded to put my make-up on. I wondered, since I forgot to ask him, if my father was going to be there. At The Grove that is. I hope to God he was. At least I would have someone there whom would keep track of all the goings on there. With me at least. When I finished with my make-up and hair, I walked into my closet and walked up and down my aisles of clothes and shoes. I chose on a Celine™ top and Dolce™ Jeans. Dolce™ wasn't yet known for their jeans but they felt so good on my body I always wore them whenever I could. As long as if it wasn't two days in a row, that is. I grabbed my choices, I walked back to my bed and got dressed. After dressing, I walked faster to my closet and grabbed my Celine™ handbag and sat on my bed, switching out my purses. When I was done doing that, I was wondering what shoes to wear. Since I was mixing Dolce™ and Celine, I decided to wear Celine™ booties. Black, since that color goes with anything. Plus, I could wear bootie-socks with them. VERY comfortable. Plus, the heels weren't too high. They were a four inch stacked heel. I grabbed my Celine™ handbag and out the door I went, closing it behind me. As I was walking down the stairs, I heard my father's voice talking to Steven. Probably, from the direction the voices were coming from, the breakfast table/nook. As I hit the bottom of the stairs, I walked over to the breakfast table; which is exactly where they were sitting. As I sat down, their conversation stopped and as I put my napkin in my lap, Steven asked me 'How my sleep was.' 'Very good, Steven. How was yours?' 'Great. Went to sleep as soon as I put my head on the pillow.' 'Great.' I answered him. I did not know if he had any sarcasm in his voice or not. Nor did I care. IF he did, it was on him and he knew what that would entail. As I started to eat my eggs and bacon, I looked at my father. He looked like he was deep inside his paper. But, I knew better. He was reading but he was also listening to everything we were saying as well. 'Who is driving me to school, Tata?' I asked. He looked up from his paper and replied, 'Steven is, Gia. Lane is doing a job for me this morning, actually.' 'Oh. Good. Lane bugs me anyway, daddy.' He looked up again and asked, looking me directly in the eye, as was Steven, how does he bug you, babe?' I thought about my answer for a bit and decided with just telling them the truth. 'He just looks at me funny most of the time. Like he is undressing me or something. I know that sounds cliché but, I think he likes me; in a way that he shouldn't.' My father looked at Steven quickly and then turned towards me again. 'Is this your *true* feeling or gut feeling, Gia? Because, if it is either, I will put a stop to it. Instantly.' 'I know you would, daddy. It would make me feel more comfortable. But I just don't want him to get in trouble is all.' 'And why is that, Gia? He knows better than that. And if he is making you feel uncomfortable, God knows whom he has told about this 'lusting' after you to other employees of mine. That is unacceptable, as I'm sure you know already. I'll handle it. In the meantime, I will have Steven drive you and be your main bodyguard as long as he is not traveling with me. In the meantime, I'll have to think about who will replace Lane as your main bodyguard. I need to be able to trust him. Steven?' Steve looked up from his coffee and replied, 'Yes, sir?' 'I would like to have a small meeting with you, after work this afternoon or early evening and have you Cassieng me some files on the other 'Detail' employees as well. I would like your suggestions as to whom you would also suggest for this job. As if Gia was your *own* daughter. Have a problem with that? Have any plans or anything of that sort?' 'No Sir'. He replied. 'I will grab some potential folders when I do get home from your office. I'll Cassieng them to...where? The conference room? The dinner table? Or where would you like to have this 'meeting', Sir?' 'I would prefer it in my room. With the door closed and locked.' 'You got it, Dominick.' 'Good.' My father looked at me and told me that, as of today, Lane was no longer my personal bodyguard. 'Awesome' I told him. 'Thank you, daddy. Thank you too, Steven.' They both said, 'No problem' and proceeded to finish their coffee. As I finished my breakfast, my father as well as Steven, had already finished their meal. Steve got up and told me he would meet me on the chaise by the door. Our normal 'meeting spot' for going to school. I also found out, from my dad, that he was riding with me to school and then he was going off to work. My father also got up from the table, gave me a kiss on my forehead and went to the chaise as well. With his Cassieefcase, of course. As always. When I finished my coffee, I got up, put my napkin on my plate and slid it next to my dad and Steven's plate's. I picked up my purse and walked over to the chaise. Steven got up and opened the front door. The limo was running, waiting for us. Steve opened the front door for us, walked to the car, opened our door and waited until we got in and then got into the driver's seat. As my father and I got comfortable, I asked him why Steve was driving. 'Because I asked him to, kitten' was his response. 'Weird, I thought.' 'Oh, ok. Why though?'

He looked at me, a little irritated. 'Do I need to give you an explanation, Gia?' 'No, of course not. It's just out of the ordinary is all. Geez, dad. Chill.' I felt his hand around my upper-arm instantly. And he was squeezing it tight as Fuck! 'Dad! That hurts!' 'Good, Gia! That was my intention. Never tell me too 'Chill.' Got that? Do not treat me like your little, stupid, followers at school. *Never* do that. Got it?' 'Yes, Sir.' I replied. Swallowing as I said the last word. 'GOOD.' He released my arm and looked out the window. 'Gia, listen to me' with anger still in his voice. 'When or how I do things, is sometimes, none of your business. Understand?' 'Yes, Sir.' 'I have reasons. Tons of reasons on why I do things. And some of them you would not understand. And some, of course, you would. Right now, you would not. Let's leave it at that, alright?' 'Ok, daddy.' As we were 'done' with our 'little' argument, Steven had pulled up to my school. Oblivious to what was said behind the closed partition. 'When you get home from school this afternoon, I will talk to you more about this Hellish trip to The Grove. Yes?' 'Ok, Tata. Will you be going?' I asked hesitantly. 'Yes, I will. I have to.' 'As I grabbed my tote-bag for all of my books and binder, I said to him, 'I would think you would also want to go because of what Harris might do to me.' He looked at me with complete surprise. As if I would even question that. 'Of course, Gia. That is the main reason why I am going. I do not go every year because of what *does* go on there. See you when you get home from school. Or, soon after. If I am not home when you are, call me and I shall leave as soon as possible. I have some things to go over with you regarding Vegas and your 'trip' to The Grove.' 'Ok daddy. I will be home at around the same time. Well, whenever Steven picks me up.' 'Alright, Gia. He'll be on time. Don't you worry about that.' 'Ok, father. See you then, Steve-o.' Steve looked over at me, smiled and gave me the thumbs up sign. I leaned in the window, turned my head over my shoulder to see if any kids were looking at me (none were...at least not now) and I kissed my father square on the lips. As I walked off, I looked after the car as it pulled away from the curb and school (thank God) and walked towards my first period. P.E. As I was dressed into my uniform and sitting on the bench, waiting for our P.E. teacher, I was looking around for Cassie. No sign of the bitch. Weird. Maybe, and this would be just like her, she took the day off just to go shopping for Vegas. And to pack, etc. That would be just like her. Mariah didn't have this class as a first period. Unfortunately for me. The only friend that I could actually talk to. Especially about our trip. Without interruptions, like Cassie would do; for example: 'How are we going to score coke?' or 'Are you going to Cassieng it, Gia?' Shit like that. Crap that I did not want to talk about. Especially at school. She is so damn stupid 80% of the damn time. In fact, I didn't even know why I was Cassienging her. Oh well. What's done is done, I thought. Next thing I knew, our teacher was standing in front of us, telling us that today we were going to be playing Volleyball. Great, I thought. Sweat and make-up issues. Oh well, Vegas tomorrow, so who cares? I will fix my face once I get back into the bathrooms/locker room. As we all slowly got up from the bench, I walked towards the volleyball net. I looked at the girls and decided that I wanted to be on the other side's team instead. As I walked towards them, the teacher said, 'Mahari? Stay where you are. You do not need to be on the other side of the net.' As I stared at her, I heard the other people where I was heading to let out a sigh of 'disagreement' and on 'my' side of the net, a sigh of 'Thank God, we may win THIS time.' As I took my place on my side of the net, the server on the other side, served the ball. Apparently, she had an 'issue;' with me because the ball came directly at me. Or, I should say, my face. All I could think of in that split second was my new nose which was done about six months ago. As I volleyed that ball back over the net, I was thinking that that chick was going for my nose, the bitch. She knew that I just had my nose done. Plus, not making any matters better, I had dated her boyfriend just after she broke up with him. One day later, to be exact. But not for 'romantic' reason's'. Hell no. He was the Principal's son and I didn't want to get after school suspension for all of the notes that I wrote, excusing me from school. When, actually, I was shopping on Rodeo Dr. with my friends. Dating him enabled me to 'meet' our Principal at his home, eat dinner there many times and not having to spend time after school. Hence, I got to graduate. Perfect, actually. As soon as I graduated, I broke up with him. We never had sex, my father knew why I was 'dating' him, and everything turned out perfect. After we completed five volleyball games, the P.E. teacher blew her whistle and off we went to the showers. As I grabbed my towel out of my gym bag, I walked over to 'my' shower that I always used. I noticed a few weeks ago that after I had used this particular shower, no one even dared use it. Hmmm. I kind of knew how my father felt. As far as 'power' went. It was an awesome feeling. I hoped that I inherited my father's company when he was gone (God? Please do not let that happen any time soon. Please?') I know. I am sure you noticed me pray to God when I did pray. Which, you're probably asking, 'Why would she be praying to God when she 'is a Satanist'? Or a 'Luciferian'? Well, I have always, when I do pray, pray to God. Why? I still do not know. I would just have to say that if you are a true Luciferian, you have to know 'The Other Side' of the story as well. And, when I learned that, He just seemed like a very gentle man. A forgiving man. Jesus that is. My father, of course, does *not* know this. If he did, you can imagine what he would do too me. As I was showering, one of the girls that was playing on the other team (a girl I did not know, really) walked up to me. 'You play damn good volleyball. What is your name, by the way?' I looked over at her and told her my name. 'You should try out for the Junior Varsity team. You'd probably make it, too. Just letting you know.' 'What's your name?' I asked her. 'Jocelyn.' She replied. 'Well, that would be awesome as well as fun, but I am only a sophomore. So, no Varsity for me. 'Really? I thought you were at least a junior. Too bad. Think about it next year, ok?' 'Sure will. Thank you.' She walked away, throwing over her shoulder, 'No problem.' As I finished soaping my body and rinsing off, I turned the water off. I grabbed my towel, wrapped it around my body and went over to my locker. I sat down with my gym bag and proceeded to dry off and get dressed. As I was finished I shoved my gym bag into my locker, spun the combo lock, grabbed my handbag and walked out of the gym. As I was heading towards my next class, I looked at my watch. Damn! I had at least 20 minutes until my class. I looked for one of the stone benches that were strewn all over the campus of my high school and sat down. I opened my purse, took out my make-up bag and my cell-phone and proceeded to fix my hair as well as my make-up. As I was about to brush my hair and put it in a scrunchy, I called Cassie to see what the Hell she was doing. She answered her cell on the second ring. 'Hey, chicky! What is up at lovely school?' 'Oh, it's lovely alright. Why the Hell are you at home, anyway?' 'Oh, I *had* to do some last minute shopping for our trip this weekend. So, I had the maid drive me and made sure she did not tell my dad. He would be so pissed!' 'He does know that you *are* going, right?' 'Of course he does, babes.' 'Good. Because my dad might call him tonight to make sure I am telling the truth that you are telling the truth' (A total lie, but I wanted to make sure she was not lying to me). 'No problem, Gia. He knows and he is letting me. Thank God! I would so die if he didn't let me. So Die!' Damn, she was dramatic. I looked at my watch and decided I better get going. I looked one more time in the mirror, closed it and put it back in my purse. 'Well, I better go. I have the rest of the lovely day to finish before I get picked up.' 'Ok, hon. Talk to you tomorrow! I so can't *wait*!' 'I know. Neither can I.' We said our goodbyes and I continued to my next class.

Before I knew it I was walking towards my school locker to get my book-bag and purse so I could go and wait for Steven to pick me up. I stood at my pick up spot and waited. I didn't have to wait long. Steve pulled up about five minutes after I got there. As I opened the door to his car, a BMW 740i, a Hell of a lot better than a fucking Limo, for God's sake! 'How was your last day until 'Gia's few days of fun' in Vegas?' he asked as soon as I got in the passenger seat. I looked at him like what he just said was the dumbest thing anyone had ever said to me. 'Fine, Steve-o. How was yours? And why are you so chipper today, anyway? I thought you didn't want to go?' 'I thought about it and I decided that it wasn't that bad, babe.' I gave him a smirk. 'My dad gave you a 'talk', didn't he?' As I asked him this question, I knew he could lie or not. Depended on his mood. Or, if I decided to tell my father or not. 'He sure did, Gia, the *all-knowing* One. Geez, man. Give me a break. I have to baby-sit a bunch of girls in Vegas! A man's playground for fuck's sake! How much fun would you have if you were me?' He had a point. But, it couldn't be that bad. After we went to bed, and we had to go to sleep at some point. My father made that very clear. Anyway, after we all went to sleep for the night, Steven could go down to the casino and play Poker or Roulette; something. He would find something fun to do. Besides, the salary HE was getting paid, anyone would find a way to have fun! Hell, he made a ton of money. He had no reason to bitch. As we rode home in complete silence, I asked 'Steve-o?' 'Yes, Gia?' 'Why did you give my dad such a hard time the other night?' Steve looked at me with a look that, to me, said, 'How do I answer this one?' 'Gia, I brought it up because I think it is wrong that he is making you do that with him. Shit, babe. Come on. You should be dating for fuck's sake. Guys your own age. You know that. Aside from your religion, you should be dating. And, I personally think that you are too young to be having sex, anyway. 'Steve, I am almost 16 years old. I know that practically all of my friends, who are the same age as I am, have already had sex.' 'But do they have sex with their *dad*?' After that statement, he looked at me as if I was completely insane. 'I have no idea, Steven! That is something no one asks their friends. It's none of my business!' 'Well, let me tell you something, Gia. They do *NOT*, ok? It is not, in any way 'normal' to have sex with your father. Hell, babe! He could go to prison for that shit! It is wrong! And I am surprised that you did not know that.' I sat there as he pulled up to the gate keypad. 'It's not normal.' Well, Hell! I knew that! What did he think? That I was a complete idiot? As Steve punched in the numbers on the keypad and opened the gate to the house, I spoke again. 'Steve? Can I tell you something? My dad already knows. I think.' 'Sure. Shoot, babe.' 'I think... or, rather, know, that I am in love with him. As in love with him.' Steven braked the car so hard that it threw me into the seatbelt to where it locked up. 'Damn, Steven! Could you please tell me when you are going to break so damn hard? What were you going to hit, anyway?' 'Gia! I wasn't going to hit anything! Damn! You're in love with him? Fuck me!!!!! As you know, He Is Your Father!' Steve turned back towards the steering wheel and continued to look straight ahead of him. But, we were still not moving. 'I know he is my father, Steve! I have had this conversation with him and I told him that we needed therapy. Or, at least, I do! I am not crazy for God's sake!' 'Dominick? Going to therapy? That would be the day. Gia, Dominick, your dad, will *never* go too therapy for 'having sex' with his underage daughter! A therapist/Psychologist or a Psychiatrist is bound by law to call the police if *any* of their patient's admit to any criminal activity! And this is exactly that!' I thought about that little bit of information and took it in. 'Well, I will tell my dad that, Steven. Just promise me that, at least for right now, you won't treat him with any disrespect? He is just as confused as I am. And you have known him long enough to know that he would never show that part of him too you. Do you promise me? At least until I talk to him?' He looked at me as I was telling/asking him this and waited, patiently, until I was finished. 'Yes, Gia. I will. Just, please, let me know what is going on after you talk to him? For me?' 'Yes, of course I will', I replied. He nodded his head and continued driving towards the house. As he parked and I got out of the car and inside the front door, I went right to my room and sat on my bed. I knew I needed to start packing for Vegas but decided to do that after dinner. I just sat on my bed, thinking about Vegas and what fun things we were all going to do there. I couldn't wait. I really needed a 'girl vacation'. Badly. Time for me to let loose and try to forget who my father was, just go dancing, and have f-u-n; without worrying about a thing. After it seemed like 10 minutes of sitting on my bed thinking, Juanita buzzed my intercom and said that dinner was ready. That made me jump a little. I looked at my watch. I realized that I had been sitting on my bed for about an hour and a half. Damn! I thought. Time flies when your life is full of freakish bullshit. Then I realized that I did not call my father when I got home. Like I promised I would. I got up, walked to my door and slowly walked down the stairs. I started hearing my father's voice. I didn't even hear him come home. That was a first. I always looked forward to my dad coming home from work. As I landed at the bottom of the stairs, I turned towards the dining room and walked too my chair. 'Hi daddy.' I said. 'Hello, my kitten. I thought you were asleep it was so quiet up there.' 'I looked at him and replied, 'Nope. Just thinking daddy.' He looked at me a little weird and then down at his place setting. 'I see.' I took a quick glance at Steven. He was just looking down at his place setting as well. But, shaking his head as he did it. Fucker! He just did not understand! Of course, who would? 'How was work, Tata?' Juanita had walked in and sat our plates in front of us. 'Work was normal, love. Nothing too exciting. Why didn't you call me when you got home?' I looked at Steve again. Again he shook his head. Ok. This has *got* to stop from him! Every time my father called me 'love', 'kitten', or whatever pet name he had for me, he had to stop shaking his head. If my father caught him doing that, he would get in big, fucking trouble again. 'I am sorry father. I really am. I remembered when I did hear your car pull in the driveway. I was thinking on what too pack is all.' He kind of laughed at that. 'Well, it actually worked for the best. I had a last minute board meeting so I wouldn't have been able to leave early anyway.' 'That's ok, Tata. Plus, I still didn't pack. All I did was look around at everything and think about what I was going to pack.' He sort of laughed at that. 'What are your plans tonight before your Vegas flight tomorrow?' I looked at him as I swallowed a mouthful of food. 'Well, actually pack this time. That's about it; other than taking a shower. After dinner I'll go ahead and pack. It won't take me long.' He picked up his glass of wine, took a sip and put it back down. 'That is good news, Kitten' he replied as he looked at me for longer than normal. I instantly got the message. As did Steven. He wanted me to sleep with him tonight. And Steve knew it now, too. I didn't fucking care. I was mad at Steve right now. I smiled at my dad and said, looking him straight in the eyes and replied, a little louder than normal, 'I will be right over when I'm done. I still need to bathe before I go to bed though.' He nodded his head. 'That should be no problem, love.' He then turned his attention to Steve and started talking to him. 'Are the dogs ready to be secured in their new kennel for tomorrow?' Steven looked up from his plate and looked at my father. 'Yes, Sir. They are *all* ready' and instantly resumed eating again. My father immediately recognized the change of tone in his voice, but ignored it, thank God. Hopefully he was going to give him some time to get used to how it was going to be between him and I. Hopefully, anyway. 'Good. Make sure that is taken care of tomorrow and that there is no way the dogs can get out. Got that?' Even though my father replied with a very stern tone,

Steven, thank God, ignored it and nodded his head in response. He then wiped his mouth clean, put his napkin on his plate and pushed it away. He stood up and walked towards the back doors. 'I'll be outside with Henreick if you need me, Sir.' Hans was our Veterinarian for lack of a better word. Since we had so many dogs, mainly the Rottweiler's that guarded our home, we did need someone to train them from when they were puppies to when they were ready to join the pack. 'Alright.' Was my father's answer. He also watched as Steven walked out the double doors to outside. 'Is he still bothered regarding our relationship, Gia?' 'Yes. That's all I heard on the way home today from school, dad. I'm getting sick of it too.' My dad finished with his last bite and pushed his plate away as well. 'Well, you won't anymore. When you are gone tomorrow, I'll have a chat with him. Hopefully, that will stop his little, back-handed comments to you. Let me know, yes?' 'Of course, daddy.' 'After you pack, love, I would like you to come to my room love. Understand? I need to make a few phone calls to Columbia and Asia. After that I should be finished for the day. Yes?' 'Sure, sexy. I will be right over after I finish packing. And, if you do not mind, take a quick bath to get the school grime off of me. How's that? Ok?' 'Sounds like a plan to me, my Princess. See you soon. Come, give me a kiss and scoot upstairs. Get nice and… well, you know how I 'like you', kitten.' I smiled, got up and gave him a very 'proper' kiss on his cheek and up the stairs I went.

After I had stood up from my bath, I thought that at this time tomorrow, Mariah, Cassie and I will be with me in Vegas. And not doing anything sexual or boring! I kind of chuckled to myself. Well, Cassie might be doing something sexual. But NOT me nor Mariah. That was for damn sure. When I was completely dried off, I walked into my bedroom, got a very skimpy nighty on and sprayed myself, lightly, with my father's favorite perfume. Thiery Mugler's Angel. I checked myself in the mirror and decided that I looked perfect. Just the way my father liked me. Straight out of the bath, anyway. I thought of something quickly that would finish the 'perfect look' that he liked. A messy, beachy, messy hair look. I ran into my bath again, took out a 'Beach Spray for my hair and gave it a good spray and messed my lock's a little that made me look like I had just woke up. But I smelled heavenly. I picked up my Victoria's Secret bag, out the door I went. I shut it and locked it from the outside. My father used to forbid me doing this but now that I was spending the night in his room quite frequently, he let me now. Thank God. I did not want anyone in my room when I wasn't in it. And if Maria tried to clean it before I awoke. It was never a big deal. She just waited until it was unlocked. No questions asked. I walked over to my father's door and softly knocked on it. I didn't have to wait long. He opened it, it seemed in 2 second's flat and pulled me in. I tried not to, but giggled anyway. He started kissing me and picked me up as I wrapped my legs around his waist. We kissed for quite a while and then he tossed me on the bed. Like a stuffed toy. I laughed even harder. He got on the bed and started to slowly 'come after me' on all fours. Now, *this* was fun!

As he was basically raping me; no, too harsh of a word because I wasn't in any pain. As he was 'doing' me hard, he was groaning and speaking to me in Farsi. Which I shall not repeat in this book. I was speaking back to him, submissively, in Farsi as well. This I knew he loved. Having sex while speaking Farsi, submissively, in our native tongue. When he was just about to finish, he rolled me over on my back and took himself out of me and came ALL over my face, hair and everywhere else he could without getting any on him. How convenient for him, I thought. I considered, for a second, about my once clean hair. I did manage to have two orgasms though. It did feel good. VERY good, actually. When he was done, I got out from under him, sort of ran to his closet, grabbed some of his old ties that I knew he never wore anymore (why in Hell keep them?) and brought them back to the bed. He didn't even know I was gone. ‘Good’ I thought. I took one tie and tied up his right wrist. In a very extensive knot. One, I knew he could not get out of. Without some help at least. I did the same to the other wrist. Then I started on his legs. When I was done, I got back onto the bed. I knew that what I *planned* on doing too him could go very bad or very good. Either way, I was willing to take the chance.

I had him tied up completely when I was done. Both legs and both arms. As he was 'recuperating' from the 'E ticket' attraction that he and I just experienced, he finally realized that his appendages were all tied up. He quickly looked over at me with such surprise that it sort of caught me off guard. 'What are you doing Gia? Or, better said, what do you *think* you are going to do?' I looked at him, hoping above all hopes that this did not go horribly awry. 'I, Father, am going to punish you for being a very, very, bad man. That is what I am going to do to you.' After I said that, I pulled out my left arm and in my hand I held a small whip. With cat-o-nine tails on the end of it. I knew, from personal experience, that this 'thing' hurt like H-E-L-L. One lovely night, Harris had used it on me. Only not as a sexual 'role-playing' game. Once I showed my father what I was holding in my hand, his eyes got a little bit wider and his mouth opened up a tad as if to speak. But... he did not. Then came, 'Are you sure you want to do this Gia?' he asked me. With a bit of sternness in his voice. Or maybe he was trying to have sternness in his voice. I couldn't tell. I also couldn't tell if he was 'turned on' by this or if he was truly wondering what the hell I would actually do with him being in this situation. Which had never happened before. 'Oh... I'm sure, Tata. I have been wanting to do this for quite some time, actually.’ I tried my very best to keep the trepidation out of my voice and try to keep my voice semi-monotone; with absolutely zero emotion in it. I slowly climbed onto the bed, never leaving his eyes, as I made sure his legs were not moving at all. I knew that he could take me down if he really, really tried. I wasn't stupid. I just wanted to see how long he would allow me to keep this up. As I left his eyes for a moment and looked down, I saw that he was actually beginning to get excited by this. But, was he excited by what I was doing? Or was he actually thinking what he was going to do to me? As usual, I wasn't sure. I don't think a woman would even consider doing *anything* like this to him. Ever. As I was now laying or straddling him, I started licking his neck and sucking on it as well. I planned on giving him the biggest hickey he had ever had in his life. Fuck it. He always wore suits to work. I am sure he wouldn't dare wear anything casual to the office. Especially when I was done with him. As I was sucking on him for about five minutes, the noises started to come. He was instinctually trying to move his hands, but couldn't. And that was frustrating the shit out of him. I could tell because he was making 'excited' noises and then frustrated noises. Back and forth, back and forth. Finally, he pushed his head as far into the pillow as far as he could and we stopped kissing for a moment. 'You better untie my fucking hands. or I will do it f-o-r you. And his voice was deep and menacing and damn serious. I decided I better; just in case he was seriously getting pissed. I didn't want this night to end up badly. Especially since I was very excited. I stopped my work on his neck and started to just nibble and lick up his neck to his mouth. Once I did get too his mouth, I started kissing him. And hard, too. He definitely reciprocated. And with equal amount of passion. I started gyrating my pelvis against his, which made him harder than he was to begin with. Which I thought was impossible. I was just glad that my body, since he was my first, was used to his size and that it did not hurt when we did have sex. That would suck. As we continued making out and me gyrating against him, he finally could not take anymore. He stopped kissing me instantly, got up to straddle me and took both of my arms. He flipped me completely around. To where I was on my stomach. He sat on my lower back and bent down to my left ear. He whispered, 'So, my dear Gia. What were you going to do with those cat-o-nine tails? Hmmm?' Since he couldn't see my expression, I sort of had a frustrated look on my face but decided, 'What the Hell.' He will definitely tell me if it was not going to happen. I turned my face a little to the right, to where he could see my profile and understand what I was going to say. 'I was planning on punishing you, Tata. For being a bad, bad, boy. That's what I was going to do.' 'I see. And how are you going to manage that? Hmm?' All the time he was talking to me, he was whispering so softly, I could barely hear him. Hell *that* even turned me on. I was very aware of the pressure he had on my lower body. And right now, at this very moment, it was hardly there. Probably so his legs wouldn't go to sleep. I decided it was now or never. I quickly whipped around and was now facing him. Unbeknownst to him, I was now straddling his stomach. This move shocked the shit out of him. I could tell by the expression on his face. 'Gia, I would be careful with what you do.' 'Oh, I'll be careful alright. You sexy, son-of-a-bitch.' He looked at me with an expression of ultimate surprise and one of the 'Complete Unknown'. He didn't know what to think. 'Now, if you would be so kind as to not move until I return?' His eyebrows both shot up. As if he really could not believe that I was carrying on this long with this 'game'. 'Why, of course, Ms. Gia Mahari. Happy to oblige.' I didn't know why he pronounced my last name louder or with such precise enunciation. But at this point, I had to go through with it. I leaned as far as I could above and over him to reach the whip. As I had it in my left hand, I started running the leather strands between my fingers of my other hand. His eyes never leaving mine. Except for that first instant when I first had it *in* my hand. As he was watching me and my hands at the same time, I slowly took the whip, my eyes still locked on his, and started rubbing it up and down his chest. The razor sharp ends slightly tickling him, I would guess, because instantly his chest started having goose-bumps on it. And then 'he' got just as hard as he was ten minutes ago. So, I guess *that* felt good to him. I then shut my eyes for half a second and slapped that whip hard. Down on his chest but quick. All the while not taking my eyes off of his. He grimaced a bit and was gritting his teeth. His eyes also got as huge as saucers. I guess he wasn't exactly thinking I was actually going to go through with it. Well, it was too late now. He whipped me onto my back without as much as a slight warning. But not before I saw the blood starting to dribble down his chest. In six straight lines. Oh shit. Maybe I hit him too hard? I never really practiced. Shit! I was in *deep* shit now. Dammit! I knew I shouldn't have done this. Fuck! As he was straddling me, on my stomach, yet again, his legs were clamped so damn hard around my hips that it actually hurt a bit. But, I dared not say a word. I looked at his chest. The blood was still slowly trickling down his chest. 'Do *not* get off of *this* bed.' He said, as he got up to get a towel. When he got back, he took both of my arms, sat me up and slapped me so hard across my face that it literally whipped my head to the left. Damn, that fucking Hurt like Hell! I forced myself not too start crying. I supposed I deserved that slap. 'What in the Hell were you thinking, Gia? Son Of A Bitch!!' He ripped the whip from my hands and turned me around. He whipped my back ten times. And not showing ANY mercy, either. My back was on fire, too. As I felt the blood run down my back, he tossed me off of his bed, onto the floor, and ripped the comforter off of the bed. 'Get up and *on* the bed. Now.' I did as I was told. 'Daddy, I really did not plan on this going this way. I swear! I wanted to do something sexy, mysterious or whatever. I swear I would never hurt you! You have GOT to know that! 'I really do not want to hear it right now, Gia. I would like to think that. So, yes I do believe you. But. If you do ANYTHING like that again, I will beat you like you've never been. Got that?' 'Yes, sir.' As I got on the bed, I laid down. Bummed out because there went our 'Romantic Evening.' He got back onto the bed and laid on top of me. He rammed himself inside of me so damn hard, that I had 'flashes' of Harris go through my head. I started to fight a little. But, decided to stop that instantly. God only knew what he would do too me IF he thought I didn't want to have sex with him. As he was inside of me, he started going in and out of me more slowly until it started to feel good to me. I knew it felt good to him. I was naturally luCassiecated enough to enjoy him inside of me. His size anyway. But my face was on fire. He slowly turned my head sideways and started to lick my neck and sucking on it too. Oh no. Now I was going to have one Hell of a hickey as well. And what the Hell was I going to tell Cassie and Mariah? After he was done with my neck, he started to lick my face. Where he slapped it. And, believe it or not, even though his saliva was not cold, it actually felt good. And he licked it gently. After ten too fifteen minutes of that, he went to my mouth and started licking my lips. I started licking his back and then I grabbed the back of his head gently and kissed him deeply. As passionate as I could. I was very wet and excited then. He could go in and out of me with no problem now. I was *very* excited. I even felt wetness on his sheets. He apparently felt 'it' on 'himself' down there, too. Which made him more excited just picturing it in his mind. He 'finished' in five minutes as I was running the tips of my fingers on his back. I felt the 'wetness' or blood, rather, on my fingertips. I felt bad. But kissing him was THE best. And, at the same time, my tongue was deep inside of his mouth. I loved having him 'finish' inside me while I was kissing him. He almost couldn't control his movements while doing both. When he was finished contorting (the best word I can describe the movement he does after 'finishing') his body and getting his breathing under control, he reached down and grabbed a towel. He pulled the covers completely off of me and asked me to open my legs for him. Which, again was a first. I did as I was asked and he started to clean me up. Being very gentle. Knowing how 'delicate' or injured I was down there. Thanks too good old douchebag Harris. He then kissed both of my thighs on the inside. I then took the towel from his hands when he wasn't expecting it. I pulled the covers back onto me and pulled them off of him. I slowly dried him off. I gently, with some pressure, spread his legs apart. I then started wiping him off there too. When I was done cleaning myself off of him, I got up and walked into his bathroom. As I was digging around underneath his sink, I found what I was looking for. I took the things I needed and walked back to the bed. Since he was laying on his stomach, I could now see the damage I had done too his chest. Damn I felt *SO* bad now. Shit, I am such a stupid bitch! Why cat-o-nine tails? 'Daddy, I am SO sorry! I swear I did *not* mean to hurt you!' 'I'll heal Gia. And get over it. Don't worry about it. Just never do it again. If you are looking to do something kinky, then just tell me. Believe me, I will come up with something. He sort of winked at me after he said that. As I put some Hydrogen Peroxide onto a cotton ball, tears were falling from my face and onto his chest. I made sure that they weren't falling on his wounds. I dabbed as gently as I could and then cut small rectangle shapes out of gauze and put them on him with medical tape. 'I am so sorry, Tata. I love you so much. I would NEVER want to hurt you. Especially since you spend so much time and energy on keeping me safe.' He looked at me, in my eyes of course, and that was when, I think, he realized just how much I loved him. I loved him like a 'Husband'. I believe that was the very first time that it hit him. He just kept staring at me with a mixture of 'Oh My God' and 'What the Hell Am I Going to Do?' When he figured that I was done with fixing his chest, he patted the bed right next to him. 'Why don't you go ahead and put those things away then get in bed with me baby. Yes?' 'Ok, baby. I mean, Tata.' I hurried that response up real quick. I saw the look on his face when I did screw up and knew he had heard every word. It was too late. He knew. Or, if he had any doubts, he didn't anymore. 'Ok. I'll hurry, daddy.' I got together all of the things that I brought out of the bathroom and then I got off of the bed and went back to the restroom. I put them back and went to the bed. As I crawled between the covers, he was on his left side, leaning his head on his left hand. As I was all settled on my side, I looked over at him. 'What's going on, daddy?' 'Gia, there is something that we do need to talk about. And it's a pretty serious talk. You Cassienging up therapy has made me think of this subject. Or 'talk' as I have said. Not counting Steven getting 'involved.' If you want to call it that.' 'Oh. Ok. What did you want to talk about?' 'I want to talk about our relationship, love.' Now I was taken aback. He had never brought our relationship up. Or the type of relationship that we had. Ever. 'Okay.' I said. Drawing my answer out a bit. 'Hon, you have said it yourself that what we do is not normal father/daughter behavior. And to make it fair to you, I think we need this to stop. And pretty soon.' 'How soon is pretty soon, daddy?' He looked down at his hands for a bit. When he looked up, I was crying, yet again. Only silently. Yes, I knew this had to happen. And, yes, I knew it had to happen soon, too. Just like he said. But he was *all* I knew. *Ever*. I couldn't not imagine not being with him and being with someone else. Besides, what about Ritual? If I had to have sex with him then, was I supposed to just forget that it happened and put it, yet again, in the back of my mind? Like it never happened? I loved him for God's sake. I knew it was wrong. Shit! He started this sick relationship too! Shit! 'Babe, come here.' he said when he saw that I was crying. When I didn't move, he said it again. 'Gia, baby. Come here.' I finally looked up at him and scooted into his arms. This time, letting go completely. All of it. I was crying, hysterically, in his arms. He was rubbing my back very carefully, around my wounds and whispering in my ear in Farsi. That almost made it worse. 'Daddy, no.

Not now. Please? Can we do this gradually? Please? Please? I love you!' 'Baby, I love you too. You have no idea, Lil G'. He then started kissing me and laid me back onto his bed, under the covers. 'Now, let me bandage you up and then we best get to sleep for you to have a semi-decent night tomorrow in Vegas, yes?' 'Ok'. I said meekly. He got out of bed, walked into the bathroom and took out the same items that I had used on him earlier. He climbed back on the bed and applied gauze, ointment and medical tape to me as well. Once all was put away, he was back underneath the covers again. Looking at me. He slowly moved closer to me, climbed onto me while his eyes were closed and was saying some sort of incantation while he made love to me again. Only, I had the feeling that this was more of a 'Ritual thing' than a 'sex' thing. When he was finished, he got off of me. Damn, it really was going to be hard not having sex or making love with him. Father or not. I wonder how hard it will be for him. I decided to ask him. Right before we were going to go to sleep for the night. 'Gia, it shall probably be the most difficult thing that I will ever do, my kitten.' 'I love you daddy.' 'I love you too, baby. And you will always be my kitten. Got that?' 'Yes, Sir. I got that.' I smiled at him as I said the last part. He smirked at me (his signature smile) and I cuddled in his arms and fell asleep. With his smell. Safe.

Chapter 16

My eyes opened_and after they adjusted, I realized that it was still dark as Hell outside. I looked over at my side of the bed. The clock read 2am. Damn! 2am in the morning? Shit! Why in the Hell am I awake so damn early? I didn't even feel sleepy. I slowly got out of bed and tip-toed out of my dad's room. I walked down the stairs and into the kitchen. I stood there and realized that I *had* to go back to bed. It was way too damn early for me just to stay up. I was leaving for Vegas today. Damn! Today! Awesome! I opened the refrigerator door and took out the milk and the Hershey's chocolate syrup. Whenever I couldn't sleep when I was little, I would always go downstairs, into my father's kitchen, and make myself some chocolate milk. It was weird because after drinking that it always helped me go back to sleep. As I was drinking my chocolate milk, I was slowly glancing around the house. At least what I could see from where I was standing. This truly IS a beautiful home, I thought to myself. I liked it better than his older one further down the hill. In front of the Hollywood sign instead of behind it. It was still considered 'In the Hills' but it was getting WAY too congested. Especially for my father. Whenever he came home from the office, whether it was from his movie studio office or his real estate office, he would always bitch about the traffic. And not on the freeway. Just on all the surface streets. He avoided the 405 freeway like the plague whenever possible. His real estate office was in Century City and his movie studio office, obviously, was in Burbank. He would only have to take the freeway if he was coming from Burbank. And he hated that ride home. That was why he rarely went there. Maybe twice a month because he had to do the payroll for the fulltime office employees as well as pick up new scripts that were ALWAYS left in his Inbox. I would remember him coming home with this stack of new scripts. And at night, I would climb up into his huge bed and while he was reading through them, I would lay on his other pillows and watch him reading. Just watch him. I would always fall asleep that way. I would wake up the next day covered up, in my P.J.'s and always glued to him; practically on his side of the bed. As I finished the last of my chocolate milk, I rinsed it out in the sink and put the glass in the drainer. As I was walking back up the stairs to my dad's bedroom, I saw a light underneath Steve's bedroom door. That was strange. He was usually zonked out at this time of night. The man had a major busy, strenuous job. I was totally surprised. I walked, on tip toe of course, towards his door and listened. I heard a woman in there. No Way!! I never knew Steve would Cassieng women back to the house! I mean, I wondered how he would go about dating or 'getting laid' as the guy's around the house called it. But after my father went to bed? Very strange. Oh well. He has to 'get laid' sometime, I guess. Maybe that accounted for his horrible mood lately. Hopefully it will work. I'll have to gauge his mood tomorrow. And tease him about it too. Like he always did me. Especially with all of this attitude regarding my father and my relationship. As I opened my dad's door, I slipped inside and turned to look at him. He was out like a light. And sleeping deeply too. He must be so tired, I thought. I may have to wake him up with a special surprise in the morning. Hmmm. I made sure my phone was still on my bedside table. It was. I walked over to my side of the bed and got inside the covers as quiet as I could. My father was a very light sleeper. Regardless of how he looked when he was sleeping. Or even if he was snoring, which was rare in itself, he was still a light sleeper. As I settled in for the morning/night, I grabbed my phone and set a vibrating alarm with music. I also set the volume on a very low setting. I wanted to wake up before my father so that I could wake him up with a very special 'Good Morning' surprise. After I put my phone under my pillow, I scooted right next to my father and snuggled right up against his back; putting my right arm over his upper body. My hand resting in the middle of his chest. I must have drank the perfect 'concoction' because I was asleep in minutes. My father moved a bit as my arm rested on him. I made sure my eyes were slammed shut, hoping he thought that I did not get out of bed at all. He tried to roll over but then realized that I was there. He stopped and slowly lifted my hand and moved to where he was on his back. He then put my hand on his chest again. He kissed me on the cheek and put his hand over mine and went back to sleep. I sighed a sigh of contentment and cuddled in more to the side of his body. I heard and felt my phone at six o'clock in the morning. I quickly grabbed my phone from under my pillow and turned it off. I looked over at my father's side of the bed. Thankfully, he was still asleep. And soundly as well. Today was Vegas day! Yes! A perfect day for my dad to wake up with a 'special something' too, I figured. I laid on my side for a while and then, once I was semi-lucid, I scooted down under the covers; careful not to let the covers to scrape my back too badly. I looked over at my father, raising the sheets up a bit. Damn! He was already hard. I guess what Mariah told me a few years ago was true. Guys always woke up with a hard-on. Unless they had to pee or something? I couldn't remember. As I grabbed 'him' gently under the covers. He didn't move. I smiled too myself. Perfect. I wanted this to be a surprise. I had never done this before. This way, anyway. I put 'him' in my mouth and didn't make a move. I was as still as a statue. He made some inaudible noise and just moved his head on his pillow. And out he was again. I then decided to make my surprise happen. As I started licking and then sucking on him, he started to move a lot more. I felt him stop moving and then move his head. Probably looking over at my side of the bed. He moved his head again but didn't lift the sheet. This is too damn funny, I thought. What was he going to do? Just lay back and enjoy the 'ride'? I almost laughed. But, that would totally ruin my surprise. I remained completely concentrated on 'the job at hand.' Hell! That was even funny! As I was thinking that thought, he came instantly. Shocking the shit out of me. I gagged *and* coughed. Totally embarrassed too. Shit! Gross! I spit 'him' out onto the sheet and pulled the sheet back down so that my face could look at him. My hair was covered in his semen. My face might as well be having a facial, too. After he had collected himself, he looked down at me and instantly started laughing. Then I understood why. I must have looked a sight! My hair was probably everywhere, semen all over my face (some in my damn eyes for fuck's sake) and in both ears! How does that happen? I started laughing a little as I said, 'Good morning, daddy.' He laughed a lot harder after I said good morning to him *and* looking the way I did. 'Come here, you silly, beautiful, goose.' I scooted over and on top of him. I laid my head on his chest. 'Damn! You are a mess!' 'Yeah! Thanks to you!' I started laughing again. 'Why didn't I even get a clue, this time, before you finished, daddy?' He looked down at me with his so handsome smile. 'Gia I do apologize. But, you had to know that doing that to me, and in the morning, of all times, I am going too cum faster than I would at night, kitten.' I looked up at him with surprise. 'Really? I had no idea. How would I know, daddy?' 'True that, love. But. It was such a *fantastic* a way to wake up this morning. This sad morning that is.' 'Sad morning? Why is it sad, father?' 'Because you are leaving for Sin City, that's why. I don't think I have been without you for this long a period of time, babe.' 'Oh. I'm sorry. It's not for that long though, daddy. Before you know it, I'll be back in your lovin' arms! Ha! What movie is that from?' I asked him. 'True Romance™.

And I know it is not for very long, G. I just worry about you. Don't worry about it though. Just call me when you get to the hotel and when you are on your way home from the Jet. Alright?' 'Okey Dokey Doggy Daddy.' I replied. Another quote from True Romance™. One of my favorite all time movies. Ever. 'You and your quotes!' He replied, as he slowly got out of bed. 'Well, I do not need a towel this morning now do I? Do you, my princess?' 'Heck, I need a shower! And bad! I feel like I have hair gel in my hair. And facial cream on my face. And in my ears!' He laughed pretty damn loud for someone who needs coffee usually to just speak in the morning. 'Why don't you just put up your hair in a clip or something and put on your robe? It's breakfast time. Unless, of course, you're already full?' 'Oh! Very funny! But I think I'll take your advice and do just that.' 'Good then, darling. I'll see you downstairs for breakfast then.' 'Ok, sweetheart.' I called him that on purpose. Just to see how he reacted. He did turn in my direction awfully quick. Like he whipped his head in my direction. But he didn't say a word. Hopefully that word will make him think how hard it was going to be for the both of us not to continue 'being together.' I walked, quickly, to my bedroom door, naked. I quickly opened it and shut the door as quick as I could. I heard my dad going down the stairs. Hopefully Steven was in a better mood this morning. Surely he was at the breakfast table too. And I was not in the mood to be dealing with his bullshit. I grabbed my robe and slipped it on. I walked into my bathroom, turned to the mirror and gasped. No wonder my father was laughing! I looked like a damn homeless person! My hair was *everywhere*! I grabbed my brush and tried to brush it out. That wasn't happening. I just grabbed the whole lot of it, twisted it up and clipped it to the back of my head. As I was walking down the stairs myself, I heard Steve's voice talking to my father in his normal tone. Thank God! He sounded like the *normal* Steven! Hopefully, he will treat me with the same joviality as my father. Like he used to. As I closed my bedroom door, I realized that I still needed to pack. I think. Nope. I did pack. Yesterday, I think. As I turned the corner, once I landed on the marble floor, I saw them both at the breakfast table. Talking and laughing up a storm. Well, now I knew why both of them were in good moods. 'Good morning, Miss Gia.' Steve-o said to me as I pulled out my chair and sat down. 'Good morning, Sir Steve-o! And how are you this fine morning?' Steven looked at my dad and said, 'Wow! No coffee yet and 'it' speaks?' They both laughed and Steve said, 'I am good, Gia. Very well. How did you sleep?' 'I slept great. How about you?' 'Fantastic. Slept like I haven't slept in Months! Thank you for asking, though.' 'No prob dude.' I smiled and winked at him when I was done answering him. He smiled back. Not having a clue that I knew that he got laid last night. Not my father, either. But, knowing Steven and how careful he was, I was sure he screened this woman and had gone out with her quite a few times before they actually 'did the bone dance.' Especially taking her to my father's home to do it, too. Hell, I was just glad that he was in a good mood again. Maybe that was his problem. He hadn't gotten laid in so long, he was becoming grumpy. I knew my father always did. We ate in semi-silence and then my father spoke up. 'Gia, honey. Why don't you, after breakfast, go over your suitcase and packing and make sure you are not forgetting anything, yes?' 'Sure, father.' I replied. Looking up at him when I spoke. 'I have to take a shower anyway, obviously. I feel like a damn mess.' I knew Steve would not get that hint. He was busy himself last night, thank God. But my father sure as hell did. He glanced at me, looking at him and smirked. 'Be sure you behave when there, hon. No sleeping around with complete stranger's either. Got that?' 'Yes, Sir. And, Gross!' 'Well, I know Cassie and *she* will. Just make sure she goes to the fellas' hotel room. Not your room. Got that? And I'm deadly serious about that, Gia.' 'Yes, Sir. I wouldn't even think about it. I haven't even thought about ‘that’ either. And, as far as Cassie goes? Mariah and I know how she is. We are going to let her do what she wants to do. And let her do it alone. She is such a slut, when we go to a club, it will probably only take her about 12 minutes to find a guy or guy’s to go back to their room. Gross.' 'Hmm. Well, let her do that and you and Mariah stay inside the club or clubs and do your thing. Leave Cassie too all of the STD's.' That comment made Steve laugh a bit out loud. My father glanced at him and smiled and then shook his head. 'It's true. She is a very, very disturbed young girl. In fact, Gia, I am surprised you are still friends with her. I looked up from my last bite of food and said, 'Funny you should say that, father. Mariah and I were just talking about this trip being the last 'get-together' with Cassie and us to decide whether we *will* continue to remain friends with her.' 'I see. Well, good then. I am sure the two of you will make the correct choice. I'm sure I will find out the whole story when you all return, yes?' 'You will hear everything, daddy. If you'd like.' 'Yes, I would like.' he replied. And then he returned to eating his breakfast and started on his paper and coffee. I knew it was time to go upstairs to get in the shower and get ready. I had to call Mariah and see if everything was set on their end. Also, what, or *if* Cassie said anything last night to Mariah. She tended to say stupid shit about me when I wasn't listening or not on the phone. If she did, she was not going. And that would be the end of our 'friendship'. If you called it that. I pushed my plate to the side to where my father's and Steven's was. 'I better go and check on my packing and shower. 'Alright. G.G. I'll see you when you come downstairs and have a talk with you in my office before you, Lane and Steven take you to Burbank. The Jet is all ready for you three. And please tell Cassie not to drink my expensive Scotch. I do not know how that girl can even drink that. If she drinks any, she or her freakish father can pay for it.' 'Yes, Sir. I will definitely tell her. I love you and I'll be down in a while. How long do I have?' 'Really, as long as you want. Remember, this is your Jet. Not a commercial.' 'True. I forget sometimes, daddy. Sorry. Be back down in a bit.' I walked over to Steven and gave him a kiss on his cheek and went over to my dad and kissed him on the cheek. Since Steven couldn't see our faces from where he was sitting, when I kissed my father, I licked his cheek a little at the same time. He looked at me and then his eyes went right down to his paper. I went upstairs, realizing that I was sore as Hell between my legs from last night, but a GOOD kind of sore. What was *not* a good kind of sore was my fucking back. Damn, it still hurt like shit. Oh well, I'll think of something to tell Mariah since she'll definitely see my back and fuck Cassie. I smiled to myself and went straight to my bedroom door and my suitcase. I opened up my Carry-All™ and checked on everything that was packed inside of it. I pretty much had everything that I needed and wanted in there. Surprising since I packed at the same time knowing that my father and I were going to have sex five minutes later. I hopped on my bed and dialed Mariah. She picked up on the 3rd ring. 'What's up, Ma Bitch?' I asked her. She laughed and said, 'Are you ready to Rock Las Vegas, Bitch?' 'You *know* I am! Damn, I have been needing a fucking vacation from home, my dad, *everything* for so long, Mariah! Fuck!' 'I know you have, girl.' Out of my *few* close friends, Mariah was the only one who knew how stressful my life was. She knew pretty much everything about my life at home. Well, except the 'having sex with my father', part and the 'Luciferian' part too. 'I am about to jump in the shower babes. I have already packed, the jet is ready and I am pretty much good to go. How are you doing in that area? Plus, how was the call with Cassie last night?' 'Oh God, Gia! She is So Fucking Dramatic! As you know! I told her what you wanted me to tell her, she was fine with that. At least that was what she said. But then she goes into 'how much drugs do you think we will be able to score? How many dudes are we going to be able to get inside Gia's suite! Shit like that, girl. So not cool.' 'Are you Fucking kidding me? Ok. That's It. From now on, no more *Cassie*. I will not tolerate her talking about me *or* my father and family like that! I am sick and tired of her bullshit! I am sick of her mooching money off of me and you. I am sick of her drug use. I am sick of her, Mariah! Fuck! I mean, yes. We have all done coke. But all of the time and as often as she does? Hell *no*! My dad would kick my ass, and you would never see me again. He would send me to some overseas rehab or something, you know?' 'Yes, I do know. I am sick of her fat ass too, girl. I say we treat her very distant this trip. Almost kind of cold. What do you think?' 'I totally agree with you there, girly. Let's.' 'Oh!' Mariah said. 'I am all done packing too and I just finished my shower so why don't you just call me when you're on your way to pick me up. I'll call Cassie after you call me. That way, maybe, she will be ready when we get to her house.' 'Sounds good to me, I'll give you a call then, chicky. And, if she is not ready when we do get to her house? I say we leave, after waiting no more than five minutes. What do you say?' 'Sounds good to me, babes. See you then!' and we hung up.

Chapter 17

As I got in my shower, the hot water felt so damn good! The water didn't even bother my back as bad as I thought it would. I let it run over my head and entire body before I washed or did anything. I then washed my hair and grabbed my body wash, while I let my hair reconstructor/conditioner stay in my hair for five minutes, and poured some onto my washcloth. I rubbed it all over my body. It was called 'Cool Cucumber' and it was my favorite smell in the world. As far as body washes' go. As I washed that off my bod, I rinsed out my hair and shaved. Took my soap, also Cool Cucumber, and washed my face and 'parts'. After all of me was rinsed off, I turned off the water and reached for my towel that was hanging just outside my shower, on its hook. I started drying myself off. I was so glad that I had finished packing plus chose my entire outfit the night before. I *so* was not in the mood to do that right now. I thought to myself. Blah. Today; right now, was the beginning of my relaxing vacation. I was so glad that Mariah was in the same 'mood' as I was. We both wanted to get massages, lay out by the pool, swim and sleep in. Go dancing until three or four in the morning, drink a little bit and sleep in as late as we wanted; in bed and by the pool. I could not wait! As I was all done drying off, I stepped out of the shower and sat at my vanity. It didn't take me long to get my 'face' on. Minimal. 'Bare' make-up with hot-pink lips and mascara, etc. The usual minimalist for me, anyway. Most girls would wear red lipstick or gloss with minimal make-up. But to me, pink *was* the new red. Always. Anyway, after my make-up was on and perfect, I stepped into my room and proceeded to get dressed. You never do your hair before you put a t-shirt on. A huge no-no, fuck-up. Screwed hair. Not thank you. After I was dressed, except for my shoes, I went back in front of my bathroom mirror and did my hair. Blew it dry and flat-ironed it too give it volume. After I put my Christian Louboutins™ on, I took one last look in the mirror and said, under my breath, 'Pretty Hot there, girl. Not bad. This hotness needs BIG sunnies. Or, sunglasses, for people that do not know L.A. slang. They still use that word to this day. I wonder if the chicks there now, knew where that word or slang word even came from. Oh well. Who cares? It's a perfect word for sunglasses. At least I thought so. As I walked back into my bedroom with a small armful of hair and make-up products, I put them all into their respective places. Not bad. Everything that I would be taking to Vegas was in one Carry-All™ bag and one carry-on; for magazines and stuff. Not that we would be looking at them on the plane but we sure will be by the pool. I zipped up my luggage and picked up my Louis Vuitton™ handbag and my magazines, snack and put all of it in my pink leather carry-on, I was out of my room in no time. Oh shit! Forgot the book I was reading as well as two more pairs of sunnies. I put my crap down and ran back inside my room, grabbing them. I put them inside my carry-on with everything else. I chose a pair of L.V.'s and a pair of Versace™ shades. Now I was done. As I picked up all of my crap and started walking down the stairs, Steven took the steps three at a time (I know. He was super-human) and took everything out of my hands, except for my handbag. He knew the etiquette on THAT. Hell. EVERY man should know the etiquette on a woman's handbag. Never take your girlfriend's handbag at all unless she hands it to you. But that does not mean that you can go rummaging around in it. Only if you are married... and for a while (maybe two to three years) depending on the two of you *and* how she feels about you touching her purse in the first place.

It's kind of like a woman going through your wallet. It is none of her business. It looks like she is trying to find phone numbers from other women, or what the hell ever. Still, respect her handbag like you expect her to respect your wallet. As I walked over to the front door, I stuck my head out, telling Stev-o that I would only be a bit. He replied, 'No problem, Gia. I have some checking to do out here anyway. The car that is.' I smiled and walked back inside. I walked into my father's at-home office. The door was open. I walked in and closed the door behind me. 'What is it that you wanted to talk about, father?' He was sitting behind his desk. As soon as I closed the door, he stood up, walked around to the front of his desk and took both of my arms. He positioned me in front of him. About two feet away, at the most. 'Gia, I am *very* serious about what I am about to tell you. So, please listen to me, alright?' 'Of course, Tata. What is it?' 'As you know, I have not been away from you in such a long time, I am feeling... very... sad, almost. It is the best way that I can describe it anyway. I will sorely miss you. Just promise me, even though I will have a lot of Bodyguards on you, and No. You will *not* see them, I will *still* miss the *fuck* out of you. So, please. Respect *my* feelings towards you and do not do anything... rash. Do you understand what I am trying to tell you?' I looked at him with honest curiosity. 'I'm sorry Tata. I really do not understand. I will *not* go and get drunk, or leave my drink when I am dancing, etc. I know all of that as does Mariah. Cassie is on the outs, by the way. I've made my decision. And, if we have to wait more than five minutes for her at her house to pick her up? We're leaving without her.' 'Well, good, Gia. But, we can talk about that at a later date. What I was trying to tell you is that I do *not* want you *sleeping* with *anyone* while in Vegas. Alright? You belong to me. And, I will know if you do or do not. Not because of your detail but because of how you feel inside. I know exactly how you feel, Gia. So, please do *not*. For me. Alright?' He looked deadly serious. Even though he was telling me this in a normal tone of voice. Or, rather, his normal tone of voice, he was dead serious. Serious enough that if I did sleep with someone, my father would know it, or, find out and kick the living *fuck* out of me. Badly. 'Daddy, I wouldn't even *think* of doing that. No way! I love you! And no one else. Ok? No worries, Tata. That thought never even crossed my mind. Ok?' He looked deep in my eyes. I knew to see if I was being honest or not. And I was being honest. I couldn't even imagine sleeping with someone other than my father. That, right there, was 'The Problem'. The 'big Problem'. I walked up to him. The two feet that we were apart. I took his head between my hands and started kissing him lightly on the lips; being careful not to mess up my lipstick. He, thank God, knew 'this' drill and softly kissed me back. Not messing up my lipstick. 'You look simply breath-taking, my love. I will make you walk so completely bowlegged when you return, you better be prepared, kitten.' 'Oh, I will be COMPLETELY prepared, father.' He looked at me with a completely satisfied look. 'Ok then, baby. Have fun and I cannot wait until you come home. BUT! I DO WANT you to have a lot of fun, my love. You deserve it. Yes?' 'Yes, Tata. We will have A LOT of fun, Mariah and I. I will call you just as soon as we get to our Suite. ‘OH, that reminds me Gia. I was able to get all of you upgraded to a PENTHOUSE. What? Thank you so much Daddy, for letting me stay THERE, as well as a limo at our service too. I LOVE, LOVE, LOVE you, baby.' He was even shocked at that word. Even though he had heard it before coming from my mouth; in regard to him. In fact, he was VERY shocked at me saying that to him. I carefully gauged his reaction in his face. And it WAS complete shock. But he was also genuinely pleased that I DID say those words. I could tell THAT just by glancing at him. I smiled at him, winked, got on my tip-toes again, gave him a quick kiss on the cheek and walked down the stairs, towards the front door. Just as I was outside of the door, before I closed it, I looked back at the upstairs landing. He was standing there and mouthed 'I love you'. He then turned and walked back into his office and shut the glass door. I stood there for a couple of seconds. Thinking about my father and what HE was thinking about. I closed the front door, got into the limo door that Steven held open for me and crawled way in back; like I normally did. As Steve got in the driver's seat, he asked me if I was ready to go. I, obviously, said 'yes', and off we went. 'Oh, Steve-o?' I asked. 'Yes, Miss Gia?' He answered semi-sarcastically. But in a playful sort of way. 'We'll be picking up Mariah first since its closer, thank God, and we've also decided that after this vacation? Cassie is gone. Forever. We're *so* sick of her shit, Steve-o. I know you have been forever, but she is just too damn much work! And she will never change.' Steve looked back at me carefully, probably to see if I was being serious or not. Then he let out a huge sigh. Of relief, no doubt. 'Oh, Thank God!! I was always wondering when you were going to kick her to the curb. That girl is a complete mess! Good decision. From both of you.' As we pulled up into Mariah's driveway, the door immediately opened and Mariah walked/ran, pulling her roll-away suitcase behind her. Damn! She was as excited as I thought. I mused. Good. Now I don't feel as bad for being so fucking excited. As she got in the door Steven opened for her, she told him hello and thank you and climbed right in. 'God, Gia! You look so damn cute! I soo wish Cassie DID NOT have to go! I wish it was just the two of us.' 'No kidding! You don't think I haven't thought THAT 100 times since I last talked to you?' 'Yeah. I bet you have, chica.' she replied, getting comfortable. 'Hey. Before we get to 'The Valley! ‘Like Oh My God!’ Let's have a glass of champagne before she gets in here. Shall we?' 'Surely. Let's!' I scooted over to the mini-bar and popped open a bottle of Crystal and poured Mariah and I a glass.' As I handed Mariah her cocktail, we clinked them together and had a cold, icy, yummy, sip. 'To Vegas.' we both said simultaneously. Since Cassie lived, literally, in the Valley (*very* not cool), we made some 'Valley' jokes until Steve pulled into Cassie's driveway. As usual, we didn't even have four wheels up onto her driveway. She was already halfway down her driveway. It was as if she had been sitting there just waiting until the car pulled around the corner. We looked at each other in complete amazement. We knew we were thinking the exact same thing. This trip is going to be HARD to contain ourselves with her. Nicely, that is. As she climbed in the car and Steven was putting her suitcase in the back of the car, she greeted us with a very loud, 'Hey Guys!' Mariah and I both said, almost in unison, 'Hey Cassie. What's up? How are you this early afternoon?' 'Fantastic! I *so* cannot wait until we land in Vegas, Bitches!' Mariah and I looked at each other quickly and then Mariah asked her 'So, what are your plans for Vegas, Cass?' 'My plans? Damn, Mariah? Haven't you heard? There is this huge convention in Vegas the same time we are there! So, totally hot guys are going to be there when we are! Which means, girls that we are going to have some drunken, Vegas sex! Hopefully every night we are there! How lucky are we? And, it's a Real Estate Convention!' Mariah and I both looked at each other and then at her. 'Cass, I don't plan on having any sex there. Unless Johnny Depp happens to show up. But, unless that unlikely event happens, I plan on having a 'Lay out by the pool with cocktails, massages every day, breakfast in bed, and again, cocktails by the pool, vacation in Vegas. And, if I'm not wrong, Cass, The Golden Nugget™ may have the same type of vacay package as well. I mean, its downtown and everything, so I wouldn't go outside after dark at all. But I bet there are a lot of low-life's that deal dope near there.' I looked at Cassie and nodded my head, yes. Cassie looked at us with total surprise on her face. She then looked at me and was about to open her mouth but then I realized that we were pulling into Burbank airport. 'Hold that thought, Cass. K?' I rapped on the partition too talk too Lane and Steve (Steven had to go to drive the Limo back to the house). Steve rolled the window down since he was driving. 'Yeesss?' he answered. And I was sure he had heard everything that was said in the backseat the entire trip here, too. 'Hey guys. Just let us know when to get out, ok? And thank you for driving, Steve-o.' 'No problem, Gia.' The guys got out first, their guns out as well as carrying our luggage. Then we got out; the girls taking my cue as to when to exit the car. They semi-understood what my life entailed. But they thought *all* of the body guarding was because of what my father did. What they did *not* know, was that after Steve Wynn's daughter was kidnapped for a ransom, my father took security too an entirely new level. All day every day. It had taken me a while to get used to it, but by now I didn't even notice anymore. As we went up the steps of my father's jet, the men were climbing behind us. When they set everything down, Steve-o gave us the last mini-speech of the day. We all agreed and out he went, after telling us to have a great time. As the doors shut, Cassie made her 'inspection' of the plane. Not asking of course. As she opened the door to my father's bedroom of the plane, I told her not to go into that room. I even added a please. She completely stopped in her tracks. She looked at me in complete surprise. 'Why, Gia? What's the big deal?' 'The 'big deal' is that it is my father's bedroom and shower and all of that. I am sure he does not want anyone going in there.' She gave me a slight dirty look and came back to the chair by the leather sofa where Mariah and I sat. 'I still don't get it. But, whatever.' Mariah quickly looked at me like, 'Oh Oh. Here we go.' I looked at Cassie and finally had had enough. 'Cass. *Please* listen to me, ok? Can you do that? Just for a second?' 'Sure.' she answered with her arms crossed. 'First of all, this is *not* my jet. It is my father's. Second of all, I will not be treated like shit or your fucking slave. I invited you. Not the other way around. Got it? I can just as easily call Steven back and have him pick you up. It is completely up to you. Now, as far as Vegas goes, you can do anything *you* want to do. You are you and I am me. I am not your mom or babysitter. But when you are on my dads' plane, and anything is, God forbid, out of place or fucked up in some way, in his eyes, *I* will be the one that is blamed. And you have *no* idea type wrath that man can rain down upon me. Ok? Look. All I am asking is while we are on this plane, just leave everything as it was. Ok?' Cassie, I could tell, was taking it ALL in. Then she (finally) spoke. 'What crawled up your butt? I was just looking around. And, per you, Queen Mahari, I will not go into your hot dad's bedroom. Ok?' I looked at her with complete hatred in my glance. 'Just be glad that we are about 23 minutes away from Vegas, Cassie. Because if you talk to me that way again, I will have you find your own way home. Got it? 'No problem, Miss Rich Bitch. No problem.' She walked back to the chair she was sitting on and I looked at Mariah. I reached into my purse, took out my phone and text Mariah that once we landed, I was going to tell Cassie to find her own place to sleep. I did not give a fuck after that little exchange. As long as she didn't sleep in our room, we would be Golden. I sent Mariah the text and put my phone in my lap. I also grabbed a magazine and put my phone on top of that. Or, rather, inside of it. She was so in shock that Cassie spoke to the very person that provided this trip. Completely free to her, that she did not know what to say or what to do. Cassie asked Mariah how much was on her credit cards. Mariah looked at her as if she was a complete stranger and said, 'Why?' Cassie gave her a look as if 'Duh! So we can get our own hotel room. Away from Gia!' Mariah replied, 'I think I'll keep the Suite that Gia's father reserved. It is really nice of him to let us have it for a couple of days. Besides, my parents know where I am staying and I don't want to find anywhere else *to* stay. And I know that if there is a convention in town, finding a suite or room as grand as ours will be next to impossible.' Cassie looked really pissed.

Since she was normally not a mad or angry person, it looked very, very, ugly on her. Granted, she wasn't the sharpest tool in the shed, but she rarely got in fights with her friends. She didn't know how to handle it when she was the odd 'man' out. 'Fine. Suit both of you. I'll find my own hotel. Am I allowed to fly back with you or what, Miss Mahari?' I looked up from my magazine and said right back to her, 'With that attitude? And still not a 'Thank You for this trip, Gia'? No. Find your own way home. I'll call your dad or mom and tell them what is going on. Maybe they can save your ass. I am done with you from now on. Got it? Lose my number while you're at it too.' She looked mortified. 'No! Don't you dare call my parent's! You have no right! I looked at her like I did not give a shit and replied, 'I don't *care*. Sucks to be on the other side or having the shoe on the other foot, doesn't it? Not caring? That's *your* motto, bitch. Deal'. I finally heard the landing gear release from underneath the plane. I felt my phone vibrate in my lap. I picked it up and read it. 'I cannot believe her, Gia! Good for you! She deserves everything she got and gets in Vegas. I Hope she is miserable.' I kind of laughed. Just enough for Cassie to hear me. I replied too Mariah. 'We will have so much more fun relaxing not having to worry about that slut. I am done with her, Mariah. It's you and I in Vegas, Beeotch!' We put our seatbelts on and continued to text each other. Wondering how Cassie was going to try and get out of this mess. Once we heard the plane touch the landing strip, we were ALL excited. I didn't particularly care about Cassie but Mariah and I sure as Hell could not wait for our relaxation vacay to begin. 'Look Gia, I am sorry, ok? I was being a total bitch. I was just so damn excited to be able to go too Vegas that...' 'Not good enough, Cassie. I don't give a damn anymore. Like I said, find your own motel or whatever, get screwed by whomever and loose whatever dignity you have left. Ok? But do not call me or Mariah. Got it?' Cassie was practically in tears as we were taxied next to our Limo. Provided by my father, of course. When she saw *that*, I could see the regret in her entire face; as could Mariah. I was completely laughing inside. The doors to the jet opened and we saw Lane stick his head in. 'Ready girls?' 'We sure are!' I replied. Mariah and I had our luggage in our hands and proceeded to walk towards the stairs. Lane instantly saw the tension and semi-tears in her expression. Thank God he did not say a word. When we walked close to the steps as well as Lane, he took our luggage and walked in front of us as we walked down the stairs and headed towards the limo. When we were completely outside and noticed that Cassie was not getting off of the plane, Lane asked us what the Hell was going on with Cassie. Mariah told him the whole story. 'Should I have the pilot take her back home then?' Lane asked. I looked at Mariah and then I looked at Lane. 'That would be an excellent idea. That would ruin her entire vacation/plans. Just make sure, Lane that you or Lane sit in back with her? She was dead set on getting inside my dads' bedroom for fuck's sake.' 'Will do' Lane said. 'I'll call your cell when I return with the jet, alright? Obviously, I know where you two are staying because that's where I'M staying as well. Just answer your phone. I'm sure your father will be calling you too, to hear the whole story. But, he may just wait until you get home. Ok? How does that sound. Just be careful and just try and stay in your hotel and/or your hotel's casino, etc. If you want to go shopping, please wait until tomorrow or at least until I get back, ok?' 'Sure, Kev. And thank you. She is such an ungrateful bitch, that I just want her BACK in Los Angeles. And, I am going to call her parents and let them know HOW rude and nasty she was.' 'Alright, girls. The driver knows to take you to The Mirage so have fun. The Suite is all set up. I spoke to your father when we landed, Gia, and he said everything was taken care of. So, you two should have NO problem.' 'Ok. Thanks again, Lane.' 'Yeah, Lane. Thanks from me too.' said Mariah. As Lane walked back towards the jet, Mariah and I waved at the plane. My dad's pilot waved back, he gave us the thumbs up sign too. We walked to the car and the driver took both of our suitcases out of our hands and asked how we were doing today. We responded with 'Just fabulous!' Which was EXACTLY how we felt. Especially without Cassie. As we got in and settled in, he closed the door behind us. As the car drove towards our hotel, we looked out of the window. I realized how tired I was. Am I really getting old at 15 soon to be 16? Impossible. Maybe it was because of all the drama and bullshit today. AND getting up at the semi-crack of dawn too. I wondered if Mariah felt the same way too. I took a look at her and her eyes were closed. Taking a 'little cat-nap'? Why the fuck not, I decided? I let my body slump over to the side and leaned against the door; my head resting against the window. We must have BOTH fallen out because our driver had to wake us up. Mariah and I looked at each other when we were 'awake'. We both started laughing like HELL when we saw each other. We both, at the same time, grabbed our handbags and grabbed our make-up bags. We touched up our make-up as well as our lip gloss. We also put on our sunnies too and gave each other the 'sign.' The 'sign' was a hand signal which meant - Time To Act Stuck Up and Better Than Everyone Else.' Everyone bought it. Especially getting out of a Limo that was parked outside of THIS hotel and had been parked there for at least 15 minutes. After we were done getting the 'sign-ready' look that we wanted, we both looked out of the window and saw that a crowd had gathered outside of our car and the hotel. Oh God! Now!? Ok. Game time, Damion (our limo driver). He knew the drill...and LOVED it for some reason. I HAD to do this because of the crowds. I was severely claustrophobic and HATED flashbulbs. Mariah just hated crowds. So, we were basically in the same 'place' so to speak. When we were both ready, hotel security, thank God, walked out and asked Damion needed any help. Damion said, 'Yes sir, I do. I have two very important young women in the car and this trip was a little unexpected, if you know what I mean.' 'Yes, I do. It happens here in Vegas – especially at THIS hotel, ALL the time.' 'Ok, good. So, you know the drill then?' 'Yes, sir I do.' 'Let's go then' replied Damion. He stuck his head in the car and told us to put our sunglasses on and any hoodies we may have too. Over our heads. 'This is SO SILLY, Gia!' 'Yeah, I know. But it WON'T bc long. Promise. The elevators are just inside and to the right. Follow whomever is guiding you. Probably the hotel dude, k?' 'At this point, I don't give a damn WHO it is. I'm lame...but I'm tired.' I looked at her and reminded her to remind ME to tell her a little story about inside the car when we first pulled up. She said, 'Ok.' and off we went. Into the great sea of the ignorant masses. As we got out, people, mainly young girls, started screaming. And loud! Who the Hell did they think we were? I really had no idea. I just walked as I was being led by Damion. Then, as we were completely out of the car, the flashes started going off. That is when my eyes started to close. And fast. I let my body be pulled this way and that; my eyes stayed completely blinded by the flashes. Thank the Heavens that I had my sunglasses on. I don't think I could have handled this without them. Next thing I knew, Mariah and I were in the elevator with Damion and hotel security. Mariah and I did not say a word. It was almost like we already had this conversation on how we were going to act once we got on the elevator. Or, when getting to the hotel. That was one of the main reasons why I liked Mariah. She just went with the flow. And, if she did not agree with something I had to say or something I wanted to do, she would say something. I absolutely hated kiss-asses. Big Time. And Mariah was not one of them. Everyone that I did know were; I believe. As we rode up all the way to the awaiting penthouse we were so tired. I knew I was. I also knew Mariah was because of how she was standing/slumping. She never slumped. Our elevator stopped at the top floor. I told the hotel security dude to please have someone monitor our floor to make sure we were not 'bothered' since, I was sure some of the people saw which floor we went up to. He replied, 'No problem, ma'am.' I told him thank you and told Damion to please tip the nice guy. He did so and the hotel security left us up there. Damn, Damion! Why do you love doing that?' I asked. Mariah looked like she had been through a five day bender. 'I don't know, Miss Mahari. Just thought that for the rest of your stay we can play with that facade a bit more while you are here. You know what I mean? Like at the clubs you two want to go to tomorrow night.' 'Oh. Well, that does actually sound fun. What do you think Shelly girl? Besides being so fucking tired, you want to die?' 'I think I want to get in our room, get our jammies on and get in bed and chiilll.' 'Sounds good to me, babe. Thank you sooo much, Damion! You will be heavily tipped for this trip. Promise on that one, ok?' 'Yes, ma'am! I aim to please!' 'Also, when we do go out? Your idea sounds fun. But, please. No flashbulbs. If you can help it, ok?' 'Absolutely, Miss Mahari. I will do my very best.' 'Thank you.' After Damion left our room, Mariah walked around the room, albeit slowly, and praised it. 'Gia, girl? Will you *please* thank your dad for such an awesome room, for me? It’s beautiful! And so perfect for a relaxing, fun mini-vacay!' 'I will sweetie. Let's order some early dinner room service and then get IN our beds and read until we crash. How does THAT sound? Or, YOU can just crash and I'll take my pills and read until I crash. Since we both brought our eye-masks, that shouldn't be a problem, right? 'No, babe. That won't be a problem at all. Plus, I know I need to take a shower? But I am too fucking tired now!' 'I was thinking the same thing. We'll do that tomorrow. Besides. The maid will change the sheets in the morning so when we end up going to bed tomorrow night, they'll be fresh again anyway.' 'Sounds good to me.' I got on the phone and ordered us a small steak dinner with a Caesar salad. With two big glasses of milk. The alcohol will begin tomorrow evening, I was thinking. As Mariah and I got our suitcases semi-unpacked; meaning our toiletries were in the bathroom. On separate sides of the counter, by each sink, we also pulled down our beds. Damn. *They* even looked good. We must be exhausted. It had been a long-ass day. The phone rang. That's weird, I thought. I picked up the phone and then whomever was on the other end of the line, hung up. 'Well, Mariah. And so it begins!' I said with sarcasm. 'Don't tell me that was a hang-up.' We both looked at each other. 'Yep. It was.' Mariah rolled her eyes. 'People are so pathetic! Did it come from an inside line or an outside line?' I looked down at the phone. 'An outside line. I'll just call the front desk and tell them no calls. Except my dad and your dad? Mom?' She thought about that for a minute. My mom I guess. My dad will be out of town so, most likely, it would be my mom.' 'Mom, it is then.' After I made the call, room-service knocked on our door. Mariah knew the drill. She looked through the peephole and saw that it WAS indeed room-service and let him in. I made sure that I had my sunnies on and threw Shelly hers. She mouthed 'thanks' and we both got in bed. I turned on the tube and pretended to watch it. The waiter guy kept looking over at the bed at us trying to figure out just who we were. He left the cart and I reached out my hand and gave him a $20. He thanked me profusely. Like I gave him $100 or something unheard of. Was $20 too much? I looked at the bill. Not so much! Whatever. We had to start thinking about who we WERE supposed to be. As Mariah and I started to eat, I brought up that very topic. 'Well, after we eat, let's look in the mirror; for both of us and we'll decide who we both look like. Or CAN look like. With the least amount of effort anyway. How's that for starters?' 'Sounds good to me. Only, let's do it AFTER we wake up? Is that cool?' I looked at her. Damn she looked so fucking tired! 'No prob, babes. You look half dead right now, poor thing. We'll just do it when we wake up in the morning.' I looked at my watch. It was 6 pm. We should definitely wake up in the morning. 'Cool. I could sleep for two damn days. Don't worry though, bitch! I won't!' I laughed a bit. 'You better not!' After we finished our food, we pushed our cart outside of our room. As we did that; Mariah holding the door for me, I heard giggling and stepped back inside. Mariah shutting the door ASAP. 'Did you hear that?' She looked at me in amusement. 'I sure as shit did! Fuckety Fuck! What the Hell are we going to do?' 'Oh God! Damion started a nightmare. Ok. We are going to need 'security' if you know what I mean. Let me call my detail and see what I can do. Then, it is bedtime. 'I picked up my cell, crawled in bed and dialed Lane's cellphone number. Which reminded me that I *had* to call my dad. After I hung up with Lane I dialed my dad. My dad answered and I told him the *entire* story. He basically cussed Damion and said he would take care of it. He also asked who we were supposed to be. I told him we won't know until tomorrow morning since we were so tired. And that we were going to bed right now. After I hung up the phone with him, I called my dad. He answered on the 3rd ring. 'Hello.' He must have not looked at his caller ID. 'Hi daddy!' 'Well, well, my Princess. How was your flight? And your room. If you're in it that is.' 'The flight was great, dad. We left Cassie at the Vegas Private Airport because she pissed me off so much. So, that's the end of that bitch.' He asked what she did THIS time and I told him everything. Mariah walked out of the bathroom then and hopped in her bed. 'Well, is she flying back home on *my* jet?' 'Hell no, Tata. I told the pilot and her that she needed to find her own way home. So, I have no idea where or how she is getting home. Her behavior was unacceptable, dad. It really was. Just ask Mariah when we get home or whenever.' 'No. I believe you, love. And trust your judgment. Like I have said one hundred time's, I never knew what you saw in that piece of white trash. I'm glad she is out of your life, actually. She'll probably call her father, he'll blame 'your bitchiness' and probably try me at the office. Since that is the only number that he has for me.' 'I know. I just used her as a 'last resort' type of friend. If you want to call her that.' He sort of laughed at that. 'Ok, my love. I know Mariah is right there, so I won't say anything 'inappropriate' or keep you on the phone any longer. Though I would like too. Be good, have fun and be safe, yes?' 'Absolutely.' I answered. Laughing a little at the last statement he said. 'Ok, dad. I'll see you in two day's then, daddy.' 'Alright, my kitten. Be safe. I miss you and, most important, have fun. Yes?' 'Miss you too. Very much. And Mariah say's that 'she loves the room and too thank you for letting her stay, too.' 'Tell her she's welcome. Now, get some sleep and I'll speak to you the day you will be leaving, baby. Love you.' And he hung up. I hung the phone up and stared at it a little. He said 'you're welcome, Shelly.' 'Sweet. Ok babe. It's bedtime!' I smiled, and pushed a button on the bottom of my lamp stand. The blinds and curtains started closing. Nice, I thought. I need this in my room at home. That would be sweetness. I looked over at Shelly. She was putting on her eye-mask. I got out of bed, walked into the bathroom and grabbed mine. Once I was in my bed, I laid down with my book. I didn't even get to the second page. It was 'light's out'; for both of us.

Chapter 18

The wakeup call scared the Hell out of me. I reached to my left, when I should have reached to my right. The bedside table in Vegas was on my right. Where, at home, it was on my left. I finally picked up the damn phone, said, 'yeah', and hung up. These damn hotel phones are fucking loud! I slowly sat up in bed. I looked at the clock. It was 11am in the morning. The next morning. Damn did we sleep or what? I looked over at Mariah's bed and she was sitting on it, reading the newspaper. 'The dead arises!' she replied. 'Damn, bitch! Why didn't you wake me up? How long have you been awake?' She looked at me smiling and said, 'Only about 10 minutes, butt -head. Damn!' 'Oh. Sorry. I thought you were the one who would sleep longer than me. I never thought I'd sleep until 11am!' I grabbed my phone. No missed calls. Good. 'I know. The way I felt last night or evening, I thought I'd sleep until at least noon. Not so much. But close enough! Let's order breakfast! I'm starving!' 'So am I, babes.' Mariah told me what she wanted so I picked up the phone and ordered. 'Ok. First of all. What do you want to do today?' She thought about it for maybe a second. 'Pool time!' 'I couldn't agree with you more. Also, before we do that? We have to decide who we are supposed to 'be'. Thanks to Damion that is.' She looked at me with an almost pained expression on her face. 'Why did he have to say something like that?' 'I have no idea. We can just go out the way we are and say 'fuck it' or we can go with *his* flow.' She thought about it for a while. 'Ok. It will be fun when we are in the casinos and the clubs. So, we might as well go 'With his flow' as you said.' 'Ok... well, you first. Let's go up to the mirror and take a good look at your face and remember; we also have scarves as well as tons of sunnies, too.' 'That's true. Ok. Let's do it.' We both walked over to the mirror. We stared at her face from both angles as well as straight on for about 20 minutes. I held her hair up and down; scarf and no scarf as well as put different sunglasses on her too. We finally decidcd that with sunglasses as well as a scarf and/or clever make-up, she could pull off a thin (with straight hair) or a brunette Ke$ha™. She decided on a thin Mariah Carey™. I was thankful. Because, Ke$ha would never go brunette. Even though that was her natural color. And she was totally blonde right now, according to my father who knew a lot about the celebrities in Los Angeles. The knock of our yummy food came at our door just then. 'Yummy!' Mariah exclaimed. My stomach was jumping for joy as well too. 'After breakfast, it's your turn, babes. I already have a couple of ideas anyway.' 'So do I, Shell. So, it shouldn't take so long this time.' We sat down and ate our breakfast. It hit the spot, too. After we were done, Mariah rolled the cart out of our room and, yet again, she heard voices and giggles again. Pathetic! She told me as I was getting in the shower. 'Sad little creatures' was my response. 'Just ignore them babe. Maybe they'll get over it. I hope to Hell they do, anyway.' After I got in the shower and washed my bod, got out and dried off, I stuck my head out of the door and asked Mariah if she wanted to go to the casino today or hit the pool. She said 'Casino. Absolutely. I want to see if I can win any money for ME with my dad's money that he gave me for this trip.' 'I hear ya there. Ok. I'll put my face and hair 'on' then. The shower is open. And I didn't use all of the hot water either, bitch.' 'Thanks, bitch. I'll be right in.' I sat in the chair that the hotel provides you IN their bathrooms. I guess only in their suites? And proceeded to get ready. Mariah pulled her covers up over her pillow/bed and put her suitcase on top of her bed. Unzipped it and started thinking on what

SHE was going to wear on her first day inside of this luxurious hotel. 'Damn, this hotel is sweet', she thought, as she walked towards the bathroom. 'Hey, girly? What are you wearing? Jeans and a cute top? That kind of 'Hot-Jeans-Day' type of shit?' 'You got it' I replied from my chair. 'Hotness Supreme is what I'm thinking. And since we seem to have 'fans', I would be wearing your 'celebrity' sunnies, too. I know it is hard as Hell to see anything in a casino with shades on, babe. But we are sort of going to have too.' 'I get it. Ugh. Hey, about that. Are we supposed to wear make-up sort of looking like the 'celebrity' people that we spoke about last night? Or what?' I put down my mascara and thought about that. 'Here's what we will do and it won't be that big of a pain in the ass, either. Swear. Even though this IS bullshit, in my opinion.' 'No kidding' she replied. 'Put your make-up on as you think Juanita would. Go through my stupid Rag Mags that I have in my carry-on? I know there is a pretty good full frontal pic of her, photo shopped, so you will not have to look as big or as tall as her, and just copy her make-up in the pic. If the pic is of her in an evening type situation, lots of make-up scenario, just tone it down a bit. Like I know she always wears brown eye shadow. But during the day, make it a more nudish looking brown, brown blush, lightly put on and nudish lipstick with a topcoat of light brown, frosted, lip gloss. How's that?' She looked at me like I absolutely knew what I was talking about. Well, I kind of did. Being around these people all the time. But I had to help her or there was *no* way we were going to be able to pull this off. 'Ok hon. Um...if I have any problem or lack of make-up required to do this, can you help me? Please?' 'Absolutely! Just jump in the shower, I'm almost done with my hair and make-up; Oh! By the way, I'm going as Gwen Stefani™. Perfect, don't ya think? Easy make-up, just finishing up curling my hair in medium curls. How perfect is that!' She looked at me more closely as she walked up to me and took a really good look; she didn't have her glasses or contacts in yet. 'Oh My God! You so look like her! I swear!!!!!!! You even have the same bone structure as her. I hadn't even noticed that before! 'Well, I did use some tricks of the trade that I learned from my father's studio. But, it totally works! Don't you think? Now look at me with my sunnies on and then with my scarf on, of which Gwen wears all of the time, anyway. Ok?' 'Sure! Do it!' I looked at my watch and thought different. 'Better yet, get in the shower and when you come out, I should be all done. Make-up, hair, clothes, sunnies and/or scarf. Then you can get the entire picture. All at once. How's that?' 'Cool beans! Let me get out my 'Juanita' jeans, top and shoes and I'll jump in ASAP. This may get out of hand.' 'Well, I have already thought of that. I texted my bodyguards and told them all that is going on and they're all for it. They have fun with this kind of shit. I have no earthly idea why. But they do.' She kind of laughed with a quizzical look on her face. 'Ok, babe. Let me get my crap put on my bed and I'll be in the shower.' 'Alrighty. I should be done in here by then anyway.' Mariah walked back to our bedroom as I started finishing up my hair. Mariah looked at all of her jeans that she brought. She picked the tightest, most uncomfortable ones' that she had. She then looked at ALL of her tops. She picked out all of her dressy or 'stand-out' one's and placed them on the bed. Separately so that she could take a good look at them. Then came her heels. She knew that all Carey wore 'out in public' were high heels. She placed all four pairs of high heels on the floor at the foot of the bed. She chose a patent leather, red, high heel as her first choice. Then picked out a patent turquoise blue high heel and put them on the floor, next to the red pair as her second choice. Her third and final choice were a crystal studded pair. They were a strappy sandal, high heel. They looked like 'rock-star' shoes so she put that pair next to the blue ones. She put on her tightest pair of jeans that made her butt look bigger but not 'huge' and then looked at her tops. She chose a spaghetti-strap metallic silver halter that had crystals on it as well. Which of course, matched her embellished crystal high heels, too. After her entire outfit was on she looked in the mirror. Then she imagined her hair done with curls and her 'new' make-up choices. This will work. I don't even have to curl my entire head of hair. Not by wearing the scarf. Just the parts that will be showing through the scarf. Perfect! 'I just better make sure I bobby pin the hell out of that scarf', she said out loud. 'What did you say...Juanita?' She spun around with a look of embarrassment and blushed. 'Sorry about that. I had to see if I could pass the 'test'. You know what I mean?' 'Yes, I do! Damn! Who do you think you are talking too?' She smiled as she started taking off her 'Juanita' outfit. 'So, what do you think? With my hair semi-curled and the 'Mariah make-up'?' 'I looked at her head to her shoes. The entire 'Mariah' package. I completely, honestly, think this *is* going to work. And, you know me, Michelle, I would NOT bullshit you about this. For two reasons. And, I would hope you would know the first one.' I looked at her, waiting for her response. 'Hmm. Because you love me?' I laughed. Well, of course! But, I was looking for more of, 'I am your best friend' of an answer. Second? I am going in disguise with you too. So. Both of our Vegas Reps are on a disguise test. Plus, it's good practice for me too.' Mariah looked at me with a big smile on her face. Then she furrowed her brow and asked a question. 'Why would you have to practice being in disguise?' I had to think of a quick answer for that question. What a stupid, fucking thing for me to say. STUPID! 'In case I want to come back here and have no one know who I am. Especially if, God forbid, (I knocked on wood at that one) my father has a heart attack or gets sick or whatever and I have to take over *his* business one day. 'Oh. I totally get that, hon; but please don't worry about that baby. Your dad is still way too young and seems to take care of himself really well. I seriously doubt you'll have to worry about that for quite some time. Ok?' Chell could be so sweet when she chose to be. That was why I did like her more than most all of my friends. 'Thanks hon. I appreciate that. A lot. More than you know.' 'Well, that's how I feel, babe.' 'Ok, let's take a look at you after you're done getting into your ‘Mariah Carey’ ™ look. Cool?' 'Coolness. See ya after my shower. She tossed her clothes on her bed and went into the restroom. I walked over to my case and took out my L.A.M.B.™ jeans, black, Dolores™, High Heels, and a black, metallic, L.A.M.B.™, backless, top that tied at the neck and at the middle of my back. 'Quite Hot', if I do say so myself, I thought. As I took one more last look in the mirror, with my shades on, (Versace™), I decided to go into the restroom where Michelle was getting her 'Mariah' on and see what she thought. Maybe have her take a picture of the both of us. Or vice versa. Whichever. We did need to take some pics. One reason was too remember this trip together and the other reason was to send them to my dad. As I walked into the bathroom, I saw her sitting on the chair, doing her make-up. I stood there. Right behind her so that she could get a good look. When she looked up, her eyes got huge! I laughed inside; hoping that was a good thing. 'Oh my God! You look just like her! If I passed you in the hall looking just like that? I would swear that you were her! I promise you Gia!' I looked back at her, in the eyes. 'Are you sure?' 'Hell, yes! You look perfect!' 'Ok. Now, will you please help me?!?' I looked at her progress. She was doing a perfect job. So far anyway. 'Ok, Shelly. You are actually looking more like Carey and less like Shelly! Which, obviously, is a good thing! Damn, this is going to work! Ok. Please hand me your red lipstick and then your scarf.' After she handed me the two essentials that were needed for us to look like who we were supposed to look like, I did her lips and then put on her scarf. Thinking exactly like Mariah would do it. She would do it perfectly. Because she was such a 'diva'; or so I had heard; that I wanted it to look like it was thought out while being put on. And I explained this too Michelle, too. 'I am so glad you are here with me, Gia. How do you *know* all of this crap? I know you don't read all of those rags for yourself. I know you read them to help out your dad. So how on earth do you know all of this shit?' As I was finishing up her scarf, I was thinking about what to say to her. 'When I do read them for my dad, things just sort of 'stick' to my memory. Things that I may need in certain situations. If they came about. Do you kind of 'get' what I'm saying?' 'I guess so. Yeah. I'm just so glad you're helping me with all of this. I would not have a clue!' 'Don't worry, Shell. Why would you know any of this crap? You shouldn't know. And, if you did? I'd seriously be worried that you were a 'Celebrophile'. And that is not a good thing. I would NEVER be friends with one of those chicks. Never in a million years. I mean, especially because what my father does for a living. And NOT the Real Estate aspect of his job. You know. 'Yeah. I totally get that. You would NEVER know who your real friends were. And that would SUCK. BAD.' 'Yes it would, Mariah. Yes it would. Big time. Ok. I think we are ready for YOU to get dressed and do NOT look in the mirror yet. Get dressed and THEN I'll lead you to the mirror. Ok?' 'No problem. You're the boss when it comes to this shit. Lol.' As she was getting dressed, I picked up my phone, sat on my bed and texted my father that we just finished getting ready to go into the casino for the night. And that tomorrow night was for clubbing. Also, I told him that we had not one drop to drink...so far. Plus, the drinks at the tables were SO watered down that it would take A LOT of them to even get a buzz. I sent it and looked at Mariah. All she had to do was get her heels on and then we were pretty much ALL done. Just as she was done with her shoes, we heard a knock on our door (a half-assed knock) and then running feet. Or, rather, footsteps. 'Oh nice. Knock, Knock, Ditch. Or what the fuck ever you call it these days.' I said. 'I'll go and open the door. Since we both look like 'Who We Are Supposed to be', why not, right? Plus, I decided, and please tell me if you disagree, Shell that since we have to fly home tomorrow early evening, we might as well have some fun here. With these kids. What do you think?' I said to Mariah. 'Lol! That's totally cool with me, babe. Just don't let them see inside our room so it's more secretive like'. 'I won't, believe me.' I said with a little sarcasm in my voice. As I did open the front door to our room, I looked to the left, then to the right. Nothing. Figures. I thought to myself. I shut the door and locked all of the locks. 'Not A damn thing. Not even a note saying 'I love you', or anything.' I laughed at that, as did Mariah. When we were done with our 'Character Changes' we looked each other over and approved. With our scarves on and sunglasses, we walked out the door. After we were in front of the elevator doors, we listened very carefully to what voices or noises we heard around us. God forbid we ran into our 'fans' while we had nowhere to escape to. That would suck. And why wouldn't 'Mariah' and 'Gwen' have bodyguards with them in Vegas for fuck's sake? Oh well, I'll just have to hope that these kids didn't even think of that. As the doors to the elevator opened up, we heard kid's voices. 'Oh Shit! Hurry, Mariah!' I said as we jammed into the elevator. I started pressing the 'Close Door' button as fast as I could. Just as the doors were closing, we saw them. There were about five or six of them and they skidded to a stop right in front of the closing elevator. As the doors sealed shut, we heard one or two of them saying, 'Dammit! We missed them! Go down...' and we couldn't hear anything else as we started moving. Down to the Lobby and the Casino. As we hit bottom and the doors opened, we saw no one in front of us. Just the familiar sounds of a busy Casino. As we walked out of the elevator though, not one or two people stared but around 20 people stared at us. Even while sitting at their slot machines. 'Damn!' I said too 'Mariah'. We are going to get a hell of a lot of attention tonight, babe. 'No Kidding!' she replied. 'How should we handle this?' I looked at her as I thought about it. 'Just keep your head down and follow me. I'll get us some bodyguards.' She did as I requested and followed me to the men's bathroom. Which was smart because about seven of the people that were staring at us, decided to follow us. Apparently thinking that we went into the Women's bathroom. Hence why I went into the Men's. I called Lane on his cell and told him what we were doing and what I wanted him and two other guys to do for us. He didn't seem to mind so I told him where we were and to knock twice, count to two and then knock twice again. He Ok'd that and I hung up. I told Mariah what was going on. 'No kidding? Awesome! That's exactly what we need!' 'No shit! I did not think that we would cause such a hubbub.' 'No Shit, babe. I didn't even think, at first, that people would even know who we were! Guess I was *way* wrong. Damn!' As 'Mariah' and I looked in the mirror to make sure we looked just as 'good' as we did was when we left our room, we heard the knocks from Lane and his other 'bodyguard to the stars.' I said 'Enter!' and in they came. 'What the fuck?' Lane said. You two look exactly like who you guys were going for! What were you thinking? Going out alone?' I looked at Lane and his buddy and replied, 'We were not thinking that we did look like them! At least that closely!' He looked at me and said, 'Well, you were *wrong*! You both look *exactly* like them!' 'Well, I know that now, butthead! That's why we need bodyguards! So, you are going to do it, right?' 'For how long?' 'Until we go in our room for the night/morning/whatever!' 'Fine, Gia.' 'Good! Let's go then. We want to gamble.' As I walked out of the restroom, it was just assumed that Lane would be my bodyguard and Lane would be Mariah's. We were stopped by a group of about 50 people deep. With flashbulbs. My worst nightmare. As soon as I turned the corner, outside the restroom, they started going off. I was blinded. Lane put his arm on my lower back and steered me through the crowd. With my head down of course. After we got through the initial crowd, we could, or, rather, I could breathe again.

'Thanks so much, Lane.' I told him. 'No problem babe. Just tell me what you and Shell want to play and I'll get you two a table. Lane looked over at Lane and he nodded. I asked Shelly what she wanted to play and I could tell, just by looking at her, that she was actually having fun now. 'Let's play blackjack first, Gia, I mean Gwen, and then we can think about what will be next. How's that?' 'Sound's good.' I replied to her. I told Lane, he and Lane found a table that was not crowded and they sat us down. The dealer, apparently, needed no 'introduction' as to who WE were. He smiled politely and introduced himself to us. I sort of kicked Mariah in the calf, shook my head at her and answered the dealer. I said 'hello' to him and he said hello back. He waved down a cocktail waitress and we ordered our first drinks for the evening. He dealt us in a hand and we took out our money and placed our bet. I brought $10,000 for these few days and Mariah brought $8,000. So, too make it fair, I only cashed in eight of my $10,000 to gamble with. As we played blackjack, more and more people were starting to sit at our table. The more we drank, the tipsier we became. We were both lightweights. That's when we knew there were a lot more people at our table but it didn't 'hit us' like it normally would if we were completely sober. Lane and Lane sure as Hell noticed and realized that it was getting out of control. Lane leaned down in my ear and whispered that it was 11pm and there was only standing room at our table; about 12 rows back. And that we either switch tables, switch casinos or head back to our room. I said, 'Let's go and play the slot machines.' 'Gwen', the Slot Machines are VERY hard to guard you at. Get what I mean?' I looked over at him and then at Mariah or, 'Juanita'. 'Ok. How about we go and play some poker and then take some pictures with our 'many fans' and then we'll call it a night?' Lane did look exasperated but agreed. I told the dealer we were done and to please put our chips in a carry-box. He did so and handed Mariah and I our boxes so that we could cash them out at the cashier. Since we were both very tipsy, we both wondered just how much we *did* win at that blackjack table. Probably not much since we were both talking up a storm, in our character's voices of course. Once Lane and Lane lead us up to the cashier's booth, we stopped and set our boxes on top of their counter. When I looked behind me, actually feeling a little tired already, I noticed that the 'fans' that did want pictures with us had followed us all the way to the cashier. I whispered to Lane and Mariah that we better get the picture ordeal over with so that they wouldn't follow us to the poker tables. I stepped back from the cashier and asked, in my 'Gwen' voice, 'Ok. Who wants a picture?' About 15 hands all raised. Most all of them were kids between the ages of 11 and 27. Maybe 30. I stood next to my first 'victim' and they took the picture themselves with their iPhone. I even had to practice on how to smile like Gwen Stefani. I know it sounds very, very weird, but that was my life. I didn't think it would get as out of hand as it did. Now I knew better. Especially for someone who did not like crowds at all. Unless my father was by my side. Then I could handle them. Well, better at least. Lane helped but he just didn't 'get it.' Thank God the cashier was being totally understanding. I hoped I had won at least $80 so that I could give her a semi-decent tip. I looked over at Mariah who was on her, I think, fifth 'fan.' I gave her a quick smile and she returned it. I knew then that she was having a hell of a time. Good. That is exactly what I wanted to give her on this trip. I kept smiling my 'Gwen' smile as did Mariah give her best 'Juanita' smile. For, I would say 90 straight minutes! Damn, we were tired! At the end of our 'picture opportunity', Lane & Sean pushed and walked us through the remaining crowd, telling them that 'Mariah™' and 'Gwen™' should be back tomorrow. That seemed to satisfy them. As we both turned back towards the booth to get any money that we won, we hoped at least, the cashier had already done her job in cashing each of us out. Plus had our money in our own separate bags. 'Good', I thought. We won't have to wait for our money plus run the risk of having more 'fans' come up to us. After she handed our bags to us, we walked as fast as we could to the elevators. As the doors closed in front of us we looked at each other, as we were at least five floors above the Lobby, we both burst out laughing to each other. 'Can you believe we got away with that shit?' I asked. 'No ma'am! Damn, that was a blast, Gia! Did *you* have fun, though? And I'm being serious.' 'Yes! I did! More than I really thought I would. Seriously!' I said, when I saw doubt creep into her expression. 'Well, good then. I really wanted you too, babe. And I was thinking about that on and off all evening we were down there. Hoping that you were having as much fun as I was. Seriously.' 'Well, thank you sweetie. I appreciate that. Out of all the friends I *do* have, which isn't many, as you know, I don't think any of them would worry about ME having fun. And 'I'm being serious about that, too. So, thank you Shelly. Love you. I hugged her. And, at that moment, I meant it. When we reached the top floor; our floor, we walked out, looked both ways and then half ran/half walked too our door. Once we opened it, the maid had obviously been there. The beds were made perfectly as well as all of our towels were switched out and clean. Perfect. The beds were turned down and a chocolate was on our pillow too. Nice touch. 'Wish it was a Werther's™ though.' I thought to myself. 'I am going to wash this shit off of my face and climb in bed, girly. Join me?' 'Absolutely babe! I'm beat!' I looked at my watch as I walked to the restroom. 2 am? Damn! The fucking pictures, plus the Cashier's Booth took over 2 hour's! Shitski! No wonder why we were so tired. I told Chelly what I found out. She couldn't believe it either. 'I'm actually glad we didn’t get drunk tonight, babe. We would feel *so* much worse right now. Especially when we had to be on the plane tomorrow evening. Yuk! Don't you think?' As we started brushing our teeth, I took out my toothbrush and said, 'Hell yes I'm glad we didn't get drunk tonight! Not only would we feel horrid, we might have said something 'not in character'. You know what I mean?' As we both put our toothbrushes back in our mouths, she looked at me and nodded her head, as in, 'Hell Yes!' When we were finished with washing off our make-up, taking our hair-pieces out and brushing our hair out, we walked back to our beds and grabbed our books. We got underneath our covers and I heard giggling outside our door again. 'Fuck!' I said out loud. 'Is this going to be happening all night?' Mariah just shook her head and gave our front door the bird and went back to reading. I got out of bed, made sure our door was completely locked. Then I saw the 'Do Not Disturb' sign hanging on the inside of our room. I grabbed my sunglasses off of the kitchen counter, slipped them on, took the 'Do Not…' sign, opened the front door and put the sign on the doorknob to our door. As I did this, I saw a glimpse of two of our culprits. Running like Hell down the hall. 'Kids, man!' I said under my breath. I shut the door with a slam and locked every lock, as usual, and climbed back into bed. 'Hopefully we don't need any ice in the middle of the night. We're screwed then.' Chelly said. 'No we're not.' I told her. 'That's when I call Lane and tell him to get us a bucket of ice. That's what detail is for. Or bodyguards'. 'True, Gia. True.' As we both settled in and started reading our books, the door knocking kept happening every 10 to 15 minutes. Finally, I had had enough. I called Lane and told him that I needed a 'bodyguard' posted outside our hotel room door all night. Until we woke up for the day. I even added in a 'Please' with that. He sighed and finally said 'yes.' I don't know why he would put up such a fucking stink about it. He knew that I would get my way in the end. OR I would call my father. What he didn't know was that I really did not want to call him because once he heard what Chell and I were doing he would tell us to absolutely stop. So, hopefully, Lane just took what my threat was as the truth and just do it. Turned out, he did just that. Hell, Stev-o wouldn't have done it. Unless HE was drunk. Which he would never do on the job. As Mariah and I were laying in our bed, reading our books, Lane was standing outside our door. I heard him trying to get comfortable outside our door. Not loudly, but loud enough to where I knew I wasn't going to be able to read with the noise. I got out of bed and went to the door, opened it and told him to please try to get comfortable. Please. I looked at him with my eyelashes batting. I said, 'Why don't you just take one of our chairs so you can sit on it so you won't be so damn uncomfortable? And I promise I will call the front desk to tell them to stop this bullshit. They will probably call their own security and then you can go back to your own room and chill. How does that sound?' Lane looked at me like I was being a lifesaver. 'Yes, ma'am. That would be awesome.' After I gave him the chair, I went back in the room and climbed in bed again. Hopefully for the last time this evening. I got Mariah caught up on what the hell was going on and continued reading... again. Thanks to Lane staying outside our room, we didn't hear a damn thing all night long. But, of course, we had our earplugs in as well as our eye-masks on the entire night as well. Nice!

Morning came and then early afternoon. The phone rang *so* damn loud that I must have lifted a foot off of the bed at least. It scared the Hell out of me and Michelle. 'What the Fuck?' was Mariah's first words of the day. Mine were not so nice either. Waking up like that. From a complete R.E.M. sleep is not recommended. OR even remotely pleasurable. As we slowly woke up, I realized what time it was and told Shelly. We ordered breakfast and I went and got myself 'ready' in the restroom. As I was looking in my suitcase deciding on what to wear for today on our ride to the airport, I decided that today, during the day, we were going to just have enough time to pack all of our belongings and do a double check around the room to make sure we didn't forget anything. Once we had ordered our breakfast and started semi-packing for the ride home, I got up, rolled my cart outside and locked our door again. I then, instantly put on my Chanel™ sweats and began packing; as did Mariah. 'I had so much fun, Gia girl. Thank you so much for inviting me, babe.' Yes, Mariah pretty much new me alright. My father only allowed me to buy one Louis Vuitton™ bag. And that's it! Oh well. Better than nothing, right? 'Yes it is, girl! Hell, with this trip and the limo plus the damn Penthouse, I don't know IF he'll let me charge anything on his card. We shall see though.' 'Good luck, btw!' 'Thanks babe.' I replied as I walked to the bedroom, picking up my handbag as I went. Once I sat on my bed, I dialed my father; looking at the bedside clock as I was doing so. 'Hello?' Again he didn't look at his caller ID. I was going to have to remind him to get used to doing that. Especially NOW with all of the sick fuckers out there. 'Hi Daddy!' I said very enthusiastically. 'Well, my baby has finally called me.' Even though his words sounded like he was sort of disappointed in me, I knew he was just fucking with me too. 'I know. I figured YOU could wait for a phone call. Especially since I am wayyy down on your 'important people' list.' He laughed a bit; more of a chuckle. 'Very funny, beautiful. How in Hell are you? Having fun, I hope?' 'Yes, we are! And we didn't really do anything! It is just so nice relaxing and doing nothing! Damn, baby, I missed you! When I said the word, 'baby', I whispered it, for obvious reasons. 'I know you have, love. That is why I decided to let you go. When Lane called me last night, he reported that you and Michelle have some 'game' going on? Pretending that you two are pop-stars or something? Why on earth would you want to do that? You *hate* attention. Especially that kind of attention, love.' I thought about that question for a minute. 'You know, Tata?' It started when we got off of the jet and you know how people stare at anyone who walks out of a private jet. Well, these people saw two very young girls/women walking down the stairs from your plane and just kept on staring.

Like they were trying to figure out if we were anyone 'famous'. You know how the 'masses' are, daddy. So, I just thought of this 'plan' on the way to the hotel. Just an extra little game to fuck with people is all, Tata. But, the main thing on my mind is you. I miss you so much! Much more than I thought I would. And that's the truth! Damn, daddy. I truly miss you! 'I do as well, my Gia.' Very much. And, as you have said, much more than I had expected as well. I assumed, which I *rarely* do, that my work at both offices would keep me from thinking about you so much when you were on this trip. I was very *wrong*, kitten.' 'Hearing him say those words were music to my ears. 'I love you baby. And just keep thinking, like *I* am, that I will be home in a few hours. That way, it doesn't sound so bad I guess. Even though the nights are the...' 'Worst. Yes, I know, love. Ok. I better get off of the phone, G.G. I feel emotion in my voice or throat, rather. Anyway, people are sort of around me and I will not get emotional in front of them. Yes?' 'Of course, father. I'll see you when we all fly home. Ok?' 'Ok, baby doll.' 'See you then, daddy. I love you and be careful. See you soon.' I blew him a kiss over the phone and hung up. Wow. My father truly missed me. Missed me as a girlfriend, wife, whatever! And, right then, I realized that I did too. Damn. Oh well, yet another 'thing' we have to deal with in therapy.

As we were waiting on Lane and his other detail guys, I walked into the living room where Chell was sitting on the couch. I instantly felt bad that we were leaving earlier than planned. Michelle looked up and I sat down next to her. Chell? Next time? I promise you that we will stay about one week, do all of the things that we can possibly do and then come home. It shall not be all rushed and stupid just because of some stupid trip my father is making me go on, ok, babe? I'm sorry, too, for all of this rushing around. Forgive me?' Chell looked at me as if I was nuts. 'Forgive you? Sweetheart, you have given me the time of my life! I would not have traded this trip for anything in the world! I promise you, hon; and, yes, I forgive you! If there is anything to forgive, that is.' 'Ok, then, babe. Let me call Lane and tell him that we are ready then.' I sat on my bed and dialed his number. 'Hello, Ms. Mahari. Are you two ready yet?' 'Yes, we are Lane. Packed and even made three walk a rounds to make sure we didn't forget anything. So, we are all yours!' I could almost feel him blushing over the telephone. I knew he was thinking about Michelle. Hell. He had been looking at her and treating her like she was *his* property. 'Alright, then ma'am. We'll be down there in five minutes then.' 'Sounds good, Lane. Did you want to talk to Michelle before I hang up or anything?' There was a slight pause on the other end. 'Um, why would I need to talk to Chelly, ma'am?' 'Just curious is all. See ya soon.' And I hung up. As I looked up, Michelle was staring right at me. 'Gia?! Is it that obvious?' 'Is what 'that obvious?' I replied. 'That I think that he is cute and all of that.' I looked up at her as I got up off of the bed and walked over to her. I sat down and took one of her hands. 'Hon. It has been obvious to me since we were in the limo when we were being driven over from the airport; to the hotel. Just as I finished that sentence, the doorbell rang. Twice and then twice again. Lane's code so that we knew that it was him. I got up off of the bed to answer the door and told her that it was, indeed, Lane. She instantly blushed and hurried to 'collect' herself in the restroom. I answered the door and let him inside. Along with three other detail guys. 'Where the hell did the other detail come from Lane?' 'After last night, since you told me that you two were going home early, I decided to call in some reinforcements. Just in case. Plus, I spoke with your father on the phone this morning too. He wanted more guys on you two as well. So, here we are. Now, the limo is downstairs. 'And you are sure you want to go back home early?' I looked down at my feet and over at Shell, whom was checking out Lane in a way like a *very* edible cream pie, I decided right then to tell Lane what was going on. 'Lane, my father wants me to get home early from this trip because we, or *I* have to go with him up north. For 'Org.' business, so I will be travelling alone. So, as you can probably guess, it is *very* important. That's why I have to go home and cut this trip off. But next time, we will go for a full week. I promise you that. And… I will, of course, be bringing Michelle. How does that sound? Hmm?' 'Ok then. That sounds fantastic, Gia. Thank you, ma'am.' He said 'Thank You, ma'am' in a sort of hushed whisper though. Probably so Chell would not hear. 'Almost ready?' Lane said. 'Yep! Just about. All we have to do is grab our purses and then we're ready. And Lane? Just have the other guys that you brought take the suitcases? They are the ones with the wheels on them so it shouldn't be too bad.' After Lane acknowledged me, he told the other detail to take the suitcases. They walked out of the door, with me behind Lane and Michelle behind me. 'Just make sure that the car is parked pretty close to the front door of the hotel. Just in case Bullshit ensues, that is.' 'I'll call Mohammed and tell him that, ma'am.' As he called Mo, Michelle and I made sure that we had our room keys or cards, more like. As we were in front of the elevator, we *all* heard the giggles and laughter that we were now getting used to whenever we left our room. We all got in and the door shut quietly as we slowly went down to the lobby. 'Any weirdness as far as 'fans or little girls or young boys in the lobby yet?' I asked Lane. 'We haven't been down there this morning yet, Gia. So, we don't know.' 'Well, I guess we'll know soon enough!' 'Yeah. In about two seconds.' Michelle said under her breath even though everyone heard her. As the doors opened, we were greeted by a *swarm* of people. I couldn't even tell how many there were! 'Oh my God!' I said out loud. Lane grabbed my arm, pretty roughly. But, Hell, he *had* too. He also grabbed Michelle and started to try and walk forward. We just put our heads down and took their lead; both holding onto our handbags for dear life and covering our faces with our hands and part of our hoodies. Which, thank God, we decided to bring AND wear. Mohammed must have seen the chaos from just outside the limo doors. He rushed inside the lobby and sternly told everyone to 'back off' and to let them 'breathe for God's sake.' Thank God for Mo & he had enough to worry about. As we slowly made our way to the limo, I lifted my eyes towards the lobby patrons as well as the front desk to see how they were reacting to this chaos. They all had a facial expression just like one of those Sex Dolls. The blow up ones. Their mouths were in a perfect 'O' shape and staring right at us. Not moving at *all*. Not that they could do anything. And I am sure it was quite a site. I was wondering, as we were going out of the front doors, if they were all going to try and follow us to the airport. I would think that airport security would definitely keep them out. As the doors to the car were shut and we pulled out, we all let out a sigh of relief. Damn, fuck, Hell that was horrid! ‘Shit guys. I am sorry you had to go through that mess. If I would have known it was going to be that bad, we wouldn't have done it. Or we would have done it totally different. 'No Shit?' was one of detail’s reply. 'Yes, whatever your name is. Problem? Except *my* apology?' I was in *no* mood to take bullshit from him. Let alone any lip from him. Hell! I didn’t even know him! He looked at me with a brief 'are you ‘*serious*’' type of look and then a more 'yes ma'am' type of look. 'That's better, Douche. And you should know better than to talk to me that way, too. Especially in front of guys that are above you in rank. 'I said that little bit on purpose. Just to put him back in his place. Michelle, put her head down, of course. Not wanting to embarrass the employee. Or looked out of the window since we were in a car. It didn't happen all of the time but it *did* happen. Especially when my father wasn't around. In fact, I was thinking that I would have to talk to my father about that when I got home. And if he asked me why I didn't bring it up earlier, I will just say that I didn't really notice it until later in the trip. And that we only had one more day left. No big deal. I took a look at the particular detail guy in question and he was looking out of his window and behind us. Probably ignoring what I said to him because of the other guys around him. He was not the type of guy to be embarrassed by a 'woman' reprimanding him in front of his 'buddies' or, what I heard *he* called them, 'his minion's'. Whatever. I knew that sometimes he was very nice to me and all. I just did *not* want him to think that he could take advantage of the position of being on my father's daughter's detail. At All. Especially in front of other detail guys that were not usually *on* my detail. This trip was just special. Not your normal trip, so to speak. As we turned onto the Tropicana Avenue, I looked out of the back window. I saw about four cars following us. Or, from my training, it looked like they were following us. 'Mohammed? Are those four cars behind, following us? Like 'from the hotel' following us? 'Yes Ma'am. They are. Just tell me which entrance you would like me to turn into, east or west for the Private Plane Gateway. Ok, Ma'am?' 'Sounds good to me, Mohammed. And thank you *SO* much for driving us. Michelle and I appreciate it. A lot!' 'Anything for you, Miss Mahari. You know that!' I whispered to Mariah and asked her if she would like to sit next to Lane on the Jet for the ride home. She looked at me like I was The Fairy Godmother. 'Can you do that without him knowing that I wanted him too?' 'Hell, yes I can, babes! No problem! I'll just tell Lane that he is now in charge of you and 'So and So' is in charge of me. To give him a little more 'intense' training or whatever.' She smiled from ear to ear after I was done speaking. 'Yes!!! A thousand times yes! Thank you, Gia!' As I told Lane to tell the other guys the new plan on who was guarding whom, they arranged themselves in the limo. Lane sitting next to Chell and 'Sean' it turned out, was my bodyguard, and sitting next to me. I leaned over, after telling Mohammed to park as close to the front of the Jet as possible, turned to

Chelly and called her a horny whore and then laughed. As I pulled away, she looked at me with such an innocent look on her face that I almost questioned my thinking about her 'wants' in a guy. But then she started laughing in my ear and said that, 'Yeah, I think he's hot. Better than the guy that was protecting me last night in the casino. 'Well good then. Glad to be of service, bitch!' She looked at me and laughed. Knowing that what she did tell me would go to the grave. I never told my any of my secrets. 'Do you want me to ask him or Steven if he has a GF and if not, if he would like to give you his digits? I don't mind.' 'Sure babe! That would be quite nice. He is totally my type. BIG, shaved bald and built like a Mack truck. I feel safe around those types of guys. Speaking of types of guys, what is *your* type of guy, Gia?' While Mohammed was parking the limo as close to my father's Jet as possible, I told Chell that I liked older guys. She looked at me and said, 'How much older, girly? Like grandpa age or what?' I looked at her and almost started laughing my ass off. I didn't know if it was the tired giggles or the possible stress of getting out amongst tons of people or what. But I told her that 'grandpa age' was too damn old. Just mature guys. I didn't really have an age in mind. Especially since I was a 'virgin' and had no clue about ages. She seemed satisfied with that answer. The car stopped and everyone was assessing the situation. Mainly Lane and his guys.

Chapter 19

As the car stopped and Mo opened our doors, we all slowly got out. Lane had both of our arms. Only on Michelle's, his hand was *holding* hers. How cute, I thought. As we started walking up the stairs, Sean made me go first, his head on a swivel; handgun out. As I was safely inside, he let Michelle go on up with him behind her. As we were tucked safely inside, the stewardess rapped once on the cabin to the cockpit once and the stairs came up silently. She closed the door, locked it and secured the safety bar. She smiled at me and told us if we wanted anything that she would be out as soon as the plane leveled off. I told her thank you and sat in my sofa and buckled in; as did Lane and Shell; still holding hands. 'Good sign.' I thought to myself. Don't blow this one, Chell. He has a *great* job, with even greater pay. And, he seems like such a nice guy I thought to myself. 'Ok. We only have about one hour in the air. And that is counting circling the airport. Remember?' I reminded her. 'Oh yeah! That's right babe! Well then, since we have so little time up in the air, I will just sit right here, chat with Lane and nibble on my peanuts until we start circling the airport at Burbank, right, Gia?' 'That is correct!' I answered. I leaned back against the couch, closed my eyes and relaxed until we did start circling Burbank Airport. I wasn't sleepy, I was just thinking about the 'trip' to The Bohemian Grove when I got back home. Just like my father told me before I left. I wondered what that was going to be like. I had heard of that place before. Mainly, only overhearing conversations between my father and Harris, but that was about it. At least my father was going to be with me, thank God. I did *not* want to go but I also knew that I did not have a choice in the matter. God, I prayed that it wasn't going to be horrible. But it was a 50/50 type thing. Even though my dad was very protective of me, if Harris said otherwise, my dad had no choice. And not every time that he would say 'No' would the choice be a beating. Harris would just get his way.

The *asshole*. I hope that The Grove was not one of those times. As I sat there thinking about my 'little trip' with my father, Mariah apparently had woken up. 'What are you thinking SO damn intently about, Gia?' 'Good Afternoon, Miss Thang! How was your sleep?' 'Good. Especially the lap I was sleeping on, huh, Lane?' He looked down at her and grinned. 'Yes, Michelle. But my leg is now officially asleep. Can I adjust?' She laughed a little and moved into the sitting position. After Lane told her 'Thank you, babe' her attention went back to me. 'So, what's going on?' I looked at her wondering if I should tell her the absolute truth. I knew she had never heard of the location. But I also knew that I should not tell a soul about it either. I wasn't even sure if Lane knew about the trip or if he was even going. 'I was just thinking about a trip that I have to go with my dad. It's going to be so boring. But, oh well. Maybe I can shop when he is in meetings. Just thinking about boring crap like that.' I took a quick glance at Lane to see if any recognition was on his face. None that I could see. But I wasn't sitting right across from him. He did look over at me when I mentioned it to Chell, though. He and I finished our mimosas and the empty glasses were sitting on the glass coffee table. 'Sounds exciting as Hell. Why do you even have to go?' she asked me. He just asked and he said he wanted the company. He also said that if I decided to go, there might be a shopping trip in the deal.' Which was a complete lie. But, I had to come up with something, quick. And believable too. 'Ah! I see. Well, Hell! I'd go for that, too. I've seen your dad's shopping trips. Totally worth it.' I laughed. It was most of the time true. Only if it were true *all* of the time. 'See what I mean? That's why I'm going.' As I just finished my sentence, we felt the plane bank and the stewardess walked in, took our empty glasses and told us to buckle up. We were getting ready to land. As we sat up straighter, we put our seatbelts back on and got ready for landing. Home sweet home, I thought. As the jet landed, smoothly as always, we sat until it was done taxing towards my father's limo. When it stopped and shut off its engines, I looked out of my window and there was Steve, sitting in the passenger seat. Waiting until our door was open and the stairs descended. As the pilot came out of the cabin, he hoped everyone had a good flight and was happy to be home. We all thanked him for a smooth and fast flight as the stewardess opened the door. As the stairs descended, we grabbed our luggage and belongings. Just as Lane was about to stick his head out of the door to look around and at the waiting car, Steve stuck his entire head inside the cabin. 'Howdy, folks! How was your trip?' 'Oh my God, Steve! You gave me a heart attack! Douche!' 'Nah. Maybe a friendly one. But nothing horrible like that, right?' 'Ok. Whatever, weirdo. You're forgiven. Now. Can we please exit the aircraft now? Oh. And I just noticed that there are two cars outside the plane. What's up with that?' 'Oh. I thought, or rather, your *dad* thought, that it would be nice for Michelle to be taken straight home by your dad's second driver? And with Lane in the backseat just so he can make sure she is comfortable. How's that, Michelle?' 'Um... sounds good to me? What do you think, Gia?' 'That's fine with me, Shell. But it's totally unnecessary since we're taking her home first anyway, Steven. But since the car *and* driver are already here, why not? Have fun you two. And don't do anything I wouldn't do, k?' 'Wow. Really? Coolness!' Chell said. We hugged and I gave her a kiss on the cheek. 'I'll call you in a day or so. Definitely before my father and I leave for his trip, ok? And you call me whenever. For *any* reason. Know what I mean?' She winked at me. 'Absolutely, babe. And, again, thank you so much for the trip, sweetheart. Love ya.' And off they went to their limo. 'Stev-o. What is that all about? Separate limos and all?' I asked him. 'It was your father's idea. He is in our Limo, babe. Plus, he wants to talk to you regarding the Bohemian Grove trip. Obviously, without anyone else in the car.' 'Oh. Alright. I get it.' He put his hand on my lower back, as usual and we descended the stairs to the ground. All of a sudden it kicked in. My dad was *in* my limo. Right *now*. I missed him a lot! I didn't even think about '*that*' when Steve said it. Now I knew why he wanted us to be alone on the way home. And, Steven was driving up front with my dad's main driver. As we walked to the car, Steve took my suitcase from me and I adjusted my handbag better on my shoulder. I never even thought that my dad would be here. Not with Michelle travelling with me. It would have made him extremely uncomfortable. But, he took care of that little 'problem'. As usual, I thought. I sort of laughed inside as I thought about my father. That damn man gets *everything* he wants. One way or another. I guess the 'sad' part is that I didn't mind when it came to me at all. As Steve opened up the car door on the opposite side from my father's usual seat, I climbed in, not looking at him (on purpose of course) and then, when Steve closed my door, I looked over at him...slowly. Once our eyes locked, it was like I hadn't seen him in months. He had been enjoying the sun out at the pool. He was more handsome than when I had left. If that was possible. 'Daddy, you look *so* handsome. What did you do? I mean, not that you don't every day, but right now. For some reason. You look phenomenal.' He didn't say a word. He just sat, staring at me. At, it seemed, every inch of my face, hair, eyes...and then my body. What he could see of it, that is. He reached his left hand up too touch and brush the right side of my face. 'You are more beautiful than I thought possible, my Gia. I missed you so much.' 'I missed you too, daddy. Very much. Come here baby.' He leaned in, apparently not surprised at me calling him that anymore. I took both sides of his face and kissed him. Soft at first and then with more passion. I was instantly 'ready.' He must have sensed it because he started unzipping his fly. Of his business suit. He must have been at the office for the better part of the day. That was obvious. As he slid his pants off of his legs, he started unbuttoning his shirt. His coat/jacket was already laying across from him on another seat. Once he was about completely naked, except for his underwear, I was down to my bra and G-string. He sat there for a bit. Just taking me all in. Almost to the point where I felt uncomfortable. Or insecure. Totally *not* me. If you haven't gotten that clue yet. 'Come here, my baby.' I flung myself into his arms. Entwined we were in less than a minute. Comfortable. Safe. Warm. Those were the words that were going through my mind as we were kissing. Very slowly and passionately at first. Then more frantic next. As we came up for breath, he said, looking at me, 'You will *never* leave me for this long again, Gia. I tried. I did. Ask anyone about my mood. After the first two days you were gone. I believe Steve was the only one who 'Got it'. 'Well, baby, I'm home now. Here with you. At your beck and call. Pretty much, anyway. Except for school.' He smiled at that and then just held me. That was when I realized. Right that moment. That he was so *lonely*. He had to be the loneliest man in the world. At least one of them. Especially the ones that had money, that were in Fortune 500, etc. Damn, he needed someone. But women of his caliber were so few and far between. 'So, daddy, tell me how you've been, the business, everything! I want to know it *all*.' He looked at me. With complete and utter surprise. 'Don't worry, daddy. I am *not* done with 'that' yet. As I looked down at his lap. 'Well, in that case...' we both laughed at that. 'God I missed you princess. But, did you and... Michelle have fun?' 'Yes. Chell and I had a blast. We never even went dancing. We were going to but then decided that we can do that at home. So we decided to have a massage after we laid out by the pool. Then we went back up to our room, ordered room-service and watched the damn news! The local news dad! It was so... oh, I don't know. So adult? I sort of giggled or laughed at that. We didn't even want to go out dancing. Maybe if I wasn't there, Mariah would have, but she sure as hell seemed like she was having a good time. And then, after we ate, we both read and crashed. Oh! And then Lane and Michelle have crushes on each other as of yesterday. And, yes. Before you say anything, I *will* talk to her regarding The 'Dating Detail Rules'. To the 'T'. Promise my sweet, handsome, father of mine.' He looked at me down his nose and replied, 'Please do, love. I do *not* want another 'detail dating' disaster. Ever again. I've had, as you know, so many. I don't need another one. 'I will do my best, father. Promise. The rest, as you know, is up to them.' I scooted over to him again and continued to kiss him. And at the same time, rubbing him gently but firmly between his legs. That made him moan. And, quite loudly at that. 'Oh God, Gia. If you keep on doing *that*, we shall have to fuck right here and now.' 'Fuck? Hm. I don't know if I'm in the mood for 'fucking.' We'll see how I feel tonight. That is, if I'm invited. 'Oh. You're 'Invited' alright. In fact, you're commanded to be in my room tonight.' 'Commanded? Well, I will be honest and say that those domineering words sort of turn me on. Don't forget that this evening…?' 'Oh, I will *not*. After all, I ***OWN*** you.' As he was telling Steve what he wanted him to do this evening for him, I thought about our little exchange just now. It was this kind of banter that I did love having with him. It did turn me on. Just like a normal boyfriend and girlfriend. But I know I was kidding myself. We were not a normal boyfriend and girlfriend. We were family. Father and Daughter. He knew that as well as I did. But until he did something, I was stuck. But since I enjoyed sleeping with him, plus the protection I received from him, I couldn't stop it. Not that I *would* anyway. Unless he wanted too and saw it as a priority. That was the problem. He was in the same exact place I was in. Except for the 'Priority' part that is. As we were driving up the long driveway, my father was looking out his window, holding my right hand with his left. 'Almost home, kitten. Did you miss your bedroom at all when you were gone? Or were you not gone long enough, Princess?' 'I missed OUR bed the most. Sleeping and cuddling/spooning with you Tata. That's what I missed the most.' And that was a true statement. Whenever I closed my eyes in Vegas at night that is what I thought about. Everything that I told him. Plus things that I didn't tell him. As the driver pulled the car to a stop in front of the house, he opened my dad's door and Steve opened mine. As Steve was getting the luggage out of the trunk, my father and I walked up the steps to the house. I watched absentmindedly, my dad unlock the front door. 'Where is Juanita, Tata?' I asked him. 'She ran to the store very quick to pick up some of your staples. Like your favorite cereal and more milk, etc. She should be home any minute, baby. 'Oh, ok. I'll be upstairs unpacking Tata. I'll see you at dinner? Or, whenever you need me. K?' 'Sounds good, babe. I have some work to do in my office. If you need anything, let me know, yes? Get comfortable too, love. Tonight, no need to dress up for dinner. For you at least. You may eat with your white gown on if you'd like. Then it is retiring too 'daddy's room' for the night. Yes?' 'Thank you, Tata. I appreciate it. I think I'll put my clothes away and then take a nice, warm bath. Will you come up personally and tell me when supper is Tata? I would really like that. Just this one time? Without the Com?' He looked at me a little funny. Then said, 'Of course, kitten. Whatever you want. I can do that. See you before dinner then. Enjoy your bath baby. Wish I could join you. So that shall be *next* time.' 'Absolutely, daddy. I would love that.' We then parted ways and I walked upstairs to my room. As I opened my door, suitcase in my other hand behind me, I visually took in all of my things. Well nothing had changed since I had been away. I knew all of my clothes had been washed. As well as my sheets changed, too. I walked in and lifted my case up onto the bed. As I unzipped it and folded the top of it back, I heard my father coming up the stairs and his office door close. Even though I thoroughly enjoyed my trip, it was nice to be home in familiar surroundings. Knowing what to expect, pretty much, at each hour of every day. As I put most, if not all, of my clothes into the hamper, I picked up my various pairs of shoes and put them in their places on my closet floor. I double checked my case, made sure there was nothing left inside, zipped it back up and carried it to its spot on the very top of my closet. I grabbed a towel off of one of my shelves and put it on the top of my commode seat top. I also went and grabbed a washcloth for my face as well. I made sure that all of my hair products were full or at least full enough for washing and conditioning my hair and sat on my towel on my toilet seat; turning on the bath faucets. As I waited for the tub to fill up, I thought about tonight. And it wasn't until just then that I realized just how much I wanted sex. And from who, too. Damn. Why did he have such a *hold* on me? I thought. It had to be because he was my first. And that we had sex at least four times a week. That had to be it. I knew it was not some perverted sex-thing, because he was my father. Or some taboo fantasy because of the exact same reason. I knew I was too young for those things. Oh well. Whatever. I enjoyed it, I knew he enjoyed it, so who cared right now anyway? Steve seemed to get over it pretty quickly so screw it. Until my father tells me '*enough*', then this is exactly what we are going to do. And if the opportunity presented itself for me to get married, then so be *that* as well. I reached over and turned off the nozzles of the tub. As I walked to my dresser, I opened up the second drawer from the top and took out one of my white sleeping gowns. A Victorian looking, long, light cotton, sheath type, nightgown. But it was sure as Hell comfortable. And, I didn't care what I looked like at dinner. Plus, my dad told me HE didn't care what I wore either. So, this was going to be it. As I slowly eased into the tub, I laid back on my bath-pillow. God, the water felt good! I just laid there day-dreaming for a while. I think. Next thing I knew, my mouth was filling up with water. Holy-Shitski! I sat up as fast as I could and spit the water out. 'Let's drown, why don't you, idiot!' I said under my breath. I grabbed my razor and soaped up my legs and shaved them. Then my arms. Now was the woman-scaping that I always deemed mandatory. When I was done with all of my shaving 'needs', I washed my face and everything else 'underwater' and then un-plugged the drain. I stood up, grabbed a towel for my hair, bent over and wrapped it up in a turban. Grabbed my other towel and started drying off the rest of my body. As soon as I was satisfied with how dry I was, I got out, folded the bath-mat over the edge of the tub and walked over to the counter. I grabbed a few things from under my sink and prepped my hair, which was now barely long enough to reach the top of the crack of my ass. 'I am going to have to get my hair trimmed.' I said. I towel dried the hell out of my hair and put my products in it. Mousse at the roots, hair protectant all over, to protect it from the heat and, finally, blow-drying it. As I was doing that, upside down first, I leaned over to the right a bit and grabbed my big roll brush. It was a kick-ass brush for any length of hair. It heated itself in the middle from the dryer and then once you started 'rolling' parts of your hair, it cooled itself and stayed that way. Until you brushed it out to how you wanted it. I loved it. Anyway, once my bath and hair was done and my bathroom was as clean as it was when I first got in there, I walked out and over to my bed. I got on top of it and started to put my other things that I took to Vegas, away. As I picked up my last object, well, next to last, my book, I put that on my bedside table. I turned back to my bed. Looking at the last thing that was left from my trip. Something that I did not mention earlier when we were all in Vegas. It was a present that I bought my father. Yes, I knew I had used my father's Black card to buy it. It was just 'easier' that way. I was going to give him the cash, this evening, when we were in his bedroom tonight for it. It was a man's necklace that was made entirely of high-end Sterling Silver & Platinum. The 'pendant' at the end of the chain was a triangle that read, on the back, 'To my one and only lover, teacher, and dearest man in my life. Love, Gia' with the date, of course. I hoped to God that he liked it. I was pretty sure he would. It was his favorite 'type' of jewelry metal; Silver/Platinum. Plus it was a personal gift from someone he cared immensely about. Or I hoped he did. More than sex, anyway. I put it back in its gift box. Another masculine touch. I had Tiffany™ wrap it for me. In its most masculine gift wrapping. A dark brown box with a black net ribbon and put inside a dark brown Tiffany™ bag. I put the bag into my closet, next to my overnight bag that I would be using to sleep in his room tonight. The only things that I did take into his room at night were my favorite pillow and my nighttime facial cream. As I put everything away that was on my bed, my com went off. 'Miss Gia? Dinner is being served. I just wanted you to know, bambina.' I laughed a little. Juanita's accent was so cute. I knew that on Friday nights she went with three of her other friends, also maids in the area, to an English speaking class that was given at the local Catholic Church. My father even had his second limo driver take her there. She was ecstatic about that. Plus, it was a lot easier on her, too. I checked myself in my bedroom mirror, decided I didn't look too bad at all and went downstairs for some yummy dinner. Juanita Style! As I descended the stairs, I saw my father and Steve sitting at the table already. 'Oh Shit.' I said to myself. 'I hope I am not late.' I looked at my watch. No, not by my count I wasn't. Weird. I walked to my normal seat at the table and sat down. I waited until they were done talking and then interjected, 'I hope I am not late. Am I?' My father looked at me menacingly. 'Oh God. Not now!' 'My dear, *you* are *not... late.*' He looked at Steve and the both of them started laughing. 'Ok you boogers. Whose lovely idea was this?' I said with a joking tone in my voice. My father looked at me in his normal gaze and said that it was indeed, his idea.' That was surprising, actually. I'm sure Stev-o agreed wholeheartedly as well. Fucker. I am so going to get him back. And I shot him a glance 'telling' him so, too. He just picked up his glass of water with his middle finger pointed towards me sticking straight out. My father, obviously couldn't see it from his chair. I flipped Steve off as I 'scratched' my left eye-brow. 'As Juanita and family put the dishes on the table and left the room to consume their own meal, my father took a bite from his salad. 'So, love. Are you finished unpacking all of your things?' 'Yes, I am, Tata. Everything is put away. Thank God. As you know, I hate putting things away after a vacation or a trip. Packing, to me, is actually fun.' I took a look at Steve and said, 'Yes, I know, Steve. I'm a weirdo.' 'Anyway, father, I am all unpacked, bathed and so ready for bed.' I looked at him a lot longer after that response, than anyone would do. Mainly because I saw that Steve was looking down at his plate; not paying attention. And my father was looking straight at me. As usual, catching the hint instantaneously. 'Well fabulous then, kitten. You should sleep pretty damn deep then. I have found that no matter where you sleep. No matter how comfortable the bed is, or how sleepy you are when you return; even if you had a massage, you still sleep the best that first night at home. I still, too this day. Do not... know...why.' As he said those words, the answer to my reply, his eyes never left mine. At that moment, I knew that I was madly in love with him. And wanted him right now. Now. Fuck. This whole sexual, sleeping, kissing, fucking my dad/father/whatever was *all* his fault. So, he was going to fix it when it needed to be fixed. Basically when I said it needed to be. Like before I moved out of his house. Steven must have been spoken to, regarding 'us', or 'this'. Or maybe my father might have gotten inside his brain. Because not once did he look up, pause eating, or seem like he was listening to us. Or me. Not even following our conversation. I kept looking at my father for a while and then finally winked at him and smiled and slowly turned to look at Steve. 'So Stev-o, what did you do when I was gone? Anything interesting? Or same shit, different day?' My father gave me a slight disapproving look. Steve looked at me and replied, 'Well, G, nothing completely exciting. Went with your father to Chicago for a business meeting. That lasted for 12 hours. Then basically same shit, different day. Not that I see it that way, of course, Gia. I love my job. And, no. I am not just saying that because your father is sitting here either.' As he said that, he looked right at me. 'I am very lucky to have this job as well as his trust. You know that, Gia.' He then looked at my father. 'Sorry about having to address that in front of you, sir.' 'No need to apologize, Steven. I appreciate your honesty. As usual.' Yep. My father had gotten into Steve's brain. Regarding getting involved in our personal stuff. 'Good!' I thought. 'That will get rid of any fights in the future regarding my father &and my privacy.' I continued eating the main course from my plate. Head down. Without looking up I told them both that I bought them each a present when I was in Vegas. 'And even though I bought them with your Black card, daddy, I have saved enough cash for both, so I will give it to you this evening. So, it *is* actually from me. Both of them are. 'Why, thank you, my dear. Very much. I had no idea you would be thinking of the people at home while you were on your relaxing get-away.' 'Yes, thanks G.' Steve said. I looked up while putting my napkin on my plate and pushing it away from me to the right. 'Of course! Just because I was on a vacay, doesn't mean I would forget my two favorite men in the whole world! Since we are done with dinner, Tata, may I go upstairs and retrieve them both and give them to you before I retire for bed?' When I said the last part of that sentence, I looked at my father. He quickly winked with his right eye, the one furthest from Steven and said that I could. 'Thank you!' I got up from the table and walked quickly from the table to the stairs. As I reached the top, I opened my bedroom door and went to my bed, grabbed both gift bags and ran out of my room, closed the door behind me and hurried back downstairs. As I reached the table, Steve and my dad had not moved from their chairs. 'Why don't we take this little soiree to the brandy room'. How does that sound, yes?' 'Sounds good to me, boss. The chair will be a lot more comfortable.' 'I was thinking the very same thing. ‘What do you think, Gia?' I looked at him and then Steven. 'That sounds fine. Yes.' We all got up and walked towards the brandy room. As my father got there first, he opened up the windows and let the slight ocean breeze into the room. Since nights in the summer were still pretty cool in the evening, it was heavenly. I sat on the small couch next to my father's chair; a black leather recliner. He loved that chair. Even when a close friend told him that they were associated with white trash, my father responded ‘not at these prices’. All HE cared about were that they were damn comfortable. That's why he had a brown leather one on his jet. Funny, I guess. Hell, at that time, he probably didn't know what 'white trash' meant. As we all sat down, Steve on the other side of the couch from me, I handed Steven his and then my father his gift. Please, these are not a big deal. Not expensive. So feel free to open them all at once. Again, no big deal. I, again said that last part while looking at my father. He looked at me with a question in his gaze. He had no clue as to what this would be. And it didn't hit me until now how Steve would react to my gift to my dad. I didn't care I finally decided. Knowing him and how Steven did feel about the two of us, he probably won't read the engraving in front of Steve. Hopefully not, anyway. As they both were opening their gifts, I sat there looking at the curtains blowing in the breeze. I loved white, lacey, linen type curtains. They were so light that they blew with just the slightest breeze blowing. That is why I chose them to be put in my room as well. Steve-o opened his gift first. His 'monogrammed' T-shirt. I was hoping he would like it. He was always saying he wanted T-shirts from my travels and he always picked them up when he was traveling with my father, too. As he pulled it out of the paper and held it up to look at it, he smiled his big old, 'Steve-Smile'. Big smile and all teeth. 'Thanks Gia! I do not have a 'dressy' t-shirt yet! At that my father exploded with a heartfelt laugh. 'Dressy t-shirt huh, Steven. I may need to give you a raise so that you can round out your wardrobe with 20-30 of those'! My father then opened his present. 'Fabulous! Thank you for thinking about me, baby-girl. Very much. I mean it. Love ya.' He leaned over and kissed me on the cheek. 'You're welcome Daddy. I love you too. And even though this gift isn't much, just know that I am so grateful to have you as a father. And Steve I am grateful to have you as a bodyguard. When we're together, that is. You're the best damn bodyguard ever.' Steve held the shirt up for my father. We all laughed at Steve as he slipped on his first new luxury tee. My father had opened his gift up to see the contents of the box. But he waited until Steven was finished first. As my father opened the box, he just stared at it. He sat there for a bit, looking at it. Steven looked at me. I just shrugged. My dad then took his left hand and turned it over, quickly read it, and turned it back facing forward. He did not let on that there was anything written on the back. Why, this is beautiful, my baby. Very nice and unique. You know I only prefer simple jewelry and this is perfect. Goes with everything. Thank you, my sweetheart. I appreciate it. And you must have paid a pretty penny for it, as well. 'Oh', I said. I reached into my sweat pants pocket, took my money and handed my father the cash that I had been saving up for this trip and the gifts I was going to buy them. 'I wanted to pay for them, Tata. Not you. Oh, Steve-o? Be sure when Juanita or you wash that shirt? Do *not* to put it in the dryer. It will shrink. And we do not want that to happen.' He laughed. Completely understanding that. 'I'll tell her, sweetheart. And thank you again, baby.' He stood up with his gift, bent down to give me a kiss on the cheek and said 'I am hitting the hay. Sorry to be the party pooper but, as Mr. F said, it was a hell of a day. See you both tomorrow, Gia. And you too, Sir.' 'Thank you Steven. Sleep well.' And we were finally alone. My father looked over at me as he sat his brandy down on the table in front of him. 'You know, Gia. I absolutely love the gift you chose for me. Absolutely love it.' 'Thank you, Tata. I wanted to get you something unique but at the same time, a gift that doesn't sit on a shelf all the damn time. You know what I mean? This you can wear. And *every* single time you look at it, you'll think of me.' 'You *know* I shall think of you when I look at it, my love. Now. Shall we retire? Or do you want... to... come over here... and... show... me how to put it on… correctly?' He lifted his head up so that he could gaze up at me with a quizzical look on his face. Doing, whatever he was doing, on purpose of course. And, it worked. I was excited instantly. 'What about Juanita or Steven?' 'They are in bed or on their way to their bed, Gia.' 'You're... sure?' I gulped. Not in fear, but in anticipation. I hated to even admit this to myself, but I wanted him so bad right now. I wondered if he could tell. Knowing him, probably. I stood up, walked over to the smaller couch he was sitting on and sat on his lap. Since he was wearing jeans and an Affliction™ t- shirt, I wasn't too worried about getting his clothes wrinkled or, God forbid, 'messy'. I took his gift in my hand and studied it for a minute. The front and the back of it. I looked down at him then. He had moved his face about an inch from my face. 'It looks pretty damn good to me, father. I think you did a... good... job.' He took the back of my head and pulled it the inch closer to his lips. He started kissing me hard. And with an intensity that I had not experienced from him in quite a while. He was already hard as a rock. I could feel 'him' underneath my thighs. 'Before we head up to our room, I would like to show you something that I just picked up for you yesterday. It's not much. So don't get your hopes up or anything. It's just a little something to remind you of me whenever you look at it. Alright? How does that sound?' I laughed at that one. 'Ah. Ok, copycat. Let's do it. I winked as I got up. He stood up a little slowly. I looked down and then I knew why. Since he was wearing jeans, it was very obvious as too '*why*'.

Chapter 20

As he led me through the main living room from the brandy room, we were heading towards the garage. This is weird... wait. NO! This could not BE! Please God, let it be! I thought to myself. My dad said to me as he wrapped a black kerchief around my eyes, 'you cannot play with this until.... later. So to speak.' 'Um, ok.' I replied. He opened a door. Most likely the door to the garage from the house. As he steered me inside the 'garage?' he closed the door behind us. As he started to untie the kerchief from my head, he turned me around. Facing, I think, the garage doors. When the wrap was off, I opened my eyes. There, in front of me with a huge red bow on top of it, was a brand new Lamborghini. 'Oh My God! Daddy!' I turned around and jumped up in his arms. He held me and whispered, 'Happy Birthday, My Princess.' He set me down and I just about let out a little scream. I was so damn excited! I knew I was going to probably get a car from my dad. But not a brand new, high end (to say it mildly) sports car! And my favorite color, too! I ran over to it, opened the driver's door and sat in it. I looked around and fell in love instantly. I noticed that the keys were in it. I turned on the car, just enough to hear the stereo. I turned that on and the sound system, was excellent (Duh!). I turned on the CD option and hoped that a CD was in there. My dad, being 'My Dad', had put one of my favorite one's in there as well. I cranked it up loud, but not so loud as too wake up Steve or Juanita. I so could not wait to go and take my driver's license test! Only three more days to go! I shut off the CD player and then the car itself, already knowing that it was special ordered from the factory, just for me. I hopped out and ran up to my father again. 'Do you like it, Princess?' I looked at him as if he were Nuts! 'Do I like it? Oh my God, Daddy! I love it! When did you buy it?' 'I purchased the car several months ago my love. 'It is so damn awesome, baby! And the color is my favorite! Canary yellow! It looks so good!' And it *did* look good, too. It was a Bright Canary Yellow with tan interior. The doors were even Gull-Wing. Meaning, they opened *up* instead of *out*. 'Wow, Tata. This is the *best* present I could receive from anybody! I so love you! But, you know that!' 'Yes, I do know that, my dear. Now, before you go into some type of excitement-stroke, let us go upstairs to bed. Shall we? We can get your license Monday and then you are free to drive anywhere, at any time. As long as I know *where* you are going and *when* you'll be back, yes?' 'Of course, Tata! Anything! I love you!' 'Plus, tomorrow, I need to fill you in on our trip to Northern California as well.' 'Oh yeah. Right. I have some questions about that, too.' 'That is fine, love. And I will answer any questions that you may have.' As my father closed and locked up the garage for the evening, we both went upstairs. Me practically skipping, thinking about after I do get my license, driving to Michelle's house and showing her the best birthday gift known to man! Yes! I had the *best* present ever! And, right now, I wanted to shout it from the rooftops! Why I was so shocked was because my father was *never* into big surprises like that. Big purchases anyway. Normally, the car purchase would have gone like this: My father, the day before the purchase of the car, would walk into my room (or wherever I was at the time) and tell me that he was going to purchase a car for me for my birthday. Since I was turning 16 and everything, it would be a lot easier on him and detail. Not having to drive me places and guarding me at the same time. Then he would arrange a time when Lane would drive me to his office so that we could look at cars on the internet and decide, between him and I.

That process would take at least an hour; maybe two. Usually, me going with HIS preference. Then he would make an appointment at the DMV to get my Driver's License test set up; the written and the driving part. Then, after that was all taken care of, and only then would he actually sit down with me and go over cars that I would actually be 'ok' being seen in. Or driving. Especially in this neighborhood. Not that my father would have made me drive an old clunker, but he would want me to be safe. Even though I took the best defensive driving classes from the best trainer's in the world. And, on the Autobahn no less. If Volvo™ made a sports car back then, he would have definitely pushed me like Hell to go with that one. Though now, they do make a sweet sporty car. That, I heard, was just as safe as their other sedan-type cars. Anyway, that is why this surprise present was so unexpected. Awesome in fact. As we got to my father's room, I flopped on the bed. My dad looked at me a little strangely and asked, 'Aren't you forgetting something? Or things, love?' 'Oh! Duh! That's right, Tata. I'll be right back. I rushed out the door and went to my room. I grabbed my brush, toothbrush and one of my short, hot-pink nighties. I skipped out of my bedroom and shut the door. I noticed that that didn't take very long at ALL. In fact, as I was walking fast back to my father's bedroom, I saw that he was still standing AT his bedroom door, holding it open for me. 'Well. That was quick, my girl. I am *so* glad you enjoy your birthday present, baby.' 'Daddy! Who wouldn't? Seriously! I absolutely love it! I didn't think that you would go about it that way. At *all*!' 'What do you mean by that?' he replied. Sitting down on his side of the bed. I looked at him realizing that he did indeed want a serious answer to that question. Which meant that he truly was clueless on how he handled buying me big gifts or purchases. 'Well Tata, normally you find me on the specific day that you plan on telling me what you're going to get me. Then you tell me and arrange for my bodyguard at the time to usually, depending on where YOU are at the time, take me to your office or wherever and we go over options on the computer. Then we would have a 'discussion on what you would think would be best for me and why' and then I would tell you what I think would be best for me. And this would go on for about an hour or so. Usually, I would just finally agree with your decision.' Anyway, that's how it usually went. Every year. But, only if it was a big purchase or required a lot of money. Needless to say, Tata'? I like this way much, much better.' He threw his head back and laughed louder than I had heard him in a long time. 'No kidding, love? How horrid for you! And I do mean that baby. I hope this birthday present and how it was presented, was much better.' When I looked at him, my eyes must have been as big as saucers. 'Heck, yes! It couldn't have been better, Tata! I absolutely love the way you presented it to me.' 'Well, good then. Let me brush my teeth; you too, crawl in the sheets and let me give you some fantastic, *much* needed, birthday love. Yes?' 'Sounds fantastic, daddy. Oh! I almost forgot. After my 'fantastic birthday love', can we talk about this Northern California trip together?' He looked at me seriously. With a kind of sad look on his face and replied very quickly, 'Yes, my love', got off of the bed and walked into the bathroom. 'That is weird' I thought as I grabbed my toothbrush and followed him. As we were both brushing our teeth, we didn't look at each other. Just both of us in our own thoughts and when we were done, we wiped our mouths and walked back into the bedroom. Him staying behind. As I crawled between the sheets of his massive California King, I realized that this is the best bed made ever. I had the California Queen. But, when I did move out, if ever, I would get the King too. It was so damn roomy! I loved it. I laid on my back and stretched out, relaxing, waiting for my dad. Just as my eyes were about to close for good, the door opened and I heard my father's footsteps walking towards me. As he got in the bed with me, I rolled over to face him.

Only this time my head was resting on my left hand. 'Ok. My questions are pretty brief, ok? So, it won't be torture for you. I promise.' He turned on his right side and got basically in the same position as I was in. Ready to listen and to engage into a conversation with me. 'Um. As far as this trip to The Bohemian Grove? What exactly do I have to do, daddy?' He put his head down and looked at the sheets. Only he knew what he was looking at, really. 'Gia. You know that I would and will do anything to protect you from physical harm and/or any emotional abuse. Right? Any abuse, actually.' I looked at him with some trepidation in my face. 'Of course, daddy. I know you would. But why would you say that now?' 'The reason that you are going to The Grove this year is for one reason only. And that reason is because Harris wanted you there.' Obviously, that got my antennae up. I asked him the same damn question. Harris replied to me, 'I would like her to 'entertain' the guests. Every single one of them.' So, my baby. That's the 'Why' of it. The reason why I am letting that happen is because I do not have a fucking choice. And that's the *shit* of it all, love.' I took all that he said in. Thinking about what I would have to do there, who I would have to '*DO*' there and shuddered. I knew who all went there every year. I also knew that women were not allowed there except Whores. Professional Whores that were flown in from different places across the world, programmed, and then, once they were finished with their stay', they were taken into another building, off of the main property, and depending on their physical health, they would just be deprogrammed. Or, if they were pretty screwed up physically and or mentally, they would be taken into a room in that building and taken care of mentally. Usually shock treatment. Depending on how 'bad off' they were mentally or emotionally. Then, false memories would be put into their brains. Or memories. It also depended on whom they saw during their stay. Once they were as 'well' as they would ever be, they were flown back to where they were from without one little memory of ever being there or going for that matter. If they were too bad off and 'They' could not fix them emotionally, they were, 'Taken Care Of'. Or, never seen again. Killed, basically. This happened every year. And, everyone in Washington knew about it as well. From the highest levels of government on down to some of the lobbyists. Their entire memory erased. Of anything to do with The Bohemian Grove. Everything. And then false memories put in their brain. 'Tata, will I be programmed and then deprogrammed as well? Like the other Whore's?' 'Absolutely not. I made that perfectly clear with Harris. You are not to be programmed, used in any weird fetishes, or any sick, perverted games that these men want to get involved in. Me being there will help as well, as far as you are concerned, love. I will mostly be in my cabin at night. Alone. And talking politics with certain people there during the day, Princess. If, and I do hope so, you are not otherwise engaged, you shall be sleeping in my cabin. Alright then?' 'Yes, Sir. I hope no one wants me, Tata. The very thought of it makes me sick. It really does.' 'I know it does, baby doll. And I did all I could to change his mind as well, babe. But, he had his mind set on making you feel humiliated. One more thing, Gia. I also made him PROMISE me as well as take a blood oath to me that you cannot and will not have any sexual relations with him. At all. 'Well thank God for that, Tata. I would rather have sex with a dog than him. Gross.' He slid under the covers and scooted closer to me. His lower body was touching mine. 'Him' on my stomach and he was as ready as any other man could be. Just add about four inches to the average man's penis size. 'One more thing, Tata? When do we go?' 'The day after tomorrow. And, just an idea. Get in 'Mode' the entire time you are there. Yes?' 'Absolutely, baby. I'll have to. Because I won't be with you.' After that statement, he rolled on top of me and started kissing me with such passion, that I did not want to stop. Boy it felt good.' I loved kissing him. He kissed perfectly in my book. Not too messy or sloppy. Not too dry to where my lips and mouth got chapped and dry. But just a little of both. It was heaven to me. But since I had not kissed anyone else to compare his kisses to, I just believed that most men kissed the exact same. I mean, how many ways can a man kiss? As we were kissing on his big, wonderful, bed, I made it clear to him that I wanted to be on top. I was slightly pushing him with my body, not stopping or pausing in my kissing. He finally 'let me' roll him over so that I was straddling him; though still laying on top of him. As we continued kissing, I stopped for a minute and pulled my head away from his for a minute. I looked at him deep in the eyes. I started brushing his hair back from his forehead too. He loved that. But not too much. Especially during sex. Doing that made him sleepy or too relaxed he had told me. Therefore, no sex. After four or five minutes of this, he took his hand off of my back and slowly pulled my hand away from his hair. I took that hand and put it under the covers, feeling for his hardness on my stomach. I took him and put the tip of it right up to the opening of 'me.' Touching. That was all he needed. He entered me very slowly. It was like something we had NEVER done before. It really surprised me. Normally, when he was *this* excited and had been waiting more than two days to have sex with me, he would normally have rammed it in me. No question. But, even his entire demeanor was different while we were in bed together this evening. As he was moving in and out of me, slowly, for a long time, I must have had four to five orgasms. That is something I cannot explain on paper. It felt *so* good that if I had to explain it, I would have to compare it too something to the extent of having the best massage and the best cunnilingus at the same time. Maybe not even that good. It was better. We continued our slow love-making for hours. I watched the clock every once in a while. It felt sooo good. I didn't want it to stop. Ever. He made love to me as if to 'prove a point' or to 'tell me' that I was his property only. He then started 'finishing', long and 'deep', if that's the correct word. He shuddered at the very end and literally collapsed on me. I didn't think he could do that, let alone any man. Unless they did a LOT of cardio. Or at least worked out a lot. But that was the *best* sex I had ever had. Ever. And I told him so. I waited until both of our breathing got back to normal. And then I whispered it in his ear. A breathy voice. And not intentional, I was damn tired. He, apparently, was too. When he was laying on me and after I whispered what I did in his left ear, he held me tighter. He stayed in that position for a long time. Not moving his head from my left shoulder. 'I want to tell you something. Right now. And we shall not talk about this again. Got it, my Princess? My Goddess? My Everything?' When he was done saying what he did, I sensed a slight tremor in his voice. Almost like he had started to cry. Or was about to *or* almost was. 'Of course, daddy. What is wrong? Is there something I need to know? Are you ok? Please say nothing is wrong with you! Ok? Please?' 'Gia. Nothing is *wrong* with me.' He replied. 'It is about The Grove. No matter whom you end up sleeping with. No matter who, go into Mode. Understand? Be submissive. Do as they ask. And then be done with it. I will erase your entire memory of it. IF you'd like. I would rather if you did. But, of course, it is up to you.' 'Baby?' I took both of my hands and put them on each side of his face. 'I shall leave that decision up to you, ok?' When I said that to him and was speaking directly to his face; inches from mine, he had a single tear rolling down his face. My God. This man is in *love*, *love* with me. He nodded his head and mouthed the words, 'Thank you.' I nodded, smiled and sat up a bit and pulled up just the sheet and light blanket that he had on his bed. Over both of us. I reached over him and picked up the fresh glass of ice-water and gave it to him. He took a few drinks from it and handed it back to me. I drank from it and then put it back on his nightstand. 'Bedtime, my love?' I asked him. 'Yes, G. I barely can keep my eyes open. I love you, kitten. You know, yes? With ALL of my heart and soul.' I looked at him right before I turned out his bedside lamp. 'Yes I do, father. More than I ever have. And...I am glad I do know. Now, anyway. And, I am glad. Because I feel the very same way about you as well. Always and forever. Regardless if we do not end up together. Do you know what I mean?' 'Yes I do, Gia. Yes I do. Always and forever.' We fell asleep in, it seemed like, five seconds. We were so damn tired.

Chapter 21

We both woke up, or rather, opened our eyes at the exact same time. I looked at the clock slowly. It was 11:45 AM. Almost Noon. I looked over at my dad. His eyes were open, though barely, looking right at me. 'Good Morning, baby doll. How did you sleep?' 'Very well, Tata.' I stretched long and straight, as I said that to him. My father and my lover. 'My lover.' I rolled that word or words in my mouth a few times. It just sounded 'right'. Even though I knew it wasn't right. Oh well. 'How did you sleep? Good I hope, because I slept the best I have EVER slept in a very, very, long time, Gia. So... thank you... my kitten.' 'You are very welcome, my baby.' I smiled and kissed him square on his lips. So soft too. I loved this man. Too damn bad he was my father. I only hoped that I would find a man just like him and get married to him. If 'He' even existed. He rolled onto his back. 'What are your plans today, my baby? Anything interesting?' 'Well, actually, yes! I am going to go and take a nice drive in my brand, new car, of my dreams, and drive and do stupid errands that I would have never thought of doing!' I laughed a little after I said that. 'So, if there is anything that you need that needs to be picked up, dropped off or bought at the store or a pharmacy or something like that, I'm your girl!' He laughed hard. And pretty damn loud, too. 'This is the most excited that I have ever seen you react to doing errands, my kitten.' I also have some cash inside your birthday card that we never got to open, so to speak. You may want to spend that today too. In your brand new car, love. When all of your driving and 'showing off' is done for today, I should be home and done with all of my crap/work things.' I looked at him, smiled and told him thank you; 100 times it seemed. I was SO grateful that he bought me my first car on my list! What dad does that? Not mine, I thought. I thought that he would buy me a nice car. Just nothing fast, flashy or potentially dangerous. And what does he do? He does just that! Damn! I couldn't love him any more than I already did. I slowly sat up in bed and stretched. Arms in air stretching all the way to the ceiling. That felt damn good. I turned a bit too where I could see my father. And I looked at him in his eyes. 'Well, it sounds like your day is full to the brim. I shall see you when I get home. And my cell will be on the *entire* time I am gone.' 'Oh, and what bodyguards will be going with me today, hot-ass-man of mine?' His eyebrows shot up as quickly as I have ever seen them. Of course I have never called him that before. Especially face to face. He is still in that position. Or expression. Whichever you call it. 'What? Did I say something wrong, Tata? I'm just calling you what I truly think of you, baby. I love you. I truly do. And I am speaking from my heart, daddy. And until we get this 'fixed' or whatever you want to do with 'this', then shouldn't I, in private, call you those things?' His eyebrows slowly went back down. 'Yes. I suppose so. Until further notice that is. I do have to think about this 'thing' we are involved in. Do you understand, baby? But, I ask you not to talk to a soul about this. Understand? And promise me?' 'Of course, Tata. I will not say a word about us to a soul. Steven already knows, but that is old news and you took care of that. So no, I do not have a problem with that and I *do* promise.' 'Good, kitten. Now, let us go downstairs and have some breakfast and then you need to go and do your errands, yes?' 'Yes! Let me go to the restroom first baby and then I will see you at the breakfast table. I do hope Juanita made breakfast now. And not lunch. She knows I love breakfast no matter what time I wake up, right?' 'I am SURE it will be breakfast, Gia. I am damn sure. Ok? Now go and do your thing. I'll see you downstairs.' As I agreed, kissed him on his lips and got out of his soft, warm bed, I walked out of his room and headed towards mine. What a fantastic night and day today, I thought. I couldn't wait to call Mariah and tell her what I got for my birthday. Maybe I should call her before I got to her house? I'll think about it after my shower, I said to myself silently. I walked into my room and then closet. I went to where my 'going out' clothes were hung up and decided what the HELL I was going to wear on the first night of MY dream car drive. My dream car! I still couldn't believe that I owned it. The best car one could ever own. I finally picked out a short, butt-skimming, silver, sequined, mini dress. I walked over and put it on my bed. Then went to my drawers and took out a silver G-string. I laid that on my bed, too. Shoes. What in Hell am I going to wear as shoes? Ah! My pair of SIX and a half inch Christian Louboutin™, sequin-looking, shiny heels. Perfect! They always looked cute. In the spring or summer with a short skirt or a pair of short shorts. Anything, really. I went into my bathroom and got my shower ready. Once the water was perfect, I stepped in, washed my hair, shaved my legs, washed my face and everything in between. As I dried off with my towel and stepped out of the shower, I dried the rest of my body off. I threw my damp towel into my hamper and combed out my wet hair and put on my club make-up in record time. Dark, smokey eyes and nudish lips; with lip-liner of course. I blew my hair dry and styled it with my hair straightener, curling iron and of course... hairspray. Not much, though. Just a light spray. Only on the top of my head. As I double checked myself in the mirror, deemed myself presentable, I walked into my closet where I kept my shoes and slipped on my Louboutin's™. Just as the Com went off with Juanita telling me that late, late breakfast or dinner was ready. As well as my father was downstairs waiting for me. I told her I was ready and on my way down. I opened my door, with my going-out purse and Chanel™ sunnies in hand as well. I shut my door and walked down the long, winding, stairs. I instantly saw Stev-o and my father. My father was even wearing jeans and a t-shirt. I believe an YSL™ t-shirt. Sweet. I stopped on the stair that I was standing on and took him all in. Since I was walking slowly down the stairs, no one heard me. I looked at his long, long legs, his combed back hair that was so straight and jet black, and his loose but tight jeans. IF that makes any sense at all. It is hard to explain. His jeans were tight in the butt (I knew the jeans he was wearing), but looser in the legs and all the way down as well. Let's just say that he looked good in them. Only tall guys could pull it off, obviously. You needed to have long legs to pull them off. As I stood up, I noticed my father turning his head in my direction. Checking me out in my short dress. My tanned legs, my chest, just about everything. And that made my day all the more worth it. 'Hello gentlemen!' I said with a smile in my voice. As I descended the rest of the stairs and made my way to the table, I did notice the smell of pancakes. Yay! Breakfast for dinner in the late evening! So far, so good tonight. 'Good morning, Gia. How was your sleep? You slept in longer than I expected this afternoon or evening, is it?' Steve said/asked me. 'Really? Why is that, Stev-o?' 'You knowing that your sweet, yellow ride is in the garage waiting for you, for starters.' He grinned as he said that. 'Oh. That little thing? It can wait. I guess...' I couldn't continue that charade. I started laughing. He smiled and looked down at his plate. Before I could say anything else on that subject, he continued. 'So, where are you planning on going tonight?' 'Well, let's see. I called Mariah as soon as I got out of bed to see what she was up to. She didn't have anything really planned. So, we decided that I was to go, pick her up, and go out to the club tonight. 'Ah. Playing it big this evening. Are we?' I'm like, he was crazy to think I wouldn't! 'HELL yes I am! Wouldn't you? I mean if you were me, that is. Michelle doesn't know about my present yet.' 'She's going to crap herself when she sees you pull up in *that* car.' My father looked at Steven and gave him a disgusted look. 'Really, Steve? Crap herself?' Steve-o looked up from his plate at my dad. 'Oh. Sorry, sir. I forgot where I was.' My father kept looking at him and then picked up his coffee and turned towards me. 'Let me know when you shall be leaving, Gia, so that I can let detail know, yes?' 'Sure, Tata. Oh! What about my driver's license? You said you 'called in a favor' or something?' 'Yes I did.' He reached in his back pocket, took out his wallet and handed me my brand new 'driver's license'. As I took it from his hand, I looked at it very closely. Steven had already took out his real one and handed it to me so that I could compare the two. As I looked at both of them, side by side I could not tell the difference. AT all. It was unbelievable. 'Thank you again, daddy! These are exactly the same! I cannot tell the difference!!' 'Well, that's the point, Gia.' He sort of laughed at that. As did Steven. 'I know, I know. I should have expected that. But, it is amazing how real mine looks compared to Steve's real one! Damn!' My father gave me a 'look' this time, pushed his plate aside and looked at me. Very seriously. 'Now, Gia. I want you to listen to me. I am being very serious about this.' I was looking at him and I nodded my head. 'Just because you now have a brand new car; a fast new car, does not mean that you are allowed to speed, run red lights or stop signs, etc. I know you know that you have a Do Not Cite, Do Not Apprehend on your license. But that does not mean that you will not get punished at home if something like that happens. Alright? Your detail will tell me those things. And, before you say anything, no. This will not last forever. I'll give you six months to prove to me that you are responsible enough to have a car like this. Yes? Do you have any questions about anything that I just told you?' I looked at him for a second and then at my empty plate. I pushed it away and then grabbed my coffee. 'Well, let's say I did get a ticket. And not trying to get one, or testing the cop or anything. A God's honest ticket. And when

I got home and told you the story, what would you do? Would you believe me that I didn't do something stupid? Like any of the things you just described?' My dad looked at me for a bit before he answered me. 'Well, babe. That would depend on a couple of things. First of all, since you have not taken the official driver's test, and you received a ticket for something ridiculous. Such as 'rolling through a stop sign', instead of coming to a complete stop, which you are supposed to do, no. I would not get angry. 'Ok, Tata. I promise to you daddy. I will try my hardest not to get a ticket. And, I will always, when driving, look for cops. No matter how close I am from the house, ok?' 'Sounds good, kitten. And, one more thing, babe. I expect *no* tickets the first week of having or driving, rather, that car. Got that? I don't care if one of your friends dares you to race another kid in a car... or, most importantly, race a boy/man/ Douchebag in another car. If you get in a wreck, that is my worst nightmare. Ask Steven. You dying in a horrific car wreck. Especially when it could have ALL been avoided. And we've already had the talk about drinking and driving, yes? That will result in your car being taken away from you. For how long? I have no idea at this point because I have no reason to even think that you would be that stupid. At this time, anyway. Do I? And I won't even go into doing drugs. That is self-explanatory. If you are too drunk to drive, you can call me or Steven. Anyone who answers the damn phone. And, if you call, I promise you, you will not get in trouble. I think the hangover, in itself, would be punishment enough.' 'I totally get it, Tata. First of all, in my defense? I do not do drugs. Yes, as Steven knows and probably you, I *have* done cocaine. But I will not do it ever again. Especially while driving. All in all? I will behave as responsible as I can. Ok, Tata?' Steven and my father looked at me. My dad leaned back in his chair; coffee in hand. 'Ok, Princess. You may go. Be careful. Please.' 'I promise! I will even valet.' Steven laughed at me then. 'What the hell are you laughing at?' Smiling even as I said that. 'You were going to Valet *anyway*, Lil G.' I looked at him, trying to pull off a surprised look and failed miserably. 'Yeah. You're right. So what?' I got up, as they both started chuckling, and grabbed my purse. 'Tata, who will be my detail tonight?' 'The usual, baby. Except David. He 'misbehaved' last night so he is being punished. But, you'll have your regular detail, plus I'm adding one more to them.' 'Ok, daddy. Oh. I would like to talk to you and you too, Steven, about Kevin when I wake up for breakfast. Is that ok?' They both looked up, simultaneously at me. 'Of course, my baby. You are sure that you do not want to tell us right now, my love?' I actually thought about that option for a minute but decided against it. It was already coming up on 9pm and I wanted to get going. 'I would rather talk to you both tomorrow? At breakfast? If you don't mind? Please?' 'Of course, babe. That's fine. You are alright, yes?' 'Of course I'm ok, daddy. Promise.' 'Alright then. You may go. Be careful. I'll be home all day, tomorrow, Gia. Be safe, be well.' I walked around the table and kissed my dad on the cheek and lips (the first time I had done that in front of Steven) and then walked around too Steve and kissed him on the cheek. 'Have fun in that hot car, Gia.' 'Oh, I will Steve-o.' I grabbed my purse and made sure my phone was in it and out the door I went. As I stood on the steps, reapplying my lipstick & gloss, one of the detail dudes rushed up to me and I told him to grab my yellow Corvette™. He answered, 'Yes, Ma'am' and raced towards the garage. I only waited about three minutes max and the car was heading towards me. 'Damn, she was pretty.' I thought. 'I am going to HAVE to come up with a name for her.' My very first car. Beautiful. My dad can be such a sweetheart. Can be. Not, by any means, all of the time. I mean, it was my birthday and everything, but a brand new Lamborghini? Son-of-a-bitch! 'Wait until the kids at school see this bad bitch!' As I saw my new car slowly pulling towards me, I just almost could not contain myself. When did my dad buy her? Oh yeah… he told me that already. How did he know that this was my favorite color? My first favorite car of *all time* was a Chevrolet™ Corvette™. Sweetness in all of its American beauty. In my opinion, America's *only* sports car. No question. As detail got closer to me with my car, it woke me up from being 'in my head'. I threw back a 'Thank You' too him as he tossed the keys to me. I looked down at my hand and saw my keys. I started to get tears in my eyes. I opened up my driver's door, got inside and sat down. I pushed the button that took the top down and kept staring at the key fob. Once the roof was completely down, I looked out of my passenger side window. Or where it be. If the top was still up. I looked to see if my father was looking out of the window. He wasn't so I picked up my phone and texted him: 'Tata. Could you please come outside for a second? Please?' I reached into my Louis V.™ mini-bag and got a tissue and dabbed my eyes. 'I swear, if my father *ever* got married, I will kill her.' I thought. As the front door opened and my father walked out, I got out of my car and ran over to him. I wrapped my arms around him. 'Thank you *so* much for everything, daddy. I love you like you will never know. Please never leave me. And you are the best father a girl could have. I love you more than anyone. Ok? Please never forget that. Please don't.' My father gave me a very tight hug and then slowly pulled me away. 'What brought this on, my love?' I stared at him in his eyes as usual and replied, 'because, in the car was the first time I read the back of my key fob. Obviously. I haven't seen my keys yet nor have read the back of the fob, either. So, I just wanted to say to you, with no one around, that I feel the same way about you, daddy. No one could be as beautiful on the inside as you. No one I have ever met anyway. Ok?' 'My darling, I understand. Just know that I meant every word. Yes?' 'Yes. Absolutely.' 'Ok then, love. Have a fun and safe night. And, no later than your normal 3am curfew, yes? You deserve it. And when you *do* get back, we shall talk about our trip to The Grove in more detail when you wake up. Love you.' 'Love you too, Tata.' I said to him as he was walking back to the house. I got back into my car and started it up again. I made sure the top was secured properly in back behind me. And then I looked at how many miles it had on it. Zero? How is that possible? Someone had to drive it back to the house! Oh! I bet my dad had it flat-bedded to his home. As I put it in 'Drive', I cruised towards the gate, which opened up as if someone were watching, with draining patience, no doubt (Ha Ha!). As I drove down the long driveway, I looked up at the overhanging trees and felt actual freedom. For the first time in my whole entire life! This was awesome! I came to a complete stop in the driveway. I dug in my purse for my phone and my sunglasses'. I put my sunnies in my glove for daytime. My 'just-in-case' sunnies™. In case I forgot them when I left the house one day. I told my phone to call Michelle. My phone, of course, dialed Mariah's number and I continued on my way. As I hit the bottom of Mulholland, I turned right on Sunset and continued until I reached the entrance to Bel Air. Bel Air had two entrances. East and West. Mariah's home was closer to the West entrance. As I stopped at the gate guard's little stand, I told the guard that I was here to see Michelle Grenier. He checked, saw that I was on the list, and let me through. As I pulled up into her driveway, I parked behind their boat. Which was a 'safe' place to park since the damn thing never moved unless it was July through September. Or the beginning of September. I got out, walked up to their door and knocked. I instantly heard Mariah's mother's voice and then Mariah. The door opened and there was her mother. 'Why, Gia! How are you!!? You look fabulous. AS always, dear. Please, come in. 'Thank you, Miss Grenier.' 'Mariah should be down in a minute. I heard you received a nice little gift for your birthday from your father!! Do you want to share? Or do I have to guess, hmmm?' 'Oh. Did Mariah not tell you what it was?' I asked her. 'Not a thing! It's like under some National Security Confidentiality Agreement or something! Haha! But I would love to see it, of course, dear.' She started looking at my hands, my neck, anything where a piece of jewelry could be. 'It's outside, Miss Grenier. Here, follow me. I was completely surprised at this!' As I walked out of the front door again, she followed and once she walked outsidc and where I pointed, her eye's got huge. 'Oh my! Your father is *very* considerate! Isn't he? How is he by the way, my dear? Still single, I heard, from lunching with the girls last week.' I looked at her with some surprise. I had no idea that my father was the topic of conversation amongst divorced women in Beverly Hills. At all! Oh My God. I'll have to tell my father that one. It will blow his mind! 'Yes, Ma'am. He is still single.' She did not turn away from the car but still spoke to me. 'You should do something about that sweetheart. That man needs a woman in his life, my dear. In fact. A man like that has needs.' 'Yeah, I *know*. And that woman is *me*, thank you very much.' That, I thought to myself, of course. But *man* did I want to get out of here. I had no clue that my father was considered The Most Eligible bachelor in this town. Bitches! All of them. 'Well, that's it, Ma'am. Not much to see really. I do love it though.' 'As well you should! Be kind to that wonderful father of yours. Maybe we should all get together and have dinner? Just the four of us. What do you think?' I was trying like Hell to come up with something; an excuse to say to this woman. 'Well, as soon as we come back from a trip that we have to take up north, that might work. I'll bring it up to him when I get home today, Miss Grenier.' 'Fabulous, Gia darling. Michelle! Are you ready? Quit dawdling my dear. And just wait and see what Miss Mahari brought over to the house my love. You will absolutely love it! After all, Gia is just like your sister.' She grinned at me like we were old friends. Even though I had just really met her a month or so ago. She was the typical Beverly Hills Divorced-Type. And, I think, she was a Cougar, too. I never asked Michelle about her mother. But I think it was prime time. Since Michelle thought it was appropriate to talk about my father in a sexual fashion, why couldn't I ask about her mother's private life? Chell came down the stairs and I gave her a look like, 'Get Me Out of Here!' Thank God she 'knew' that look. 'Well mom, we better go now. The clubs are starting to get busy as Hell right now and Gia always wants to get to her glass, V.I.P. booth before there are crowds everywhere, mom. Ok? You understand that mother, right?' 'Well, that's absolutely understandable.' 'Ok and thanks mom. I'll be home around 2-3am like usual. Ok?' 'That's fine, Chelly. I trust you with Gia, Hun. She's like your sister after all. Have fun girls. I'll see you in the morning, Chell.' 'Bye, mom.' And then she closed the door. 'My God, Michelle! I don't mean any disrespect but no wonder why your mother is divorced! Damn!' 'I know. She is a piece of work. My father's new wife is a completely different person. So nice!' 'Oh My God! Is this your fucking present?' She ran over to the car and ran her hand, with the sleeve of her tie-top covering her hand, (thank God), over the front fender. 'It is fucking beautiful! I want, I want, I want! It is beautiful, chicky!' 'When my dad showed it to me last night, I practically cried! Get your butt inside. And let me show you two awesome fucking things. K?' 'Hell, yeah!' I opened the doors with my fob and she got in the passenger seat. As I walked over to the driver's side, I saw her rub the supple leather. I got in and started the car. 'Seat belt on Miss. We are almost ready for take-off.' We both laughed at that. She put her seatbelt on and I turned on the CD player. As Depeche Mode™ started blasting in the car, I hit the button for the convertible to go down. Mariah just sat there and watched it move. Not saying a fucking word. 'Oh My God! Let's go baby! I cannot wait to see the looks we get when we pull up too valet!' I, personally, couldn't give a shit about the looks we got. I just loved my car, loved driving my car and was thrilled that we didn't have to go in a limo like I always had too before. As we drove off and sort of bopped to the music, we hit the last light before we turned onto Sunset. As we pulled up to the line for valet, I could see all of the people in line staring at us. Most undoubtedly, the car. But maybe us, too. Who knows? I was just glad that we were here. Traffic was brutal this weekend. As Michelle turned up our music, I pulled up to the valet line and waited. I put my car in park, grabbed my L.V. 'going out purse' and re-applied my lip-gloss; as did Michelle. 'How do I look, babe?' I looked at her and gave her the nod of approval. 'Awesome!' 'How do I look, sweets?' She looked at me from side to side and replied, 'As gorgeous as usual. Sometimes I am so damn jealous when I go out with you bitch.' I looked at her with a "Yeah, right' look. 'And why is that? Are you just fucking with me?' Michelle cleared her throat and looked at me pretty seriously. 'No. I am not kidding. You always look so damn ‘put together’! Always, girly. And that's a compliment.' I, all of a sudden, felt bad. I knew she was attractive. In a weird way. Not in a bad way. Just a different way. Hard to explain. 'Hon, *you* have no reason, at *all*, to feel jealous or whatever you are feeling when you and I go out together. Ever. You are beautiful. With your long-ass legs, your pretty hair... I could go on and on. But really. You do not have to feel that way, ok? Too me, we are equals. In a different way, I know. But never as in an 'Oh, I am 'put together' or 'prettier than her' way. Alright? So stop feeling that way. Ok?' She looked at me for a while. Then smiled and gave me a hug. 'I love you so much, sweetie. Not in a gay way. Obviously. But you know what I mean. In a ‘sista' kind of way... bitch. Now let's go and rock this club.' As the valet walked up to my door, he smiled his 24-27 year old smile and I gave him a grin as if to say, 'I know you think I'm hot... but I'm too expensive for ya'. As he ripped off the green tag for my car, I told him to make sure he parked my car in front, leave the top down and to please keep an eye on it while we were inside? Plus, if he and his buddies kept their eyes on it, he would get a Hell of a tip. He promised his very soul to keep an eye on it the entire time we were in the club. I thanked him and also told him that I knew the exact mileage that was on it too, as we both walked to the front of the line and showed our ID's to the huge, black, dude at the front of the rope. He looked at us up and down, finally smiled, and said 'deez are some fine-ass women.' And let us through; with *much* protest from the line behind us. As we walked inside, me in front, I was met with the manager. Someone must have let him know that Mahari's daughter was here. Usually *that* only happened *if* my father was with us. It was nice to know that it happened when I was here 'alone' as well. I looked back at Michelle before I started talking to the Manager. She smiled her 'I'm so fucking excited, I could faint' smile as I turned towards the manager again. 'Nice to see you again, Miss Mahari. Would you like your usual booth this evening?' 'Yes, we would. Thank you.' As he led us through the club, he said, 'So your father couldn't make it tonight I see?' 'No. He could. He just wanted to stay home and go through his pages upon pages of bank statements tonight. So, I decided to give him some peace and let him be.' 'I see. Well, I imagine how many and how long that would take the poor man. Tell him 'Good Evening' for me, will you, Miss Mahari?' 'Of course I will!' Like that would ever happen. He would be like... 'Who?' Haha! As he walked us up the stairs to my glass booth, which looked over the entire club, we sat down. He handed us the menus and asked if we would like any appetizers or any cocktails. We ordered cocktails and Calamari. Our usual. I always ordered a Buttery Nipple Shot and one Amaretto Sour with a single cherry on top. Mariah ordered a Tequila (Patron) shot and a Whiskey Sour. He thanked us and continued down the steps. I said Thank You again after he started to leave the table. 'You are most welcome, Miss Mahari.' As we got comfortable in our glass booth (there were only 3 in the entire 10,000 square foot club. PLUS you had to own them. Like *buy* them. And there was a waiting list for them 3 pages long. But they *were* the coolest. The music that was blasting downstairs in the club was piped into our glass booth at a descent level where you could actually speak and not yell at each other. That was *the* selling point when my dad bought it for me 3 years ago for my birthday. He also did business there too as well. So it was a win, win for both of us, really. It was only $2,000 a month so it wasn't that big of a deal for him. Plus, an excellent tax write off for him, too. We received our cocktails minutes later and then, our 2nd sip from them and ate the cherry, one of our favorite song's came on. We looked at each other, smiled, counted to 3 and then did our shot. We got up and went downstairs to go dance our asses' off. As we both were out of our booth, I turned around and locked it up. That was the selling point for me. You could lock the door to your booth, keep all of your belongings in there and not worry about your drink getting spiked. Awesomeness. As we walked down the semi-short stairway, eyes were locked onto us. I made my way to the dance floor and started getting into my 'dance-zone'. Which, basically was that I was totally into the music and was *not* aware of my surrounding's. I was completely into the music. Usually the dance floor cleared when I was on it. Sometimes, I was told, since my eyes were usually closed or I was not paying attention, a single girl would stay on it but would soon give up and walk off. I never understood it. But it did happen. The weirdest thing. I decided that tonight I would watch and see if it happened this evening. It would have to be a kick-ass song though. After the first song was over, and Michelle and I were about to head up to our booth, the best song ever, at least too me, 'Bizarre Love Triangle' by New Order, came on. This was one of my favorite songs in the 80's. I danced my ass off with Chell. Once I get 'going' as far as dancing is concerned, I dance. I don't care who looks, who stares, or who does whatever. Why? Because I am not. I am 'In the

Zone' I guess you would call it. I still dance, go out, the same way. And I STILL can clear a dance floor at 48 years old. Anyhow, as I told myself to keep my eyes open, I DID. And I SAW with MY own EYE'S people leaving the floor! WHILE watching ME! I tripped OUT! I looked at Mariah and I mouthed, 'I told you so.' I completed dancing until the song was over. That was when Mariah and I walked up the stairs too our booth. When we sat down, I asked her if THAT happened ALL the time when we would go out. Dancing, obviously. 'Yes it does, babe. Pretty much ALL the time. It's NO big deal so don't start apologizing for ever about it, ok? It REALLY does NOT bother me. I mean, Hell! It draws attention to me too, babe.' I looked in her eyes. Deep into her I and realized that she was telling the truth. 'Ok then. I was just curious, Miss Butt-Stain. We both looked down at our drinks just about simultaneously, and realized that we had been here a LONG time. I looked around the club and it had thinned out quite a bit. I looked at my watch and told Mariah, 'Why don't we just sit here, chat, catch up, whatever, and then decide when we want to leave. How does that sound? Plus, it lets the club thin out a little so when we *do* leave, there is not a long ass line to wait in. That SUCKS!' 'Sounds good to me sweetie.' 'Cool Beans.' We sat in our glass enclosure for a while and said not a word. Out of nowhere, Michele sounded out a very 'out-there' question to me. Something I was NOT expecting. 'Babe? What exactly DOES your father do for a living? I don't think I've ever asked you after all these years that we've known each other.' As she asked this question, she was looking over her right shoulder. Out over the dance floor. Almost deep in thought. 'He does A LOT of entrepreneurial work; overseas, mainly. Why do you ask now, babe?' She slowly turned her head and THEN her eyes followed. 'Well, he has this HUGE house, maid and tons of bodyguards; hell, YOU have bodyguards. So, I was on my laptop the other day doing an OLD homework assignment and I decided, when I was done, too Google him. I was pretty damn sure he would come up somewhere, ya know? Making ALL that money, owning all of these places or properties, and owning TONS of expensive cars. I was just curious. When I Googled him, not 1 mention of him turned up. His name was NOWHERE. I just thought that was REALLY strange is all.' I sat there for a while without looking at her or saying a word. THIS was NOT something that I thought I was going to have to address tonight. Or, for that matter, EVER from her. 'Well, Shell, he is just SUCH a private person that he even pays people to *KEEP* his name out of the papers. Or the media, actually. He HATE'S paparazzi. And he HATE'S attention. So, that's probably why. I have never Googled him. I WILL on the other hand, ask him tomorrow though.' She was looking at me the entire time I was talking about him. 'That's cool, hon. If it's not 'Top Secret', will you tell me what he say's?' 'Yes silly! I will! Now let's get the Hell out of here. I'm beat. Plus, my father, no doubt, wants to talk to me tomorrow about our trip up North. Yuk. I am not in the mood to go anywhere with him at all.' 'I get it. Let's go. I'm beat too. But I had a Hell of a time and thank you so much for going! And taking or sharing your fabulous automobile with me, k?' No problem! Anytime, hon.' As we walked downstairs and towards the exit, I was thinking about what I was going to tell her what 'my father told me about what he did' for a living. Which he wasn't! I was in no way going to ask him shit! I'll just tell him what she asked me, out of nowhere, and tell her what he told me to tell her. As we waited in line for valet, I took my ticket out of my purse and stood really close to Shell. Looking around for my Detail. I spotted them with no problem. One was to the right, one to the left and the 3rd person in line for the valet was my detail as well. Coolness. They did their job perfectly. I didn't see them when we were in the club either. Which is the point. We waited only 5 more minutes and then it was our time to get my damn car.

The valet dude grabbed my keys after he took my ticket and ran like Hell to go and get my car. My *sweet-ass* car. Loved it. As he pulled it up...right in front of everyone in line, everybody stared at it like it was a work of art. Which it was; too me at least. God I loved this car. My car. As Michelle made a big 'deal' walking towards it, I just walked faster than normal so we could get the Hell out of here. I was tired and wanted my bed. Or...my father's bed. I had too 'properly' Thank Him for this piece of art under me. I put the car in drive and we roared out of there at 40 miles per. Sweet. I looked in my rearview as I waited to turn right on Sunset, and I saw all the valet people, in line, all talking too themselves. No doubt about us. Oh well. Get used to it, bitche's! I'LL be back. As I made my turn and turned on the CD player, we started dancing in the car and had a great time driving to Shell's house. As I pulled into her driveway, her mother obviously was waiting up for her. That was a bit much. Mariah was 16 for God's sake. Damn! As she walked towards the driver's side of the car, I put the car in park and waited. 'So! Did you two have a fun time? I bet you did! Especially in this baby! Am I right?' Michelle looked at her mom and rolled her eyes. She was still smiling though. 'Mom! Don't be so damn embarrassing!' 'I was just asking, babygirl!' 'Yeah, right.' She turned to me and thanked me again. 'I'll call ya tomorrow, k? Love you.' She kissed me on the cheek and got out. As she and her mom walked towards their house, I put the car in reverse and started my slower than normal drive back to my house. I turned up my music and was lost in my own thoughts as I thought of The Bohemian Grove. I also wanted to ask my dad what the name of the man was that I sacrificed the other night. I didn't know if he would tell me. But, the more I thought about it, the more I thought that he just might. There was no reason why he wouldn't. He was already dead, obviously. And he obviously did something that really pissed off The Brotherhood. I already forgot what Harris said he 'did'. All I remembered was doing the Sacrifice. Yes. I'll definitely ask my father 'what' exactly he did to deserve 'Death'. According to the Illuminati/The Brotherhood. As I turned left onto Mulholland, I drove towards home. And 'a' comfy bed. Whichever bed I was sleeping in tonight. At this point. I did not care. Actually, come to think of it, I preferred to sleep with my dad. I just felt safe, and all of that. But I loved to cuddle. My father's 'rep' was that he was *not* be a 'cuddler.' Well, regardless as to what his rep was, he *was* a cuddler with me. Ha! And, hopefully will always will be. Unless, of course, I got married. Which I did want to do one day. And have a child. And obviously that could not happen with my father. So, one day we will just have to see who that lucky son-of-a-bitch would be. Actually, if he was like my Tata, I would be the lucky one too. I pulled up to the gate and punched in the code. The guys who were manning the gate looked in my car, gave me the 'thumbs up' sign, and said, 'Nice car, Gia!' and the gate started slowly swinging open. I mouthed 'thank you' and gave the thumbs up sign back to them and drove on in. I pulled around the statue and put my car in park, pushed the button for my roof to come back up over me. As it was swinging back up, I looked at my watch. It was 4AM. A detail dude ran up to me and I asked him if he knew if my father was still awake. He told me he had no idea but he thought that he saw a light go out about 30 minutes ago. 'Thank you!' He opened the door for me, said 'you're welcome. I grabbed my purse, smiled at him and walked up towards the house. I used my house keys to open the front door and silently walked in. Instantly the light came on. And I knew it was my father. 'I heard you had a great time. And thank you, Gia, for texting me the updates that we talked about the night before last, baby. I do trust you now to go out on your own, in your car and from now on, I promise, I shall not wait up for you. Unless there is an emergency of course. Which, obviously, I hope does not happen.' He was standing there, in his jeans, but shirtless.

Damn, he was fine. At that very moment, even though the thought itself made me jealous, I knew he deserved a normal relationship. Not tomorrow, not next week or month. But someday. I walked up to him, threw my purse on the couch and walked into his open arms. I started kissing him. Not stopping either. After a few minutes; not even 3 minutes, I felt him against my tummy. I started kissing him harder. He then returned the favor. Making himself harder. If *that* was possible (which, from experience, it was). He picked me up and carried me up the stairs. I guess I knew where I was sleeping tonight. No argument here. He laid me down onto his bed and started kissing me again. But with a lot more intensity this time. Obviously because we were in the privacy of his room. I started working on his jeans. Which, I found out, was pretty damn hard. Considering his tummy was hitting the top of my right hand and the button to his jeans was intertwined in my fingers. He finally, slightly, rolled over a tad onto his left side so that I could have an easier time unbuttoning them. Once that hellish task was over and done with, he started kicking and pushing them down with his feet. Finally, between the both of us, we got them off. Thank God they were not tight fitting and just semi-relaxed fitting, or we would have never gotten them off that way. Once they were on the floor, he started on my outfit. He took a lot more care of my outfit, probably knowing, too the penny, just how much it cost him. Typical dad. We were laying on top of his comforter. Which, usually, he did not like to 'mess up'. Apparently, he wasn't thinking too clearly right now. So, I decided I wasn't going to remind him of his comforter. In fact, I wasn't going to think about anything except what we were doing right now. At all. He took both of his hands and put them on either side of my face and looked deep into my eyes. 'Gia. I have been thinking a lot about what we had talked about earlier. Before you left. And, all I can say... is, um. All that I *can* say is that I honestly do not know how I can let you completely... go.

Do you understand what I am saying, my love?' I, of course, was looking at him as well. Not leaving his gaze. I knew that for him too actually stop what he was doing; completely. It was going to be something serious that came out of his mouth. And, it turned out, that it was serious. 'Father. I know. I completely understand. I have been thinking the exact same thing. I don't know what to do about 'us', father. You havc got to be the love of my life. You have to be, if I feel like this?' 'Baby, what you and I feel is called, simply, 'First Love's'. We are each other's First Love's. And I take complete responsibility for that. I did NOT have to take advantage of you when you were 9 or 10 year's old. But I DID. So, we will have to get 'over' this in time. Like the beginning, which is now. The 'beginning' of your adult life. Since you have a car, you shall be meeting people. Men. Other 'Men' that you will take a fancy..... too. Which is perfectly normal and natural. So… with that being said... I shall have to get over you. Now. Let's please not talk about 'this' right now, yes? I will only get emotional. And, as you know. Best. That is not my favorite emotion to share. With anyone but you. Even sharing it with you is hard on me, my beautiful, talented..... baby.' I looked in his eyes and they were getting very wet. Or maybe, misty. I couldn't tell. But it made me sad. I instantly started kissing him. After about three hours of sex and kissing, I asked him, during our love-making, if this was the last time we were to be sleeping together. 'No, no, no, baby. I just wanted to get you mentally prepared for when it does happen, is all. As am I. Yes? Now, come here, you.' He reached for me and we became entwined once again.

Once we were finished, I slowly turned my head and looked at my bedside clock. It read 5:30am. My God! I needed water and bed! I looked over at my dad and he was deep asleep. His body turned towards me, left arm laying over my waist, and snoring lightly. More like heavy breathing. I knew he was out. I reached for the glass of water on my bedside table and took a long drink; knowing that when I did wake up, I would have too majorly pee. Oh well. I needed to sleep. I laid back onto my pillow, shook off part of the sheet that was covering the right side of my body. Just removed it off of my leg up to my waist. Just in case some fool decided to walk in here without announcing through the Com or knocking. That would be something. And a 'something' that I didn't want any part of. As I scooted closer to my father and very gently took his arm that was on my waist, I put it back where it was. Now that I was completely snuggled into my father's body and felt completely safe, I knew that I could sleep deep; no worrying or sleeping with one eye open. No, I did not sleep that way every night at home. But tonight, for some reason, I felt very insecure. I didn't know why. Maybe it was just a 'gut feeling' that I had from years or months ago. Who knew? I closed my eyes and fell asleep. Feeling my father's breathing against my left cheek. It was, as usual, like heaven too me.

Chapter 22

Morning, for the first time in years, came *too* early this time. I woke up fully refreshed though. THAT in itself, was a first. I DID finally get the sleep I needed. I looked over, fully expecting my father to be out of bed and probably, downstairs with Steve having breakfast. I looked at my bedside again. Damn! Only 8AM? That was a *first*. Then I heard him. His heavy breathing. Someone whom was fast asleep; and in REM still. Awesome. For once, we can wake up together. I loved that more than anything. In the morning, waking up with your 'man' or 'boyfriend' in the morning made me feel safe, and completely taken care of. I had always felt that way. Well, with my father. The only one that I obviously had slept with. Or, slept overnight with anyway. I closed my eyes again. Half sleepy and half awake. I knew I had enough sleep for the day. But the warmth of my father's body, plus his breath on the back of my neck made me sleepy again. Well, sleepy enough to lay there until his stomach or bladder woke him up. I also knew that today was the day that he was going to tell or talk to me about our trip to the 'lovely' Bohemian Grove. Also, I just remembered that I wanted to talk to him about the man's name whom I sacrificed the other night. What. Two weeks ago? Three weeks ago? Something like that, anyway. As I was thinking my thoughts, I felt my father stir. He yawned in his 'asleep' state and rolled over. Facing the ceiling. I slowly and quietly rolled onto my back. Eyes wide open. Nope. No more sleepy for me. It was weird. He was always up before me. I wondered what day it was... Sunday! That's why he is sleeping in this morning. We did go to bed late last night. No wonder he is sleeping in. I turned my face to look at him while he was sleeping. He looked so peaceful when he slept. Yeah. I know it sounds so cliché. But he did! Hard to believe, I know. But sometimes, he didn't. He would, on occasion, look like the weight of the world was on his shoulders. And, it usually was. At least, tonight, and this morning, he looked peaceful and 'happy'. Whatever happy was for him. Whatever it was, I was happy for him. I kept staring at his face. After an hour or so, I couldn't help myself. I kissed him softly on the nose. Instantly, his eye's opened up. I jumped a little. He slowly smiled. A lazy, sexy smile. 'I'm sorry, daddy. I swear I did not mean to wake you up. 'That's alright, kitten. What time is it?' I turned my face and looked over at the clock. Only on his side of the bed. '9:30, Tata.' His eyebrow's arched up. '9:30? That's all? Fuck. I wanted to sleep in at least until noon.' I looked at him then, when I saw that his face was not changing expression, I worried. Oh shit! I am so sorry, daddy!' 'I'm kidding, Gia.' 'Huh? I mean, what?' 'I said... I am kidding. Now is fine. I slept perfectly. And, I need to use the restroom. Quite urgently, actually. And, I am famished. What about you, love? Did you sleep well? Had enough sleep?' 'I slept better than I had in forever, actually, Tata. I am hungry as all Hell, too.' He looked at me. Probably wondering if he should correct me on my language or not. I guess he decided against it. He walked into his bathroom and shut the door. I got out of bed, looked around for my white nightgown, finally found it in a pile underneath my father's jean's, grabbed it and pulled it on over my head. I walked over to the closed restroom door and gave a slight knock. 'Yes, Gia?' 'Daddy? Do you mind if I go to my room and slip on some light sweat pants and a halter top AND pin up my hair? Today is a non-make-up day for me.' 'No, kitten. I do not mind. I will see you downstairs then. Yes?' 'Absolutely, baby. I'll hurry, too.' 'Alright then. See you soon.' As I slipped out of my father's room, I heard nothing downstairs. Steven must be outside in the garage with the rest of detail, I thought to myself. When I was in my room, getting my sweat pants on, I also went into my bathroom and brushed out my 'bedhead'. I put my hair up into a high ponytail. I also peed and then walked out my bedroom door, closing it behind me. I stopped right at the top of the stairs and looked down at my feet. Damn it. Forgot footwear. I walked back to my room and into my closet. I chose some flip flops and went out to the stairs again. Thank God I had a pretty new pedicure going on. Or no flip-flops would be allowed. Yuk! I started walking down the stairs to the breakfast table. Just as I hit the bottom of the stairs, I heard my father's door close. I paused for a second but decided to keep walking towards the table. My prayers had been answered. There was the smell of freshly fried pancakes in the kitchen. Yum! That meant warm syrup too. Double Yum! 'Good morning, Juanita!' 'Good morning, bambino! How was your sleep last night? You and your father? That stopped me in my tracks. 'Well, I slept very well. I would think my dad slept well too. I haven't really spoke to him yet this morning.' 'I see, bambina. Ok. Sit down for some pancakes. Si?' "Yes! I have been waiting for these since I woke up! My father and I had a long night last night. Business until 4 in the morning. Yuk!' Juanita looked at me with a 'stern' look on her face. 'That does not sound so good, Gia. Not at all.' When she was finished with her 'scolding' of my father, I heard him close his door and proceed down the stairs. I started eating when Juanita was finished putting two pancakes on my plate. I grabbed three pieces of bacon on my plate, too. As my father sat down, I noticed that he must be hungry. He had showered, but he was, with one hand, putting pancakes on his plate as well as bacon from the same big, serving spoon. His hair was completely undone and laying down his back. I loved it when he wore his hair loose and hanging down like that. It looked so sexy on him. He looked up quickly and caught me staring at him. He smiled at me and continued putting the rest of the food on his plate. I put my head back down. Feeling myself blushing. And badly. Both my cheeks were hot. I knew he knew I thought he was hot. But I also knew he thought I was hot. So, we were even. I looked up quickly. Low and behold, he was looking at me. Ha! Busted. Just like I was. We were even steven. Speaking of 'steven', he came inside from the garage no doubt and sat at the table. He leaned over and whispered something in my dad's ear. My dad whipped his head in his direction and said to him, quite harshly, I might add, 'And *why* wasn't I *told* about this *when* it happened, Steven?' Steve got up from the table and motioned for my father to get up and follow him. 'No. I am eating. If you cannot see that, you must be blind, Goddamnit. Go and take care of it yourself. It is your job, Steven.' I instantly put my head down. I always did whenever Steve was getting yelled at. Out of respect or some sort of 'friend-thing'. Steve did it for me, too. Even though I didn't know what was said between the two of them, I knew it was pretty serious. My father did not utter a word for the entire time we were eating our breakfast. And he kept his head down. Every once in a while, shaking it back and forth. Ever so slightly. I wondered if I should ask what was going on. Or... maybe I should just ask Steve. Text him about it. I finished my breakfast, told my father that I was done and got up to carry my plate into the kitchen. My father still not acknowledging my words. That's it. I'm going to ask him myself. Fuck it. Why pussy-foot around and go through Steven? We were fucking for fuck's sake. Why couldn't I know something that, apparently, was only prive for my father's ears? 'What's going on, Tata?' He continued eating, chewed, swallowed, sipped his Orange Juice and then finally looked up at me. 'Apparently, Someone Came onto Our Property/Backyard and was Shot in the Fucking Head, Gia. He got as far as the back doors.' He looked at me for a few more minutes and then continued eating the rest of his breakfast. 'Oh My God! What about all of the guys? What's going to happen? I thought we were safe here?' I was almost in tears. My father got up from his chair and walked over to me. 'Honey, you *are* safe. I'm here. Ok, baby? Now. After your breakfast/lunch, please come up with me to your room. I would like to speak with you regarding our trip. Like I said last night, yes?' 'Of course, Tata.' I continued with my meal. Only not as enthusiastically. As I finished, my father had already finished and was outside speaking to the detail that was awake for their shift during the day. As I watched Juanita walk in and look at me and probably the expression on my face, she walked towards me, picked up my plate, not saying a word and kissed me on top of my head. She gave my right arm a slight, loving squeeze and picked up my plate and glass and walked back to the kitchen. I finally got up and walked over to the double door's that looked out over the backyard. I noticed a white, plastic, sheet-type thing laying over a 15 foot area. Right over the stone rail that led to our steps up to the doors. My God! He did almost make it to our double doors. Shitski! I hope my father is telling these fucker's too pay fucking attention! We could have all been killed! My dad, Juanita! Me! Everyone in the damn house, for fuck's sake! All of a sudden, I felt a little nauseous. I was not in the mood for even a drink of water. Nothing. Not even 'liquids'. My father walked in from outside and saw that I was done. He then motioned for me to go upstairs with him. I got up and followed him up the staircase. Straight to my room. I opened my door and sat on my bed. He walked in right behind me and closed and locked my door. He sat on the bed right next to me. 'I have only 1 question about last night, Tata. And then I really do not want to hear anything more about it: Unless I have too, ok?' 'That is fine, my kitten. Go ahead.' I scooted closer to him, turned to him and asked, 'How did he get by the dogs?' He looked at me for a minute, looked down at his hands and then looked back up at me. 'Love. Whatever I tell you right now, you have to promise me that you will not get freaked out or scared. Ok? Even if it will make you feel better sleeping with me for a few nights. Alright?' 'Yes, Sir. I will try, Tata. But I will take you up on sleeping with you for a few nights.' " He sort of laughed at the last part I said. 'Unfortunately, he shot a few of my dogs. Yes, fatally. So, we are ***all*** having a meeting tomorrow morning; All of us. Steve, Detail, Juanita, Me, of course, and I would like you to be there as well. Right after breakfast. Alright?' I looked at him and refused to think about the Rott's that got killed by that fucker. 'Of course I'll be there, Tata.' He put his arm around my back, up to my neck and started slowly rubbing my neck. 'Good, love. Now I would like to talk to you upstairs. I know it is not the Happiest of Conversation's for you but it does have to be done. And the time is getting upon us. Tomorrow afternoon, by God. Shit. And here I thought it was after that. 'He stared off into space for a bit and then looked at me with a serious look on his face. 'As you know, The Grove is for the most influential men in the World, kitten. Women are *not* and never have been, allowed there. Except for entertaining the guests, that is.' I looked at him with trepidation. I thought I knew what that meant. But to make sure, I asked him anyway. 'Tata. I have a pretty good idea what 'entertaining the guest's' means. But I want to be sure that what I think, is correct. So...what does it mean, exactly?' He continued looking at me in the eyes, of course, as always, as if he was still listening to me speak. But since I wasn't talking, I knew he was rolling around in his mind exactly how to tell me. 'Gia, this entire trip, for lack of a better word, was Harris's idea. Meaning, both of us going. Personally, I have NEVER had the desire to go to this place of debauchery and sickness. A tad more than half of the men that ***do*** go are Deviant, Homosexual's. In *my* opinion. As well as Pedophiles. They go to fulfill their sick little fantasies and end up hurting; emotionally and physically, little boys, for the rest of their lives. It is a sick, disgusting, 'endeavor'. And, as you also know, it happens every year. Anyhow, back to your question. Sorry that I digressed. 'Daddy, that's ok. Go on.' He leaned over to me, kissed me on the cheek, stood up, walked over to my bedroom door and locked it. I had no idea what that was about. Oh well. He sat back down where he was before and answered my question. 'Harris asked, or rather, told me that YOU were too go so that you could... sexually... pleasure those that... do NOT prefer little boys.' When he was finished, a single tear started running down his cheek. 'I told him...no, no way were you too go. But he would *not* have any of it. He wouldn't even beat me. I even offered or asked him too. Begged him too, kitten. I'm... so... sorry baby.' At this point, he was full on crying. Tears were pouring out of his eyes. I instantly scooted as close to him as I could and held him in *my* arms. I petted his hair and talked to him softly. Comforting little words that he used to do too me when I was upset. Finally, after I put some tissues in my lap, he grabbed them with his right hand and cleaned up his face while still laying in my lap. After he blew his nose, he sat back up. 'Gia, I promise, since I will be there, and he wants me there, he is probably going to have me watch you get raped or God knows what. I will do everything in my power to keep you from getting injured. What I cannot promise you, my beautiful baby, is that... is that I won't be able to *stop* you *from* getting raped. Or from who. Do you understand, honey?' I thought about everything that he told me. Then I just put all of that information inside my 'huge box' and put it deep inside the dark recesses of my mind. 'Tata? I will get through this. I promise you. No, it won't be easy'... I noticed that he was about to open his mouth and say something but I lifted up my hand and put my pointer finger and put it onto his lip's. He actually stopped what he was going to say. To actually hear me out, so to speak. This *was* a first. 'It will not be easy, as I was saying, Tata. But, I can do it. And I will do it. Not giving that son-of-a-bitch any satisfaction *at all*. Then, once we do get home? I will totally let you take care of me. In your bed. Please? That's all I ask. Let me stay in your bed and you take care of me. Can I daddy?' He looked at me completely in awe. Totally surprised. Almost like that was the last thing hc was expecting to come out of my mouth. 'Hon... of course... yes. Yes, you can. Of coursc you can. I will take care of you, but you have to understand. These people are evil, ruthless, assholes. I cannot stand them. I Tolerate Them. These people can, if they so choose, hurt you, darling Gia. My baby Kiddo. You understand that I cannot and will not be able to stop them if they decide to hurt you, so, before saying anything else for the moment, please listen to what I have to say to you. Yes?' Right at that very moment, I realized just how serious this was. I HAD to listen to everything he said. Or, I may not make it out. Literally. Hell, no one would even know I was there. Per say. Except my father and Steven. But, since they were so powerful, they might just kill them to keep the entire 'experience' under wraps. Like it never happened. I'm sure this wasn't the 'first' time something like 'this' ever happened, neither. 'I'm listening, daddy.' 'Good. Now, whomever Harris 'puts' you with, I am sure he will have some sick, perverted, fantasy or fetish.' Looking at my dad's face, I could tell that he was having a very hard time telling me this. Or even talking about it, for that matter. 'My suggestion is to do anything this sick fucker tells you to do. Because if you do not, it will get back to Harris, as I'm sure you know. And since it is you, and he will be the only one who knows this by the way, if you don't do what is 'expected' from this pond-scum, creep, Harris will take you and in a separate part of the Grove, he will completely punish you. To the extreme. And not beat you like you are a 'delicate woman', neither. He will beat you within an inch of your life, baby girl.' After he told me this part of my lovely trip to the infamous Grove, he had to stop for a minute, take a sip from a glass of water and take a few deep breaths. 'Alright... once you have completed whatever it is that you will be asked to do, you are at LEAST allowed to sleep in my cabin. I made damn SURE of that. Do you think you can do this baby? Because if not, we will go away. Forever. I do not know where. Maybe Dubai. But let me know now my love. And, IF you can ACTUALLY do this, you will completely 'blow' Harris's mind. As far as how strong you are. See, love. He absolutely thinks that he can break you. Beyond repair. That is HIS goal. As of this moment, anyhow. I received this just a few hours ago this afternoon. ‘I CAN do this, Tata. And I WILL blow his fucking mind. Pardon my language, but I cannot think of that...SCUM without saying words like that. Sorry.' For once, my father grinned. Not much, but it was there. 'No need to apologize for that, my kitten. In this instance, you may say that word in front of me. Especially... maybe ONLY in regards to him. I took a deep breath, as did he and we both looked at each other. I gave him a sideways grin as did he. Sort of. His was more serious; as I would have guessed. 'So. When do we leave then, Tata?' 'Tomorrow morning, love. I will let you pack your suitcase. I will also let you take a moment, if you'd like, before you write down what you NEED to bring and then what you can and cannot bring. It's up to you.' 'I'm ready now, baby.' Whenever I called him that word, it always threw him for a loop. I didn't say it too get that reaction. And I knew it was getting too comfortable for me to call him that. So, I better get used too not calling him that. 'Alright then, baby...' he said in response. 'I know I have to stop calling you that. I just had a conversation in my head about it.' 'Alright, Kiddo. It is for the best. In the long run at least. Ok. Why don't you get a pen and something to write on and I'll be back in a minute.' I watched him walk out of my bedroom door and heard him descend the stairs. I got up, walked into my closet. Towards some drawers that were stackable. They had all of my computer supplies in them. Paper, ink, pens, markers, etc. I took a sheet of paper and a notebook too write on, got in bed and waited for my father. This trip was going to suck badly. Probably the worst experience of my life. So far, at least, I thought. As I sat there waiting for my dad to return, I started thinking about how bad it really was going to be at The Grove. If my father was as 'weirded' out about it, it probably was going to be bad. Fuck. I will just have to be in 'Mode' I guess. Yet again. I thought to myself, as my father walked back into my bedroom and sat on my bed. Close enough for me to touch his knee or his leg but far enough away to where he could look at me and look *in* my eyes while he spoke to me. 'Alright, kitten, this is the basic low-down of The Bohemian Grove. What you have to take and what you can take. Write the first, yes?' 'Ready, daddy.' I said; pen poised over my piece of paper. He swallowed and then looked at me. 'Alright. What you *need* to take are these things: 2 of your white Ritual gown's, your little 'Indian outfit', the outfit that has the short, blue and white mini-skirt that has the matching 'bathing suit top' and your long, see-through, pink, gauze gown that has the rhinestone's on it. Those are the so-called costumes that you must take with you, yes?' I looked up at him as I finished writing down everything that he had told me to bring. He, I am assuming, turned his head away as he said the last 'item'. 'Are you ok, Tata?' I asked him. 'Of course I am, baby. Just trying to remember what you should bring is all.' I nodded my head at him in response, even though I knew deep down inside of me that it meant more than that; him turning his head away from me. 'As far as toiletries, no make-up is allowed. Except just your basic...what do you call it? Your 'no make-up look'? Or something to that effect. Do you remember what I'm talking about, baby?' As I finished writing that down, I looked up at him and nodded my head. 'Yes, father. Go on.' 'Alright. A hairbrush, your shampoo, your hair product's, as far as when you take a shower or bathe, as well. Two pairs of jeans, with *no* holes in them; nice jean's love. 3 to 4 nice shirts or tops that you normally wear with jeans. And that's about it, kitten, Understand? So it can be a small suitcase or just take your Louis Vuitton™ Carry-All.' As I was furiously writing down everything he was telling me, I finally finished. I looked up at him and said, 'That is it?' 'Pretty much, sweetheart.' I sat there thinking, looking down at my list. 'Where will I be sleeping at night, Tata?' My father looked at me for a bit and again swallowed as he was staring at me. 'Well, it depends. It depends on if...if you are needed or not.' He, again looked away and down from me. I finally 'got it'. I was basically being brought to The Grove as a fucking prostitute. Because of Harris no doubt. Nice. 'Never mind, daddy. I 'get' it. As I said that he turned away again. Only, as I looked at his facial expression, he had a few tears coming down his face. I put my pad and paper down on the bed next to me and scooted right next to him. I put my arms around him and slightly drew him into my chest. To give him a hug. I don't recall if I had ever done that to him before. Surprisingly, he did not offer *any* resistance when I drew him towards me. When he was in my lap, practically, he took one arm (the arm that wasn't holding his body up) and put it completely around my waist. His face buried into my chest. And NOT in a sexual way. This entire 'trip' truly was hurting him emotionally. I guess because of the idea of someone other than him, having their 'sick, perverted' way with me, to his property, was too much for him. I didn't blame my dad one bit. It was 'hurting' me as well.

'Tata. It's ok. Really. I'll be alright. I can get through this. Promise. As you know, I've been through a lot worse. You, above *all* else, knows that I have been through a lot worse. He kept his head buried in my chest for a few minutes more and then raised up. He looked into my eyes. I did not waver. I stared right back into his. 'It's not you, particularly, that I am 'worried' about, my love. It's me. I do not know how I'll be able to take it. Do you understand what I'm saying, baby?'

'Yes, I do, daddy. Hopefully, no one will 'ask for or want me' much. We can always hope. Right? Since Harris is orchestrating this entire fucked up thing, let's beat him at his own game. When we walk in that place, I will try too not act afraid or depressed. Let alone angry. That will really get him. Don't you agree? And you can act like you normally would. Like how you would act at a Ritual. Or a meeting with him. Just act normal for the situation at hand. Or 'accordingly', more like. How does that sound?' He continued to look at me, eye's a little red and swollen. Almost like he had been trying to keep tears from falling. My top was just barely wet. 'Are you sure that you can do this, my baby? It shall not be pleasant.' 'I know it won't be, Tata. But I know I will be able to handle it. Look at all that I have handled, father.' He gazed at me and finally got it in his head that I did mean what I said. 'Alright, Gia. I trust what you say. Now all I have to do is get through it.' He sort of grinned at me sideways. As all of 'his grins' were. I grinned back at him and then glanced at my list. 'I will get the little that I have to pack, packed. And meet you... at the pool? In your room? Or do you need to do some work?' 'No, love. I am done with work for today. After the meeting, entailing the household tomorrow, we shall drive to where the Helicopter is and fly to The Grove. Alright? So, why don't you pack and finish with that. It is getting to be dinner time and Juanita is cooking. I, in the meantime, will tell Steven everything that I have told you. For the most part. When you are finished, Steven and I will meet you for dinner. Yes? How does that sound with you?' As I was looking at him and was just about to nod, I remembered one question that I forgot to ask him. 'That sounds fine, father. But I have 1 more question for you.' 'And what would that be, sweetheart?' he asked, as he was getting up off of my bed. 'What will Stev-o be doing or where will he be staying when all of this shit is going on?' When my dad was standing at my bedroom door, he turned around to speak. 'They have special quarters where the bodyguard's stay when all of this shit is going on, baby. I will see you downstairs.' And he was gone. I stared at the back of my bedroom door, as I found myself doing a lot more lately, and thought that when we do go to this *Bohemian Grove*, it was *not* going to be 'fun'. I stood up, walked into my restroom to get 'cleaned up' for dinner.

After I looked at myself in the mirror and was satisfied with how I looked, I glanced at my watch. I definitely had time to pack the few things for our 'trip' tomorrow for The Grove before dinner. I hurriedly walked into my closet and grabbed my Carry-All from my top shelf in my closet, put it on top of my bed and then picked up the list my father had me write up regarding the 'trip'. I walked over to my drawer's and took out the things that my father said I needed to bring. After that was done, I put all of those things on my bed next to my Carry-All too. I stood there just staring at those things on my bed. Not moving. I don't know how long I stood there, but when I glanced at my watch again, I realized I did not have much time until dinner. I decided that I was going to take some things that I wanted too as well. I rushed into my bathroom, grabbed my shampoo & my conditioner, my perfume that my father loved and the body lotion dad also loved. And bought me as well. In hopes that I would be lucky enough to sleep in his cabin, with him, at least for one night. Thank Fuck this horrid 'trip' only lasted four days. After I grabbed all of those item's, as well as a pony-tail holder and my brush plus hair dryer, I put everything inside my bag and zipped it up. I walked into my closet and once inside, my Com went off. 'Ello, Gia? Dinner is almos ready, ok?' Then the Com went off. 'Thank God I hurried doing all of this crap. And at least it is done', I thought. I quickly grabbed my most expensive jeans and a blouse that I only wear for 'special' occasions. Special, meaning that I wanted to scream that I had money and that I was better than everyone else and that I was *not* supposed to be there'. Wherever 'there' was. In this case, at The Grove. 'I was not a Prostitute!!! I knew it was immature and pathetic but it was the one thing that I could do too feel better. I walked out of my bedroom door and quickly took the step's two at a time. Until the first landing, that is. I heard my father AND Steven talking in a hushed tone. I peeked down and over the rail and saw the two of them sitting down at the dinner table talking, with their head's close together. 'I wonder what they could be talking about that is SO secretive, in a 'hushed tone?' I thought to myself. I descended the stairs and walked over to the table. I quickly looked at their plates and saw that indeed they waited on me to come down before they started to eat. That was cool, I thought. 'Hi everybody. Sorry I'm a little late. I packed too, Tata.' My father and Steven both sort of jumped when they heard my voice. That, in itself, tripped me out. They always knew, well, where I was anywhere! At any time! What the Hell was up?' They both stared at me and both said something to the effect of 'Hello' or 'good evening. Something like that. Completely caught off guard. For the very first time. Which only meant one thing. They were both talking about me. I looked away from both of them, sat on my seat next to my father, put my napkin on MY lap and started to eat. For the first time, NOT waiting for my father to start eating. I was glancing at my dad every few seconds to gauge his expression, as I started eating. He definitely noticed that I did start eating without his 'cue' and gave a sort of surprised, pissed off, look. 'Fuck it.' I thought to myself. And continued to eat. He did not speak to me the entire meal. He basically ignored me. He either ate his dinner or spoke to Steve. If he wanted to 'fight' over this pathetic little fucking thing then so be it. I had so much stress regarding our little excursion that I just didn't give a damn. Not at that moment I didn't. I continued to eat my dinner and once I finished, I took one last sip of my milk and was finished. I pushed my dinner away after I put my napkin on my plate to the center of the table. I looked out through my peripheral and saw that my father and Steven were done with their dinner but had not pushed their plates away yet. I sat there for a minute, stood up, and excused myself, making sure that in no way I was being rude, picked up my father and Steven's plate and took them to the kitchen. I walked back, picked up the glasses and my plate and walked back into the kitchen. Then I walked back up the stairs and into my room. I grabbed my overnight bag, put my nightie, brush and robe inside it, shut my door and walked into my father's room and climbed in his bed. I grabbed my book (also in my bag) and started pretending to read. I realized that if they were going to pretend to have a 'normal' conversation without even acknowledging me, then I would eat my dinner, and not acknowledge them. I will also 'read' my book, 'fall asleep' in my father's bed, and hopefully get away with it. I seriously doubted that I would, but it was worth a try. Regardless if I got 'in trouble' or not. I was proving a point after all. And, if he slapped me? I was going to slap him back, dammit. Well, maybe not 'slap' him but I was going to do something! I started reading my book and realized that I was actually in a great part of it. After about maybe, 30 to 40 minutes of reading, I heard quick-paced walking up the stairs. But it was so in the 'back of my mind', I didn't pay much attention to it at all. The next thing I knew, my father's door opened so hard that it hit the opposing wall. It actually left a smallish hole in it. The door bounced back as I must have jumped in bed about two feet above the mattress. 'What the fuck was that all about, Gia?' Yes? Speak!!!! Now!' The thought of slapping him was quickly fading away. And, fast. I knew I had to stand up to him. I had too. What was what about dad?!!!' I replied. Screaming back at him. He honestly looked, for a few seconds, completely shocked. 'Good.' I thought. 'You know the fuck what I am talking about, Gia!!! Now, Speak! Now!' 'You both completely ignored me through the entire dinner.

Not to mention, when I was walking down the stairs, whispering about me. And no explanation!!!!! Not fair since I am the one whom is taking all of the abuse on our little fucking little trip!!! Excuse me, Dominick, but I am a little fucking stressed out!!! FUCK!' 'Oh!' he said, still screaming, ' You're a little stressed out, are you? What about me, Gia?? I have to know that my little girl is most likely getting raped! At the very least!!! How do you think that would make me feel, Gia? Or are you too Goddamn busy thinking about your shiny new Lamborghini or your new Chanel outfits, Louis Vuitton Luggage, bag's, etc., etc., etc.?' 'That is not fucking fair, asshole!!!' and that was all I remembered.

Chapter 23

I woke up laying on my father's bathroom floor. My mouth was KILLING me. Not to mention my cheek or cheekbone, rather. I slowly got up, stumbled, and did the 'Thorazine Shuffle', to my dad's mirror. 'OMG! I looked like I got in a punching match with Mike Tyson!! Did I *have* to go to The Grove looking like this? Maybe I wasn't going, I thought. GOOD! My father kicked my ass but at least I probably didn't have to GO!.... someone knocked, or more like, 'rapped' on the door, once or twice, and then in walked my father. Of all people. 'Get your face presentable for our trip, Gia. We are leaving in 10 minutes.' I slowly turned around and looked at him with HATE in my eyes. He met my stare and I saw him look at the damage that he did to my face. I felt my cheekbone, or that area, start to swell. 'You really want me to go looking like this?' I whispered at him. 'Yes, I do. I need the company. I get *bored* easy. Get ready. Now.' And he walked out of the door. I looked at my face again and took a white washcloth from HIS drawer and put it under the faucet and let cold water run all over it. I squeezed it out and took it with me as I walked out of his room. Since I was already dressed in a skirt and crop-top, both Chanel, I walked downstairs. For some reason, I started silently crying. HOW could my daddy beat my face like this? Fuck! As I hit the bottom of the stairs and looked around for my suitcase, I saw Steve at the front door, sitting on the chaise. He looked at me, grimaced and opened his arms. I tried to run but half ran, half skipped towards him. I sat on his lap and let him hold me. I made sure my face wasn't touching his freshly pressed suit. As Steven was rubbing my back; up and down for about 5 minutes, my father yelled, 'Where the Hell is Gia, Steve?' Steve-o answered, 'She's down here! Already too go, Sir.' He pulled me away from me and looked me in the eyes. 'Now, hon? Do yourself a favor and try to be at least, nice. Can you manage to do that for me? G.G., please try to act 'normal'. As in try not to complain in front of your father how much your poor, face feels, ok babe?' I looked at him, with a pleading in my eyes. 'Do I really have to go, Steve?' 'Unfortunately, you do, baby, yes.' I sat up and got off of his lap; on the hard wood. As we both sat there; Steven looking at his watch and I looking down at the floor, my father, in jeans and a golf shirt, hurriedly walked down the stairs, passed us and went out the front door. Steve got up and hurried out the door, glancing behind him and motioning me to follow him. I got up and slowly walked out the door as well, looking at the car. Deciding which door I would be getting into. As I kept the washcloth pressed against my face, I pulled it off and looked at it. Bloody as hell; as expected. I got in the car, in the opposite side from my father, who was already sitting inside, looking at his laptop already. 'Asshole', I thought. I reached into my purse, took out my phone and started texting Michelle. I told her I had to go on that business trip with my father. Who was being a complete asshole, by the way.' And sent that off to her. I checked to see if my phone was on silent so as to not have my father hear it when she returned my message. I leaned back against the seat of the car and let my eye's close. I heard my father's soft typing stop and his laptop closing. I kept my eyes closed. I then grabbed my purse, which was next to me on the seat, took out my sunglasses and put them on. Though very slowly. 'Damn! Even that fucking hurt!' I sighed and just tried to let it go. My father put his laptop on the floor, next to his feet no doubt. I just knew that from memory. My eyes were slammed shut. I just decided that IF

I had to go through this fucking horrid experience, I would just be in Mode. Starting NOW. Fuck everybody. Even my asshole father. 'How fucking *dare* he?' The soft movement of the car as it was rolling on the pavement, probably on new tires almost put me too sleep. No such luck. I couldn't, for the life of me, go to sleep! Shit! I opened my eyes and just slowly turned my head to look out of my window. Noticing that at that very moment, my father was looking at me. 'What the hell was going on in his mind?' I thought to myself. I really didn't care. As I was looking out of the window, traffic whizzing by me on the other side of the freeway, I wondered what this whole thing would be like. What Harris, the Prick, would think when he saw my face? Not that I particularly cared what he thought. But who, in their right fucking mind, would want to have sex with a woman who looked like she was in a punching match? That was the key word though. 'In their Right mind'. I must have eventually fell asleep because the next time I opened my eyes, the car was slowly driving up this winding dirt/gravel, road. Oh my God. Are we truly here *now*? Shit! 'Go in MODE, *GIA*!' I told myself. Out of instinct, I turned to my right and looked at my father. He was looking at me as well. I was *not* expecting that. *At* all. I must have had, for that 1 second, fear in my eyes. Dammit. My dad, after brushing his hair back with his hands, he was wearing it completely loose, (I noticed for the first time this afternoon) grabbed my right hand pretty damn quickly, before I could take it away, no doubt. He squeezed it in a 'fatherly/it will be ok' type of squeeze. I just kept staring at him. With zero expression on my face. I didn't even squeeze his hand back. My hand was limp the entire time. He kept looking at me and then his eye's wandered over to my cheekbone. His face did a little twitching motion. Like *he* was even surprised that he did this to me. 'My cheek must look worse now.' I thought. Hell, it *had* too. The car stopped. All of a sudden, people we didn't even know, were opening doors, taking hold of our arm's, and leading us towards, I was assuming, our sleeping quarters. I kept rapt attention to where I was going in comparison to where my father was going. Thank God we were headed the same way. These 'robotic type people (they were *not* saying 1 word) took us to a large wooden door. As we stood in front of it, one of the 'robots' opened it up. It swung open to a huge room. Like a giant, spacious, ski resort, type room. Only when my eye's looked up. Straight ahead. Sitting at an oversized desk was Harris. The 'Devil' himself. '*Prick*! He thought he was so damn High & Mighty!' I swallowed so loud, I was surprised the robots didn't look over at me. 'Well, well, well. If it isn't Mr. and Mrs. Mahari. *So* glad that you could make it.' My father ripped his arm from one of the male robots and replied, 'Quit the crap, Harris. Just show us our room and be done with it. I *know* the drill.' You do, Mahari. But your beloved does not. I just want to make sure that she is given extra special attention is all. I glanced over at my dad. His face was filled with two emotions that I could tell. Anger and regret. He looked at Harris with such hatred, I was surprised that he didn't fly over to the desk and beat the crap out of him. 'Yes, I am sure you will. Now. Can we go to our rooms?' 'Shit. Rooms?' Harris looked at the both of us and then squinted at me. Then, for that split second, I remembered my face. 'What do we have here? Sweet butterfly, what did happen to that beautiful, flawless, face of yours?' I just stood there and looked back at him. 'I really do not think it is any of your business now. Is it?' I was surprised that I even spoke to him that way. 'Oh, but it is, Ms. Mahari. Your face looking like that, I doubt our *Very* important customer's will want to play with you over the next 3 and a half days or so. What should we do about that, hmm?' He then looked at my father. 'If you would so desire, Prick, she will cover her face with make-up. If that is, it is not too obvious to the customer's.' Harris looked at my father with a hateful look and was thinking about what he had just said. 'Well, Mr. Fahari, I will have to think about that overnight. He motioned for his 'robot's to take us to our 'rooms', as they walked up and pulled us backwards. They closed the big, wooden door and led us to our room. 1 room. Thank God, I thought. I was infuriated at my father, but I really did *need* to sleep in his room/bed while I was here, overlooking the giant, 70 foot tall owl that was to be burned at the last night of our stay. The 'Burning of The Owl' ceremony is called the 'Cremation of Care' Ceremony. 'It was 'quite fucking *lovely*' that he put us in a room overlooking that monstrosity during our stay. Nice touch, Asshole.' As I put my bag on what I thought was my bed, my father had his bags on his bed. My father went into the restroom. Apparently to speak to Steve. I would assume to see where his cabin was in comparison to ours. As he came out of the restroom, I picked up all of the toiletries that I *thought* I would be using on our 'lovely vacation'. I walked towards the bathroom when he was completely out of it and set down my 'dry' hair products on the sink. My shampoo and conditioner went inside of the shower. As did my razor and a fresh washcloth. I left my father's bloody white washcloth in the middle of his bed. On top of his comforter. I really was at the point where I did not care anymore. I honestly thought at that moment, I was the only one on my side. That I was the only person that had to watch out for *me*. Sure, Steven was on my side and would protect me. But when it came to my father or me? I truly do not know what he was told to do. Probably too protect my father. But, Hell, I wasn't sure about that 100%. I sat on my bed and a soft, satin, pillow from my Carry-All and put it on *our* bed, where *we* were sleeping. Tonight. No matter what my father wanted or not. I *was* sleeping in *his* bed, with him the entire trip. As I finished rubbing body lotion all over my body, I pulled out my silk robe and wrapped it around my body. My father entered the room from his shower and his hair was loose and clean. I bet it smelled good, too. I thought. 'Damn! It was even hard to stay mad at him for God's sake! SHIT!'I was SO frustrated. My father slipped on his bathrobe as well since he was planning on not doing anything the whole time. 'Could you please tell me how this whole thing is supposed to work, Father Sir?' He raised his eyebrows. 'Very professional are we Gia?' 'Father, after this late morning I really do not know *how* to act with you. It is almost like losing the love of your life. I never expected you too close-fist punch me like that. It will take a while to swallow that one, Father. So, sorry if I seem a little detached. I'm just trying to figure it all out, I guess.' 'Gia. I apologize to what I did do to you this late morning. Hitting you like I did. That was wrong of me. Do you accept my apology, my kitten? I truly love you. You must know *that* my Kiddo. Oh, my baby. You are my life. You really are. I did a complete 'life-check' in the shower just a minute ago in the restroom, obviously, and I realized that you are truly the only person that I *do* have. The one that I trust with my life. Of course. Yes. I trust Steven with *that*, too. But *you*, my sweet, are the only family that I have. I never want to lose you. Ever. I will *never* hurt you like this again, my Princess. NEVER. And I swear on my life with that statement. I do. Do you accept, Kiddo?' I looked at him, deep in his eyes, yet again, and I did believe him. From deep inside my heart. This man knew everything about me. He slept with me, knew every square inch of my body. Yes, I forgave him. I always would. No matter what. 'Yes, Tata. I do. I *do* forgive you.' He leaned over just a bit and softly kissed me on the lips. 'I really want you right now baby, but I do not know what Harris has in store for the both of us. So, with that in mind, I better not sleep with you tonight, love. 'But I will sleep in here with you if we don't hear anything from Harris, yes?' He looked at me, looked down at his shoes, and then looked up at me again. 'Yes, my love. Yes, you will.' Inside I let out a mini sigh of relief. 'Ok then, Tata. That was all I was really asking. I would feel a lot safer sleeping in here. Also, I have a couple questions about...this...place.' He looked at me with some hesitation in his expression. 'And those would be?' 'What sort... of things will these pigs ask me to do? Do you even know?' 'Let's just suffice it to say, that *anything* goes here, my love. Anything. Alright? So, if some...' He turned his head away and 'fake' coughed into his hand. '*Pig* asks you to preform something absolutely... dreadful, then just go into Mode and *do* it. Unfortunately, that is what Harris wants. Too '*break you.*' I looked at him with surprise in my expression. 'And you would be 'ok' with that?' 'I will *never* be '*ok*' with it, Gia. It is right now, alright? In fact, I don't even want to talk about 'it' right now. Please. This time, I am begging *you*. Yes?' He looked SO damn desperate right then that I knew, in my heart that I had to get through *this* for him. I *had* too. I grabbed his left hand, as we were standing right in front of each other. He looked at me with such a surprised look on his face just then. Almost as if I had just slapped him. His look was that surprised. I kissed his open hand as I was looking directly at him, put it against my right cheek, and said to him, 'Yes.' And that was all I said. He looked at me in surprise and then gave me what I wanted. His 'I love you' grin. We started kissing then. Still standing but kissing just the same. He pulled away first, took both of my arms and whispered 'Now let me take a look at your face. Tell me where I hurt you baby.' I thought about that for a minute. I took his hand and led him to the restroom. I am sure he thought that I was going to show him where it hurt and give him the ice water, plus cloth, too work with. Instead, as we entered the restroom, facing the mirror. I lifted up my skirt, pulled my G-string down over my non-existent ass and slowly looked at him over my left shoulder. 'This will make my cheek feel better, Tata.' He was still, loosely, holding my hand. He looked at my face, in the mirror. Probably to make sure that I was 'ok' with this whole act. Both of his hands on my hips and he started kissing the back of my neck. Not so gentle, but not rough, either. Sort of in-between. Then he stopped, unbuttoned his jeans, pulled them half-way down and entered me. He stared at my face the whole time in the mirror. I tried to do the same, but couldn't. It felt too damn good. Since he was watching us in the mirror for the entire act, looking at it taking place in the mirror turned him on so much that he only lasted 4 minutes! Damn! That was a definite first! A record for him no matter where we were. As he came inside of me, he shuddered and almost could not keep standing up. As he came out of me, he hurriedly grabbed a towel hanging up and cleaned me up first. Then himself. As I was adjusting my panties and he was pulling up his jeans and arranging 'himself' in them, he stood there looking at me. Every inch of me. When I was done, I turned around and looked at him; at the same time walking towards him. I walked into his arms. I hugged him *so* tightly that I did not want to ever let go. In fact, I wanted to go home. How could I sleep with these perverts after that? Right then, the phone in our room rang. Loud and proud. 'Shit!' I yelled. I just *knew* what that meant. My dad answered the phone. Not a word was spoken by him. After he was 'on the phone' for about 5-10 minutes, he hung up. Still in the restroom, making sure I was all cleaned up and 'out', so to speak, I did not or didn't hear what he said. I was *hoping* that was the case, anyway. I walked out of the bathroom, first making sure that it was cleaned up somewhat. I just saw my father standing in the bedroom part of our suite/cabin looking down at the phone that he just held in his hand. 'Who was that, father?' 'It seems that Mr. Harris has already pimped you out for part of the evening. Apparently a 'customer' saw your picture in Harris's booklet. He picked you for part of the evening. Please come and sit on the bed while I walk you through this evening. Yes?' 'Of course' I replied, with hesitation in my voice. I sat down next to him on the bed. 'Yes, father?' My father looked at me in the eyes. Then he looked quickly at his hands. Again he looked at me and said 'When you go too this sick, perverted fucker's room, regardless of whom he is, I will have to tell you to do exactly as he tells you. *Except* if it is something that not even an animal would do. Do you understand?' I swallowed and loud too. I knew he heard me. 'Honey. I know this is going to be so very, very hard on you. I can't even imagine how hard. But, you just *have* to get through this, this one time, baby. Can you do that? Or, I should say, do you *think* you can do this without killing him or severing his arteries?' I knew he did *not* mean that to sound funny. But for some sick reason, I started to laugh. He looked at me in a very weird way. As if to say, 'Why in hell are you laughing for fuck's sake?' 'Father, it was just what you said. Or, how you said it, is all. Definitely *not* the subject. Trust me.' He understood instantly. I saw it in his face. 'Alright, my kitten. I understand. And I did not mean for it to sound 'funny' at all. Nothing about *this*, is 'funny'. As you, of all people, know. You better go and bathe and then go then my baby. I'll wait in bed for you until you get out of the restroom. I will not be leaving this cabin until you return this evening. I *swear* to you on that baby doll. Yes?' 'Ok, father. I understand *and* I do not blame you. What do I wear for something like 'this', anyway?' He looked at me as he was slowly unpacking. He picked up his laptop and put it on the bed as he answered me. 'Wear an, um, negligee if you brought one baby.' I thought about that one for a moment and then replied. 'Father, I did not bring anything like that. I did bring my ritual gown though. What if I wear a G-String underneath that? Or a G-String underneath my fur coat?' He whipped his head around too me with a sad, depressed or severely angry look on his face and then looked back down at his luggage. 'That will be fine, Gia. Go and get ready, yes?' When he said the last couple of words to me, his voice cracked a little. I walked over to my Carry-All and took out my shower things plus my hairdryer and set them on the bed. I walked over behind him and wrapped my arms around his waist and put my head on the lower part of his back. 'Tata. You know *damn* well that I do not want to do this. I am trying to make my voice sound 'neutral' for you. *Not* me. I am *dying* inside. You know I only want to be with you, daddy. Only you. Forever. This is killing me. What if his fantasy is too beat women when he fucks them? What do I do? I can't do *anything*. That's the problem, my baby. I would love nothing MORE than to crawl inside that bed. Right there and make love to you. ALL night long. Kiss you, hold you, love you. I do not want this! And you know that. Right?' He answered with complete emotion in his voice. 'I know, my baby. This is just so fucking hard on me! Fuck Harris! And I WILL kill him baby. Mark my words, kitten. Now, go before I lose it completely. Please.' I nodded my head and picked up all of my thing's, walked to the restroom and closed the door. I turned on the shower and put my shampoo, etc. inside the shower. I plugged the hair dryer into the wall and grabbed a towel. I got in the shower, took a deep breath as I let the water run all over me. I knew I was taking a shower when I came back to my father. My father was literally 'dying' inside over this whole entire fucked up 'arrangement'. And Harris knew it, too. The FUCKER. I *HATED* him with a passion. More than anyone in a long time. I stepped out of the shower and dried myself off as I thought about what was in store for me this evening. I wondered if Harris spoke to this dirtbag before he picked me. And, I also wondered if he told him to be extra evil with me. Or brutal. Whatever. I just wondered all of this. I walked over to the door and called out my father's name to see if he was alright. 'I'm here, baby.' Well, thank God he wasn't crying or anything. Maybe he should get wrapped up in work when I was gone. After I finished my hair, I put on my deodorant and cologne; just a little so that only I could smell it. Definitely *not* for the scumbag that I was supposed to 'pleasure' this evening. Nope. Fuck him. I walked out of the restroom to see my father, undressed, inside *our* bed. Under the covers. 'Well, I better go now, my love.' He turned to look at me and looked me up and down. 'You are so damn beautiful, kitten. Even without make-up on. No one will ever say that to you except me I bet. In your entire lifetime. Now. Remember what I said, before you got in the shower. Just do as the prick says and then come back to me, sweetheart. Yes?' 'I will. I promise, baby. I cannot wait until I get to come back to you Tata. I hope *you* know that. I'll see you, hopefully, semi-soon, my Tata.' And I walked out of the door. I didn't even manage to cover up the part of my face that was all fucked up. As I got closer to the main building, where I was supposed to meet Harris, I felt myself getting angrier and angrier. As I was getting closer and closer to the main room, where I was supposed to meet Harris, I was now getting nervous. What if this scumbag man/guy was fat and hairy? What if he smelled so horrid and was fat and hairy, that I threw up right *on* him? What would Harris do too me then? As I opened the door to the building, the first person I saw was Harris. Standing front and center. Right in front of the Check-in desk. 'Well, well. Gia Mahari. I thought you would be 'fashionably late'. I am glad though, that you chose *not* to be. Our guest, or *your* guest, is a **VERY** important member of our Organization. As well as holds a chair on our Board of Directors. 'Like I gave a shit' I thought to myself. 'Follow me, Gia. I'll show you where you shall be 'entertaining' him' for a while.' As he said those last words, there was definitely a menacing tone to his voice, the asshole. God! I SO could not wait to get rid of this sick, perverted, parasite. For good.

He led me down a hallway in a building that was attached to the main building. It was connected by the hallway of which we were walking down right this minute. He finally stopped in front of a big, double-door. Made out, it looked like, of pure Oak. Well, 'They' sure don't waste spending our tax-payer's money' I thought to myself. As I stood there with 'Asshole', I knew by the look of it, that it was a private cabin. It even had the number '1' above the door. I had no idea if 'their' number's had anything to do with how important the guests were. Harris knocked on the big doors. It took about a minute or two before the occupant opened them. When he did, I about had a damn Heart Attack. The man standing in front of me was a very influential man in the government. Everyone whom was *anyone* knew who this man was. I used to actually 'Like' this man. Well, not like, like, him. But I respected him for his intelligence and knowledge of Foreign Affairs as well as just THE Government and how it ALL worked. Then, after about almost a decade. And doing some research that only my father had through HIS contacts, I began to hate him. Even though he belonged to the same 'political party' that I belonged too. IF there WAS such a thing as a 'political party' anymore. Or political parties, I should say. As I stood there as Harris was introducing me to his 'Very Important Guest', I was going over inside my head what the Hell this man would want me to do too him or with him. Hell! Thinking of *his* past health issues, he could very well have a heart attack on me! Then what? The very thought of doing anything sexual with him made me sick. 'Well, I shall leave you two to get to know each other, then. Good evening.' And off he went. But not without giving me a slight, but *very* noticeable smirk as he turned around to walk back to wherever he had to be. The Son-of-a-Bitch.

Chapter 24

I stood there, outside his door. I guess waiting to be invited in or something. Me being hesitant for that 1 second or so made him realize that I was definitely not one of the 'regular' whores that worked here. I assumed, anyway. He gave me that famous smirk of his. The one that all of America knows by seeing it on television. 'Come in. Have a seat... anywhere you like.' And he disappeared into another room. I walked in over the threshold of the front door and closed it behind me. I looked around the room and took in a normal looking 'living-type' room. I sat on the biggest sofa; my heart beating faster than it ever had in my life, I think. As I sat there, I remembered that 'He' was wearing a bathrobe. One of the robes they give you here at The Grove but charge it to your bill anyway. When he walked back in, he was holding two glasses. One holding a brown liquid; about half-way up to the top of the glass. The other glass was just about to the top of the rim of the glass. 'I didn't know if you drank or not. I assumed you did, so I made you a Screwdriver. Is that alright?' 'That's fine, Mr…?' 'Just call me 'Bill'. That will be fine.' 'Mr. Bill?' I pretty much laughed at that; expecting *him* too as well. Not a peep came out of him. 'Figures.' I took the glass from him and said, 'You know. Mr. Bill from Saturday Night Live? In the '70's?' I saw zero recognition in his face. 'This is going to be lovely evening.' I took a sip from my drink and set it down on the glass coffee table. 'Well, Mr. Bill. What can I do for you this evening?' He looked at me with his cold eyes that stared at me for quite a long time. Just enough time that, for a normal woman, it would have made her feel extremely uncomfortable. Me? Hell! I was used to that shit. He finally, after taking 4 sips from his drink, and I *knew* that he couldn't drink much or, let alone, *do* much in his condition. He put his drink on the table too, looked up at me and reached out his hand. I took it and stood up. 'Oh God. This? Please, *No*. Anything but this.' I said to myself. I followed him to his or the master bedroom. His hand felt cold and clammy. At the same time. But the grossest part was that it just felt old. Like my great Grandpa's hand. 'Get on the bed, please.' I did as I was told, obviously. He stood in the middle of the room, my head turned away from him. Not for him but for myself. G-R-O-S-S. I did *not* want to see anything more than I had too. That was for damn sure. As, I assumed, he was finished removing his robe, he replied, 'Are you not going to get under the bedcover's?' 'Sorry, Bill. I was not told to do so.' I got under the damn bedcovers. What an old fucking fart. The whole, entire time I was speaking to him, I kept my head down. He got onto the bed and instantly went under the covers too. As if he was embarrassed about his body. Well, he should be. Damn! Of *all* people that I would have to be stuck with for my 'first' encounter at this place, it had to be an Ex-Vice President for God's sake. As he got on top of me, which took about 5 minutes, he reached his hand below the covers and grabbed himself. He started to rub 'himself' against my 'parts' and then shoved himself all the way in. And rough as shit, too. Thank God he was about 4 to 5 inches long *fully* hard or erect. The whole act took about 10 minutes. And that was because he stopped and started about 8 or 9 times. Too try and kiss me. Tongue and all. I fought him off, or rather turned my head to try and get his mind off of kissing me. No way. He wanted to kiss. And tongue kiss at that. Do or die. Once he thought that I was ‘pretending’ to play ‘hard to get’ or something absurd, he punched me square in the face. And hard, too. Once my nose started to bleed, he reached up with his finger, wiped some blood from my nose and licked it. Making sure that I *saw* what he did. So, I went into instant Mode and let him. So as not to raise any suspicion. After about 3 to 4 hours of half screwing, punching, half raping, half 'normal' missionary, 'tongue-kissing', and him kissing, fondling and licking my breasts, he 'finished' and told me to stay on the bed. No certain emotions coming from his voice. Just like a monotone, flat and distant type of response. Whenever he spoke to me. And that wasn't a lot. Thank God. He came back after 10 minutes. Maybe a few minutes less and climbed back on the bed. He tossed what he brought with him onto the bed. To the side of me to where I could see some of it. What I saw instantly made me go into Mode. A whip, a cat-o-nine tails, (oh *shit*!) and a ball gag. 'Great!' I thought to myself. I am going to be whipped and gagged. Just what I *always* wanted! Not! 'Help me get through this God.' I prayed. After I was done accepting what was going to happen to me, I felt the ball being forced, pretty roughly, into my mouth. And then the straps being fastened behind my head. He roughly took my hair and wrapped it around one of his hands. I couldn't tell which one. I was too busy panicking and wishing this would be over in two minutes or that he would have another heart attack. He roughly pulled my head back, twisting my hair tighter and tighter around his hand. While he was doing this, he grabbed the Cat-O-Nine tails (a Hellish whip) and started whipping me, *hard*, very hard; until, I just couldn't take the pain anymore.

I must have blacked out for a minute. Or an hour. I did not know. I did know that he was done. He, of *COURSE*, finished inside of me. The screwed up part was what he said after all was said and done, so to speak. 'My Dear. That was the best fornication I have ever had in my life.' 'Fornication? WTF?' Are we living in the 1800's?' Plus, they never whipped or gagged women in the 1800's. Did they?' I thought. He was breathing so damn hard that I thought for a second that he might have that heart attack right then and there. But, no. He was actually just catching his breath. After he was 'finished', he rolled (literally) off of me, sat up, grabbed his robe and then leaned towards 'his' side of the bed and reached inside the table, took out his wallet and handed me a wad of cash, and said 'Thank You; you know where the door is. Oh, by the way little whore? You have a really tight… well, you are really very tight 'down there'. For a woman SOOOO damn young and working herc. That's nice to have… in your profession.' And then he was gone. He walked to the back of the cabin somewhere. I slowly got up off of the bed. Wondering at the same time, what had happened when I was 'out?' I reached my arm around to my back, once I had managed to stand up and felt how bad my back was. That even hurt too much. Once I was sure that 'He' wasn't coming back, I walked over to the living room mirror and slowly turned around; back on fucking fire. What I saw looked like something from a bad B- movie horror flick. As far as prosthetics go. My back was ripped up pretty bad. Little lines, about 25 to 50 of them, in total. But I was just guessing. There was quite a lot of blood. Just slowly dripping from my back. Down to my butt. I hurriedly (if you could call it that) to the guest bathroom, just too grab a hand towel or something. I quickly saw one, grabbed it, grabbed the money the bastard gave me and was out of that room as fast as I could move. Since I did not have a cellphone with me, I couldn't text my father but at least I had memorized my way back to my father's cabin. I looked around before I hit the lobby area of The Grove and threw the bloody towel in some bushes on the way there. I grabbed the handle to the door that opened up into the lobby and saw that even though it was close to 2am in the morning, there were still a lot of people (losers) awake and doing… whatever they were doing IN the lobby. 'Sick Sons of Bitches' I thought. I now felt my back burning pretty bad now. Damn. I didn't think that I could keep this up for 2 more days. I walked through the lobby very quickly where only a few people saw me. I finally found the trail that led towards my father's cabin. Once I saw his or our door, I tried to pick up the pace a bit. But with my 'injuries' starting to hurt and burn with quite a bit of intensity, I didn't make a good job of 'hurrying'. Not at all. Once I stood in front of the door, my tears that I had been holding back for three to four hours, started slowly falling from my eyes. I knocked, I think, only twice. The door instantly opened. It was my dad. Thank God. I just fell into his arms and closed my eyes as I just let myself cry. And I let it all out. Because I knew that I was finally *safe*. At least for a little while. My father, once he took in all of me; except my back, of course, couldn't believe what he saw. He caught me as I fell into his arms. He called out to Steven. All I remembered that evening was being moved around by Steven and my dad. And then a small prick in my hip and then nothing. When my eyes finally did open, I was in the Master Bedroom, in bed. I felt absolutely zero pain. All I did feel was a leg or another person's body part touching my legs. As my eye's moved around a bit, I saw that my father was in bed with me and the sun was shining, or trying too, through the curtains. What time was it, I wondered. I looked over at my father again and I then saw that he was sitting up in bed, only under the covers. Looking at me with a sympathetic smile on his face. 'How does my baby feel right now? Hmm?' he asked me. 'I feel ok, actually, father. My back should be killing me though. Did Stev-o give me a…' 'Yes he did, kitten. I then helped him attend too your back babe. Which animal did this to you, hmm?' He asked me that question very sing-songy. Like he didn't want to speak to me with any anger in his voice. Including tone. After I told him the Asshole's name, my father's eyes became darker and darker as I explained, bit by disgusting bit, what he did *too* me in that room. 'Well, my love. I will tell you this. Nothing like this will ever happen to you again. We are going home. As soon as Steven gets the car pulled around and parked closer to this cabin. It is pretty busy out there right now, so I thought it was the perfect timing to do so. People upon people are arriving, moving their cars, etc. So, one limo will not cause any distraction. Once it is in place, we will get the hell out of here and go home, my Princess. How is that?' 'That sounds almost too perfect to be true, my bab… Father.' My dad laughed a little and told me that I was getting so good at catching myself, that he was going to have to practice more. With his word's; when it came to me, that is. I smiled at him and slowly crawled towards his lap. I laid my head in his lap once my body reached him. After I laid there for about fifteen minutes, him petting my hair and us making small talk, Stev-o walked into the bedroom and told us 'It's Go Time Folks'. My father instantly lifted my head gently off of his lap, got up off of the bed and I, slowly, got up, in the sitting position. I gauged my pain level and then got slowly off of the bed. My back was on fire. So bad that I sort of yelled a little at Steven for a shot. He turned around and looked at me. He nodded and told my father to please wait a second. That he had to give me a shot. A minute later, I was in zero pain. I thanked him profusely. 'No problem, Princess. Now, let's get too the car babe.' He helped me get off of the bed. Once I stood up, I walked, a little faster than earlier, out of the bedroom and out the front door, behind my father. Who was walking beside, and sort of in front of Steven. One door was open to the Limo. Steve held the door a little wider for my father to get as low as he could, as did I. We both practically kneeled while we crawled inside of the back. Once Steve had shut the back door, he got into the front seat and instantly locked all of the doors. He started up the car and slowly pulled the car in line behind all of the other cars that were exiting the encampment. Mostly limo drivers or bodyguards. 'I would get down on the floor, guys. There are guards up front. Before the exit driveway checking inside windows, for some reason. It will only have to be for a minute. And please try to put your jackets on top of you, too. If you can of course. 'Harris said that this year's guests were at an all-time high, so he was having all of the limousines park down the street and inside a dirt covered parking lot type of thing. It was just too crowded for all of the limos, I assume, for all of them to fit. Thank God for us.' My father replied from his very uncomfortable spot. 'Thank god for the Morphine', I thought to myself. 'Ok, guys. We are 1 car from the guards. Just don't move… right now'. We heard Steven's front window slide down. 'Just you in the limo, Sir?' 'Yes. As always. I miss all of the fun stuff, man.' Steven said as he sort of chuckled. 'Yeah. No kidding. You know where to go. Have a good afternoon.' 'You as well, guys.' And off Steven drove, at first, behind the other cars. Then, about 3 minutes later, he split off from the pack and drove leisurely, in the other lane, towards the main road and to the freeway; or freedom. 'Ok, my Precious Cargo! We are free! You may now get up and get comfortable.' As my father slowly got out of his very uncomfortable position, he finally sat up, buckled himself into his seat and helped me get out of my pretzel position. Damn! We made it! I was so happy I almost couldn't contain myself. 'Thank you for your excellent lie Stev-o!!! A *Million* thank you's!' 'Yes, Steven. You did an excellent job, I will say. And, just *for* that excellent lie, you shall be getting a Hell of a bonus this year.' I looked over at the back of Steven's head and I could tell that he sort of smiled. By the muscles that moved. I could see them move from looking at the back of his head.

Chapter 25

As my father and I was sitting in the back of the car, each in our own thoughts, I turned to him and said, 'What are you going to do when Harris calls you at home, Tata? Are you going to get in a lot of trouble? I would guess so, right?' 'I do *not* give a shit what Harris does to me, says to me, or whatnot. He can beat me for all I care, baby. After what he pulled on you? No way. And I am sure Steven would do the same, Gia. Now just rest and when we do get home, he will change your dressing on your back, yes?' 'Ok, Tata. I love you.' 'I love you too, baby girl.'

We drove the rest of the way home in silence I assumed. I do know that I was asleep for most of the drive. And for the last bit, I had finally fallen into a semi-sleep. Not R.E.M. but just enough to where I could not hear anyone in the car nor my father's phone. As I 'sort of' felt the car come to a stop, I opened my eyes just a little. I saw the familiar wrought iron gate to our home. Right in front of us. Damn, I was so happy! I slowly turned my head to where I was facing upwards, looking at the roof of the car…or, my father's face. He looked down at me. Once he knew that I was awake enough to speak, he quietly asked how I *did* sleep. 'I slept ok, daddy. I never reached REM but I rarely do in the car. But, at least, when the Morphine wore off, I was asleep enough not to feel my back and face start to hurt again.' My father looked at me with sympathy in his eyes. I loved him so much. Dammit. 'Steven.' My father knocked on the partition window. It instantly rolled down. 'As soon as we get inside, could you please give Gia her Morphine shot? It has apparently worn off.' 'Yes, Sir. I shall. I'll just have Don take in all of the luggage and put the suitcases in their respective rooms. How is that?' 'That shall be fine, Steven. Thank you.' Steve put the partition back up to where it was before. 'Well, love. You shall have your shot sooner than later. Sound good, yes?' 'Oh Yes. Absolutely yes. It hurts horribly, daddy.' 'I know, my baby. And I am *so* sorry for all of this, my lov…Gia.' 'Tata! I give *you* the Academy Award! Good for you!' I made sure as shit too sound sincere so as to not make him think I was being condescending to him. 'Thank you, my dear. I have been mentally practicing. And, I will *only* get better.' I smiled up at him and then turned my head back to where I was staring at the seat in front of me. 'Crap' I thought silently to myself. 'IF only!' As Stev-o pulled the car around the statue and in front of the house, Don got out, opened our doors and my father got out. He stretched and then popped his head back in the car. 'Let me walk in the house, and see what is going on and I will be back to get you darling.' 'Ok, baby doll.' I smiled after I said that to him. 'Watch it, G.G.' and he was gone. Door shutting. As I laid there, my back was beginning to hurt more and more. Damn I wish everyone would hurry up! I wanted my shot, some dinner and then my father's bed! I waited for around ten minutes and decided to sit up. As I did so, I saw our front door open and my father walking out. I unwrapped the blanket from me and grabbed my purse. He opened the door and told me to scoot as far as I could towards the outside of the car. As I did so, he swooped me up in his arms and walked into the house and up the stairs. 'What about food, Tata?' I asked him. My tummy was gurgling like crazy. 'We will have an appetizer plate brought up to us with all sorts of goodies on it, Gia. Both of us shall eat from it. Before that though, you will get your shot from Steven. Yes?' 'Sounds perfect. I need that shot so bad, father. You have no idea!' After that I put my head back down against his upper shoulder. 'I know, kitten. I know'.

He said with a heavy sigh. He then kissed me on top of my head. As he opened the door to his bedroom, he laid me in his bed on my side. Juanita must have turned down his bed this evening before we got home. I didn't wait long for what I *really* wanted. As I just finished getting settled in my dad's bed, I couldn't lay down. My back hurt too much. 'Dammit!' I said under my breath. As I just semi-sat up and rested my head on my knees. Steven knocked once or, it was more of a 'rap' using just his knuckle on his left hand. In his other hand was my shot! 'Oh joy!' I said. And quite loud, too. 'I thought you would say something to that effect, babe. I also have a medical bag in my room. I want to take a closer look at your back and tend to it after I give you this shot. Ok with you, hon?' 'Sure, Stev-o. That's fine.' I lifted my gown up slowly to my waist and leaned to my right as I bared my left hip too him. As he stuck the needle into my skin and slowly plunged the medicine into my bloodstream, I felt the liquid almost go to every place that was 'on fire' from the pain. And 'poof!' It was gone. In seconds! 'Oh, God, Steve! A million Thank Yous!' 'You are welcome, Princess. Now, let me go and get my bag while you take your gown off, ok? Just cover yourself with the sheet. Ok with you?' 'Sure, Steven.' He left as my father walked in. 'I see that Steven gave you 'your savior' for the night.' He laid a large serving platter on the bed right in front of me and as he sat across from me, we both smiled at each other and started eating. We didn't say a word while we ate. We were too hungry and tired, I guess. Instantly, the phone rang. After 5-10 minutes of silence, and then hearing that, I jumped a little. Thank God the shot was already in me. I thought to myself. My father took another bite and heard Juanita say that the phone was for him. He responded that he would pick it up in here and then got off of the bed. He swallowed, dabbed the napkin too his lip's and then picked up the receiver. 'Hello.' He must have waited, listening to whomever was on the other end of the phone for five minutes before he replied. 'Harris you Cocksucker!!! What the *fuck* did you think you were doing? Taking my daughter too him? Anyone but him. And you knew *that*!' Oh Hell. It was Harris. Why didn't I even *think* of that? It was getting close to 1PM. My father was literally yelling at the top of his lungs into the phone. As he waited while Harris was speaking (I assumed), Steven had walked in once he heard the yelling. 'Yes, I *am* aware of that. I was there! Fucking Dick-Sucker!' Harris said something back. I heard his voice on the other end of the line. 'You want a war, you sick, fucking, degenerate? You'll get one. Just let ***me*** know, mother-fucker.' And then my dad hung up on him. 'Daddy? Aren't you going to get in *a lot* of trouble? It sure sounds like it, daddy. I just don't want you to get beaten for this, Tata.' 'Love, if I do get 'beat' for leaving early with you? It will be well worth it. Plus, that's what parents do to protect their children. No holds barred. Nothing is considered 'Too far across the line'. Not when it comes to *you* or anyone in my close-knit, family.' He then looked over at Steven and started preparing him for the blowback from Harris. 'As you probably already know, Steven, Harris will not 'sit this one out' so to speak. So be prepared for anything, yes?' 'Yes, Sir. I'll go and secure the house now, Sir.' And then he was out the door and going down the stairs; already on his cell with the top-dog of the 'Detail' Hierarchy. That's when my father and I heard the first shot. And then right after that, a horrible, whining, bark, yell sound. 'Daddy? Was that a gunshot? And one of the dogs, too?' 'Stay *HERE*, babe. And do not leave this room until I tell you too. Got that?' 'Yes, Sir.' 'Good girl'. And then he was gone too. Since I was used to feeling safe in my home, especially with my father home; with Detail beside him, as well as Steven too, I just continued eating, thinking my own thoughts. Just as I was chewing my last bite, two gun shots rang out in the early afternoon air. I jumped a little again, but not as bad as the first time. I just wiped my mouth after finishing my milk and picked up the serving tray with both my father's and my 'dinner/snack' and put it on top of the dresser. I just 'knew' that everything was going to be fine because it had always *been* fine *before*. Not once did I think anything could or did go wrong. I, like most young girls, thought that their daddy's were invincible. Especially mine.

The sun had come up and somehow, Harris's guy's or Harris or whomever got here before we did. I didn't know how *that* was possible. Then I started hearing men, outside, yelling back and forth at each other. That was when I got scared. Because with *those* voices, came more gunfire. I instantly got up, not feeling any pain, thank God, and ran out of the bedroom. I then stopped still in my tracks. My father told me to stay *in his bedroom*. What do I do? Shit! Screw it! I was scared as Hell! I continued running/walking/hopping and down the stairs I went. I knew I was a site. I instantly saw my Daddy. I ran over to the big white couch and practically leapt into his arms. Completely surprising him. He was talking on the phone and to Steven and Don at the same time. 'Kitten. I told you to stay in the bedroom. Why are you down here.' 'Daddy, I was scared. Why are they shooting at us and why early in the day?' My father as well as both Steven and Don were looking at me too. Juanita was even in here. Sitting on a chair and *knitting* of all things. Knitting? I put that in my 'ask about this shit later box' and filed it away. 'Because Mr. Harris is an idiot. That is why. After my dad said that, we heard the sirens. 'Now, all of you?' And he looked at all of Detail, Don and Steven, as well as me too. 'As far as the gun shots? We have 'no idea what is going on'. If they knock on the door, or, rather, buzz at the gate, let them in and if they ask to speak to me, *let them*. Steven? Secure all of the guns away right now. Are the Rotts alright? He asked Henreick. 'Yes, Mr. F. Fine are the Rotts.' 'Good. Then let's all get back to what we would be doing at this time of day. Except. *Stay* in the house. That is what normal people are doing, I am sure, hearing what is going on outside. Understand?' Everyone nodded or said 'Yes, Sir' and continued on their way. Juanita looked at my dad and asked if 'we would like some little breakfast. Like pancakes?' 'Juanita, that sounds *fantastic*. You are the *true* angel, Juanita. You really, truly are.' She blushed. I smiled at her as she quickly looked at me and nodded. As if to let her know that I agreed with my dad as well. 'Gracias, Senor' she answered as she got up and went into the kitchen. I looked up at my dad and smiled at him. I was so excited for pancakes that it almost... *just* almost... made me forget about the gun shots. 'I am so hungry daddy.' 'Me too, Lil G. Me too. Let's go upstairs and wash our hands and I want to have Steven fix the dressing on your back before we eat. We just have enough time. Why don't you go and Steven and I will be up in a little bit after you. Yes?' 'Ok, Tata. I'll be waiting for you guys.' 'Alright then hon. Go on now.' As I slowly walked up the stairs, looking at my nails, I thought to myself, 'Damn, I need my nails done.' I walked into my father's room and got back into his bed. Thank God the police didn't knock on our door. I looked up and waited for Stev-o and my dad. After a minute or so, I decided to go and get my book. As I got up from the bed, once again, I walked as fast as I could too my bedroom. I saw my book on my bedside table. After I picked it up, I went back to my father's room. I then saw that they had beat me to it. They were looking around like, 'Where the hell is she?' I called out that I just needed my book. My father, for some strange reason, looked relieved. As I got to his door, I slipped past them and got on his bed. 'Gia. Please. For just right now, or, a couple of days, rather? Tell me where you are at, all times. Yes?' 'Of course, daddy.' I said to him when I was perched in my spot on his bed. Steven then apparently had his cue to walk up to me and put his med bag on the bed as well. As he was opening it and taking things out and placing them on a towel on the bed, my father walked over to me, kissed me on the lips and sat down next to me. I looked at him and smiled. For some reason, I blushed when he returned the smile. When Steven was finished, he looked at me and asked how my pain level was right now. 'It's great, I suppose. I don't feel my back at all, really.' 'Good, then babe. I need to check your dressing so that means that you have to lift your nightgown up and over your head. Then cover your front with the bedcover. Ok hon?' 'Ok, Stev-o.' 'Why don't you turn around so that your back is facing me. Ok?' 'Ok.' I took off my white nightgown and covered myself up, while Steve turned around and waited. 'I'm ready.' I told him and waited patiently while he stuck the syringe into the small, clear, bottle of Morphine and sucked up the medicine with the syringe. I was so lucky that Steve was a licensed E.M.T.; especially for the guy's that did not have a high tolerance for pain like I had. But *this* pain? No thank you! I felt a prick in my lower hip/butt area and almost instantly, zero pain. 'There we are.' I said too no one in particular as he stood up and started picking up the little trash and items that he *did* take out of his bag. 'You are very welcome, Lil G. Take it easy for a couple of days. Alright? Seriously. Your back is by no means close to being healed.' Steven must have looked at my father because my dad looked over at me, took his hand and lifted up my chin with his index finger. 'Listen to Steven, kitten. I am serious about that as well. No over doing things as you are accustomed to do. Yes?' 'Alright.' I replied with some disappointment in my voice. 'Like father like daughter is all I can say.' Stev-o replied while looking at my dad. I looked over at him with a grin. I knew he was right, too. My father looked right back at us and just shook his head as he got up off of the bed. 'Thank you Steve. I'll see you in the morning some time. We are beat as Hell. As I'm sure you are too. As soon as you make sure Detail and the dogs are taken care of, you may get some sleep as well. Alright?' 'Yes, Sir.' He smiled at both of us and kissed me on top of the head. As he started walking out of my dad's bedroom door, he stopped and said one more thing to me. 'I will change your dressing first thing when you wake up. The more I think about it, Gia,

I believe it really is too soon to change it right now. I believe tomorrow will be better. How's that, Lil G?' I looked at him with a 'Thank God' type of happy smile. Sounds fantastic to me, Steve. I am *so* hungry!' 'Ok then. I will see the both of you at the dining table. Does that sound good Sir? I don't know about you two, but this growing boy is starving.' My father and I both laughed a little and told him we would both be down there. And that *we* were starving as well. As I got my robe on over my nightgown, my father went to his room to retrieve his. We both met at the top of the stairs again, took each other's hands and walked down to the dining room table to our seats. As usual, Steven was there too. And practically looked like he could drool over what Juanita was bringing out and placing on the table in front of him. We sat down and *once* my father's napkin *hit* his lap; it seemed anyway, we dug *in*. My dad didn't even seem to care at our urgency. He knew how famished we were. Hell, he was too. As we ate, we ate in complete silence. Through the entire meal. From start to finish. And that was a first, I might add. There was always *something* being spoken about. But not this late afternoon. The best part of being home? Aside from the obvious familiarity, shot and how I felt safe, was that Steven and his guys were always prepared for *whatever* decided to happen. At any given moment. Like today, earlier. Regarding the gunshots. Steven grabbed his Walkie that was *always* attached to his belt, too his jeans or on him when he was wearing a suit. And spoke into it. Softly barking orders on *how* to handle the situation. A *Lovely* situation. I guess that's why he was my father's number one guy. His right, left and *all* hand's sometimes. He was seriously irreplaceable to my father. I wouldn't know what to do without him either. I trusted my life to him as much as my dad did. As well as just… trusting him. Regarding anything. *Anything*. As did my dad. Steven must have a lot of room in his brain to hold all of the 'secrets' or 'information' that we have told him. As I thought that, a little laugh left my lips. My dad and Steve both looked up, chewing, of course. 'What's so funny, silly goose?' my dad asked. 'Nothing major, father. I was just thinking about how stupid Harris must be feeling. Or, hopefully, looking *to* his so-called parishioners. That is it, father.' 'I do hope he looks like a damn idiot. Among other things not suited to say at a dinner table. If you know what I'm saying.' 'I can guess, daddy.' Steve piped up, as I knew he would. 'No kidding, Dominick. I hope to *Hell* he looks like an idiot to *all* of them. But I'll never know I guess. And Sir? *IF* you do hear anything as to that regard? Will you please tell me? It would make my day. And, probably a few days after, as well.' My father laughed a little and replied 'yes, he would'. When Steven had left the room with his bag full of tricks and things that made you feel no pain, my father turned to me, both of us with a *very* satiated tummy and asked, 'Why don't we go upstairs and go to bed, kitten? We are both exhausted and we need to get some sleep. *Now*. What do you say, love?' 'Sounds good to me.' I replied. He stood up, walked into the kitchen to make sure Juanita wasn't still up. I guess she wasn't because he came right back. 'Let's go, babe.' I stood up, grimaced, looked up from a stooped position at him and said, 'I'll be there in a minute, Tata, ok?' He walked over to me, shaking his head and looking angry all over again, picked me up and carried me up the stairs; shutting off lights as we went. As he walked into his bedroom, his suitcase was already on his bed. Probably from Juanita. Trying to help as always. 'Do you want me to get anything out of your room, love? For bed?' He laid me on top of his bed, waiting for me to answer. 'Yes, please. Just my toothbrush out of my Carry-All? It should be on my bed too, daddy.' He winked at me and smiled a little as he turned and walked out of his room too mine. I scooted towards the top of the bed and got under the covers. Thought better of it since I had to brush my teeth. I got back on *top* of the covers and waited. He walked back in with toothbrush in hand. He handed it to me and I thanked him. I got up and walked into the bathroom. Noticing that my father had watched me limp all the way there. As I was stooped over, brushing my teeth, he walked in, in his robe, and started brushing his teeth as well. When we were done and both in bed, I asked him if I had to go to school tomorrow. I heard him right behind me. He was so tired and probably almost asleep when he answered, 'No baby. We'll both take tomorrow off, yes?' And the 'lights' went out.

Chapter 26

We slept until 2PM the next day. The time didn't surprise me. What *did* surprise me was that my father was still in bed with me when I woke up. I rolled slowly over so that I was facing him. I watched him sleep. He looked so peaceful and 'normal' when he was sleeping. And so damn young too. It was no wonder that I was in love with him. He took such good care of me. Yes, he could be such an asshole sometimes. And during those times, I hated him. But most of the time? He was just my dad who did his best to take care of his family. No matter how 'small' his family actually was. But for him, his family included Steven, most of Detail and Juanita of course. As I was looking at him, I felt my face start to throb. Shit. That's probably what woke me up. That was because of my dad being an asshole. Oh well. The good *was* better than the bad. I will say that. I slowly scooted out of bed and walked into his restroom. I looked in the mirror. My face actually didn't look so bad. Not as bad as I thought it would look like anyway. Thank God. I didn't feel like making up yet another false story for when I did go back to school tomorrow. I walked back into the bedroom and quietly got back into bed. I closed my eyes again just to see if I could fall back asleep. After 10 minutes of that, no go. My body was definitely awake. I had to pee and I was hungry. Oh well. I tried. I was feeling a bit selfish though. Even though I knew that my father probably needed the sleep, I moved closer to him and cuddled up as if I was still asleep myself. As I was just feeling comfortable in my 'safe place', (his chest area), he started moving, though slowly.

'Shit', I thought. Just as I got comfortable. Figures. 'I hope to Hell I didn't wake him up.' I laid stock still. The position his 'sleep body' decided on staying in was on his right side, facing me but his left arm went over my waist and the entire middle of my body. So, basically, there was no way I COULD leave the bed without waking him up now. Hmmm. I will just have to either lay there wide awake or move out of his embrace, wake him up a bit and go downstairs. I decided on the latter. I picked up his arm very slowly; the one that was over my waist/body and put it closer to his face. On his pillow that was right by his mouth. Once I got out of the bed, I would make sure I moved it further from his mouth. As I put his arm back down, he opened his eyes. Looking right at me. Though sleepy looking, he was very much 'awake'. 'How did you sleep my kitten?' I smiled a big smile. 'I slept wonderful. And you're not going to believe what time it is either, Tata. He furrowed his brow a bit. 'What time is it?' '2:30PM, baby.' He sat upright so quick that it freaked me out enough that I sat up too. 'What, daddy? What's going on? What's wrong?' He slowly laid back down on his pillow. 'Nothing, Gia. Sorry I frightened you. I didn't really know where I was for a second. 'Oh! Damn! You scared the shit out of me!' 'Watch your mouth, G.G.' 'Sorry, Tata.' He was more awake now. 'Damn, we sure did sleep in, love. And it felt'… and he stretched really big… 'wonderful. We both needed it baby. How are you feeling?' 'I feel almost 100% 'down there' if that's what you mean. My face is throbbing a bit but everything else is, I think, back too normal.' He smiled. 'That is wonderful news kitten. Wait right here for a second, yes?' 'Of course, daddy.' My father got out of bed, walked into the restroom without closing the door, (weird that he didn't close the door for that), opened his medicine cabinet, and walked back to bed. He showed me a syringe in his other hand that wasn't bracing him up on the bed. 'This will take your facial pain away for 6-8 hours. Want it, G.G?' 'Of course! That is what woke me up in the first place. Thank you.' He took my right arm in his hand and stuck me in my upper arm. Once the medicine was in me, he set the syringe on his bedside table and laid back down, facing me. 'So. What do YOU want to do today? You and me.' That was a total *first*. Me and him? All alone? Together, doing something? I absolutely loved doing things *alone* with him! I knew, obviously, bodyguards had to come, but I didn't give a damn about that. I was used to that. 'Hmmm. How about we have breakfast outside. Overlooking the pool and the backyard. Then relax by the pool and get some suntan going on. And Yes! I know. No more than an hour. I know you do not want to be too dark. Then we can go to the gun range or shopping for you or a drive. Whatever *you* would like to do. Since you *NEVER* get a day off. Ever, Tata. It makes me feel sad. It really does my baby.' My father slowly rolled on top of me and started kissing me. He stopped and looked me in the eyes. 'Why are you so... so... *nice* to me Gia? Why do you 'love me *so* much' as you say? Why? I certainly do *not* deserve it, sometimes. That I *know*. Regardless if it is right or wrong, obviously. Why?' I looked at him incredulously. 'Why, Tata? Seriously? You seriously do not know?' 'If I did know, I wouldn't be asking you. And asking you while on *top* of you.' He replied. Very seriously. 'So he was dead serious with this question. Wow. I thought he always knew' I thought to myself. 'Father. Or, rather, Dominick, Tata…? Whatever you prefer or feel more comfortable with. I love you so damn *much*, it literally scares me. If you left me, passed away, got killed or just disappeared, I do not *know* what I would do. Seriously, father. I do know our relationship is 'wrong' by society's standards. But, at this point, as I am becoming older, I do *not* give a damn. You know what I am trying to say?' As he was listening to everything that I was saying, he nodded in agreement. 'Ok, then. I will just say that I love you as I would a husband, a serious boyfriend *and* a father figure. I know it sounds literally impossible to love you in both ways. But it is the damn truth, daddy. It is. And I seriously do *not* know how to 'get over it' or how to deal with it'. Nothing. I have NO clue, Tata. Do you? How do you seriously feel about me? As far as… love or what to compare it too?' He put his head down. Looking at the sheets or his hands. I did not know *what* he was looking at. After he did look back up at me, he said, 'Gia Mahari. I fell in love *with* you the day you turned 6 years old. I know that sounds absolutely disgusting. And too people that do not know *ABOUT* our relationship, I understand their feelings. But, I also know that '*it*' is *none* of their business. No, I am not going to go around in public with you, kissing you, holding your hand or any public displays of affection. Nothing like that, Gia. I want too. Don't get me wrong. But I do know that it would garner unwanted attention. That we do *not* need, as you know. I am sure you understand that. Yes?' 'Of course.' I replied. 'So, I keep my hand's too myself. When I do touch you in public, I make sure it is on your lower back or in appropriate place's. You understand, my dear' 'Yes, I do, Tata.' 'Good. As far as 'Do I *LOVE* you? As in a wife or in a girlfriend sort of way? Babe, I have asked myself that question for many, many years. All I come up with. Every damn time. Too that very question is the same answer. Every time. And that answer is yes. Period. No other way too look at it. I am *IN* love with you. In *love*, Gia. And, I do not know what to do about it neither. So, too make you feel better, I am in the same predicament as you are. Ok? Does that make you feel a little better?' I looked at him and looked down at my hands. Just like he did. 'Yes, I guess it does. Thank you for telling me the truth, Tata. I know that you will one day *have* to let 'go' of me and find someone closer to your age and someone with their own money, etc. to be with. But, damn, it will 'kill' me for a while. You know what I mean?' 'Oh yes. Yes I do, Lil G. The day I have to give you too another man will be the hardest day of my life. That is a certainty, my kitten.'

We both stared at each other for a bit and then I took his face in my hands and kissed him. Rubbed his body all over with my hands and continued kissing him. We must have stayed in bed for a couple of hours. By the time we were finished, it was near dinner. My father, once dried off and breathing normally, pushed the Com in the kitchen and talked to Juanita. 'Dinner will be waiting for us in a few minutes, my girl. Let us eat, then take a shower. Together. And crawl back in bed and I'll give us an 8 hour sleeping shot. 'Sounds good to me, Tata.' As he got out of bed and grabbed his jeans off of the chair by his bed, I got out of bed too. I was sore. But a good sore. Sore by him. 'Yummy', I thought. I felt completely 100% safer than I did 24 hours ago. I probably could go to school today but I wanted to make sure my father and Harris were all squared away and that his goon's were gone. Back to where they came from, the fucker's. God, what douchebag's! Messing with my dad like that when Harris knew how much that would piss him off. Plus, Harris knew there would be blow-back from my dad. Damn! My father killed people for less. A lot less. As he was dressed in jeans and a t-shirt, he put on some socks and his tennis shoes, brushed his hair and tied it back. 'I'll see you downstairs in a minute, kitten' my dad told me. 'Ok, Tata.' When he was gone from his room, I stood there, in the middle of his room. By myself! This was the first time that I was ever let, by my father, to be alone in HIS room. By myself. Pretty unbelievable. He never trusted anyone in his room by themselves. At least without him in here with them. Things are going just the way I wanted with him. Maybe we never will have to go too therapy, I thought. 'Of ***course*** we will. Don't be an idiot, Gia.' I thought to myself. I started moving towards his door and headed towards my room. As I shut my door behind me, I decided to take a shower. I picked out the jeans I was going to wear and a crop top. Both Dolce & Gabbana. As I set them on the bed, I half-assed grabbed a pair of pink, leather, flip-flops and tossed them by my bed as well. I got in the shower and the temperature was perfect. I quickly washed everything and got out. I didn't want to waste time in the shower when my father was waiting for me downstairs. As I was drying off, my cell rang. Had to be Mariah. I took my towel and laid it straight out. Towards my bedroom from the shower. I walked on the towel, reached over to my bed and grabbed my phone. 'Hello?' I answered. 'Hey girl. What's up?' It was Michelle. 'Not too much. Just got out of the shower and am drying off. What's up with you?' I asked as I walked back into the bathroom and sat down at my vanity. 'Oh! I'm sorry. Want to call me back when you're all done?' 'I can. What's up though?' 'I just wanted to know what you were doing today. You're not at school. I am waiting to be picked up. And I wondered if you were ok. That's why I'm calling you. Do you want to go to the mall today? Call me back?' 'Sure, chica. The mall sounds good. But I have to eat and talk to my dad to see what the plan is for today. He didn't go to work today either.' 'Oh. Ok. Well, call me back then babe.' 'K. Talk to you soon.' I hung up and took out my hair dryer. I blew dry my hair and hung it back up when I was done. I put the after products in my hair, looked at myself in the mirror and decided that I looked pretty good. Especially with zero make-up on. Ever since I had my eyebrow's dyed as well as my eyelashes, I didn't need much make-up. Especially for every day type things. Or outings. It saved *a lot* of time. Worth every penny of my father's money too. As I walked down the stairs, I saw my dad. Sitting at the breakfast table all by himself. He looked up as he saw me coming up to the table. 'Decided to shower, hmm? Not fair.' I laughed and explained that I just felt…dirty. And no, not because of what *we* did, but just because of 'you know what and who'. 'I understand love. Just giving you a hard time is all.' As he spoke to me he looked me up and down as usual...well most of the time he did. I loved when he did that. Because when he did that, I knew he always approved.

I sat down at my seat and looked at him. Even though he was dressed, he still looked like he had just woke up. Well I think that you look,' and I leaned in to him, 'handsome as Hell.' He looked at me with an embarrassed look. A look that I wouldn't, in a million years, think he could make. Embarrassed? My father? No way. But he managed to do it. That, in itself, made me feel pretty damn good, actually. Yep... handsome as Hell. ‘Do you know what's for dinner babe? Or is it a secret?' I assumed, when he was sure he wasn't 'red' in the face anymore, he composed himself. He answered, 'I have no idea what is for dinner, Gia. But, knowing Juanita, it will be fantastic. Oh. And since you took a shower already, I guess we're...' And then he leaned in to *me*. '..not taking one together after dinner, yes?' 'Dominick, I am sure we shall think of something.' I whispered. And in Farsi, too. 'Don't you?' My dad looked very surprised at me calling him 'Dominick' as well as calling him his name in our native tongue. I don't think I have ever called him by his first name before. 'I am sure we will. And please don't call me Dominick, Gia... that just seems too… weird to me. Alright?' 'Yes, Sir. Sorry. I didn't mean to make you feel weird. At all. I promise.' 'Alright. Just don't do it again, please.' At that moment, Juanita came in and set out our dinner. ‘I promise I won't. I had no idea, Tata.' He looked up at me as he was putting his napkin on his lap and winked at me. Damn, he was so sexy.

As my father and I were eating, Steve walked in the kitchen from outdoors. 'Did I miss the good portion?' My father and I looked up at him and both sort of laughed. 'No. You did not 'miss the good portion.' Whatever that means.' Steve sat in his seat and put his napkin in his lap. 'The good portion part of the meal is the part of the meal that is left intact. The best part of any meal really. Don't you two know what I'm talking about?' My father looked at me and me at him at the same time with a completely clueless look on our faces. 'No.' we both said at the same time. 'Boy. You two both need a lesson on 'The 'Meal'. A Really good meal.' He started on his dinner that he very carefully took out of the serving dish from the table. My dad and I looked out of the corner of our eyes and he smirked a little. One thing Steven took *very* seriously was his food. In the morning he ate, or rather, drank a protein shake (gross looking), and if he ate any snacks, they were *all* from the closest GNC store. It is a store for health nut's or people really intent on building muscle, losing weight or working out. I, at the time, had zero appreciation for GNC. I would find out much later that GNC was a part of MY daily routine. As we were eating our dinner in absolute silence, I figured out that we all must be starving. I knew I was. And I NEVER was 'starving'. I had a pretty small stomach. I worked out regularly with Steve and/or my father and that kept me hungry. But not hungry like eating everything in the house, hungry. Just hungry enough to survive. If I knew I would be going on a job, I would prepare myself 3 weeks before said job with my protein shake's and meal supplements, etc.

As we were finished with our dinner, we pushed our plates into the middle area of the table and leaned back in our chairs. Damn that meal was good! I mean, really good. I mean Juanita's meals were usually always good, but tonight, for some reason, it tasted extra good. We all just sat there saying not a damn thing. Steve was picking his teeth, though discreetly, with a toothpick. My dad was lost in his own thought's and I was wondering what my father had planned for 'later' this evening. 'Oh, Mr. F? If it's alright with you, I am going out tonight and probably won't be back or home until tomorrow morning. After breakfast. But not TOO late after breakfast. If that's ok with you, of course. ‘I don’t have a problem with that, Steven. What is the special occasion? Or is it just a random booty call?’ I actually choked on my own spit when I heard *those* words come out of his mouth. Damn! My father saying, Booty Call? Too *DAMN* funny! Steven even looked at my father very strangely. ‘Well, sir, it is indeed a date if that’s what you mean.’ Now Steven was red as shit from his neck on up to the top of his bald-ass head. 'This is priceless', I thought to myself. Priceless. I'll *have* to tell Michelle when I call her back before I go to bed tonight. School tomorrow and then the weekend. Pretty awesome having to only go to school 1 day this week. But I also had to pick up any missed schoolwork too when I was let out for the day tomorrow. That sucked. Juanita walked in and took our plates off of the table. I decided to help her tonight since her daughter wasn't here for some reason. As I set down some plates and a glass I asked her how her daughter was doing and if she was alright. Juanita looked up at me and said 'Bueno' very fast. And then put her head back down to start rinsing off the dishes. She also, without looking up, said thank you, in Spanish, to me for helping her clear the table. I replied and said 'Denada'. Which meant your welcome in Spanish… and walked back to the dining room table. 'Tata? I think something's wrong with Juanita.' My father instantly got up from his seat just as I was about to explain myself. 'Dad. Wait. Let me explain what I meant. I do not mean physically, daddy.' 'Well, what *do* you mean, Gia?' 'I asked her how she was doing and you know how she is always really chipper? All of the time? Or, *most* of the time?' 'Yes. And?' 'Well, she looked at me really quick, answered, 'Bueno', and then put her head back down and continued doing the dishes. And that was it. No conversational question's like she *ALWAYS* does. At least with me. She will always ask me how I'm doing or what I want for breakfast in the morning or whatever. Even, how is school going to be when I go back tomorrow. Something. You know?' My father *and* Steve both looked concerned after that bit of information. 'I'll go and talk to her right now. In private. In her room or house. You two can stay here and wait for me. Or, if I take too long, I'll find you two and tell you what I find out. But, when I tell you, tell *no one*. Obviously she wants this to be kept secret or private. Or, at least, it is very private to her. Got that? The both of you?' We both nodded our head's in agreement as we looked at him. I knew that all three of us were *so* attached to Juanita that sometimes we *did* take her presence in our lives' for granted. We wouldn't know what to do without her. I just hoped to God that it was nothing wrong with her or her daughter's. That would be a bad deal. For her personally of course. But, if something were critically wrong with any of her immediate family that would mean that she would, of course, have to leave for a while. If not permanently. As my father got up from his chair and walked towards the kitchen, Steve and I just sat there and stared at our napkin's, fiddled with our clothes', or just stared at each other. 'God, Steve. What if something was terribly wrong with Juanita? Like Cancer or something? Damn! What would my father do?' 'Well, I feel or had the same question as you did. But then, G.G., I realized I was being a selfish prick.' 'I know. I did too.' I said back to him. 'Well, *if* there *is* something physically wrong with Juanita, you *know* your father would pay 100% of the medical bills. But I just cannot or *do not* want to believe that it is anything related to that. I just HO that we are horribly wrong is all, G.' 'I know. Me too, Stev-o.' We waited for about 15 to 25 minutes, making small talk, and then decided to go our separate ways. Steve to the garage and me to my room. As I opened my door, I walked into my closet and went through every piece of clothing that I had that was hanging up and decided if I needed to donate it or not. Meaning, if I hadn't not worn it in 6 months, I will not wear it. No matter how much I liked it. I started taking a few pieces off of their hanger's and threw them on the floor. After about an hour and a half, I stopped at the end of my closet and looked at the pile laying before me on the floor. I bent down, picked up as much of the pile that I could and walked it to the middle of my room. I dumped it in the middle of my floor and walked back to get the rest of it. As I returned and dumped that pile, I sat down with the semi-giant pile and sorted them. Pants, t-shirts, blouses, shorts, shoes and accessories. I grabbed some lined paper from my desk and wrote down what was in the pile for donation. My designer piece's I would take to a great consignment shop that I used for all of my clothes' that I did not wear anymore. This consignment shop was awesome. If they sell any of my pieces, I get 70% of what the item sold for. After I was done with that, I walked out of my room and down towards the kitchen. As I turned the corner, I saw Juanita and then my dad walk out of the pantry. They must have had their conversation in there, I thought. As I grabbed a couple of trash bags out from under the sink, I tried to ignore everything that was going on with them. As I took the bags and closed the cabinet door, my father took hold of my left arm lightly to hold me back as Juanita continued to walk into the dining room. Probably to finish the dinner dishes. 'Alright. Thank god it is *not* what you assumed young lady.' And he didn't say that in a tone stating or letting me know that I was in trouble. Thank God. 'Juanita's granddaughter is pregnant. At 13. So no wonder why she is freaking out. Or out of sorts. I told her that I would take care of anything she needed financially or anything else. Time off or whatever. She finally told me the story in its entirety. The girl was being a typical teenager and was fooling around with her boyfriend...and well, you know the rest. She's pregnant. And, as you know, Catholics do *not* believe in abortion. So, it will probably be a lot of 'grandma taking care of the baby'. Meaning more time off for Juanita. She did tell me that her sister will take over for her if she needs to take off more than two days in a row; which is nice.' I breathed a sigh of relief that it wasn't a health issue for Juanita. I mean she was coming up on becoming 70 years old. Damn! In fact, my father had asked her a month or so ago if she would like to retire. She adamantly said 'no way' or something like that in Spanish. My father even told her that he would still pay her regular salary if she wanted to retire. Even still live on his property. And she still said no thank you. That was an awesome employee. And my father knew it. I knew he was regretting the time when she *had* to quit because of age. She was the closest thing to family, besides me, that he had. He did pay for her health care though. She went to see his doctor for her check-ups as well as female shit too. So, I would guess that she was the healthiest soon-to-be-70 year old woman on the planet. Speaking of 'womanly issues' or a period.... when did I have mine last? I tried to remember when I had mine last. I needed to look at my calendar in my room. That is where I marked it down. 'Well, that's good news daddy. VERY good news. When is her granddaughter due, anyway?' 'Not for 5 or 6 months she told me.' I looked at him. Up and down. Slowly... and replied... 'very good. So you have time to make the... change in personnel... right?' As I said all that, I took my pointer finger and traced my finger from the top of his shirt down to just below his belt. And when I was finished with speaking, I looked up into his eyes. 'What do *you* think you're *doing*?' He tried to say that with a bit of anger in his voice. But couldn't quite pull it off. He sort of laughed and put his head down. 'Father, you do not have to put your head down whenever you laugh. At least in front of me.' He looked up at me and slightly grinned. His normal lopsided, lazy grin. One that I have only seen. And I knew that for a fact. He took my chin with his left hand and drew my face up towards his. We slowly kissed. Very slowly. That, in itself, turned me on. Very much so. I needed to go to the bathroom. That's how turned on I was. The man knew how to kiss. That's for sure. We stopped. Probably too fucking breathe. We stared at each other and I leaped into his arms and, thank God he caught me. If not, my ass would be on the floor. We were really kissing; and hard. In the middle of the kitchen, or house if you wanted to be technical about it. Him leaning against the stove. Then we heard Juanita pick up some dishware or silverware. I don't remember. We instantly stopped and both wiped our mouths dry. Juanita walked in to see us in the kitchen. Doing absolutely nothing. I picked up my trash bags at a normal pace and said to my father, 'ok, then. I'll do that.' I turned to Juanita and told her I loved her.

She said the same back to me in Spanish. We smiled at each other and I walked towards the stairs with my trash bags. 'I'll speak with you in a bit regarding what we were talking about.... a minute ago, love.' I turned my head over my shoulder. 'Ok, Tata.' And I walked back to my bedroom. As I sat on my floor again, I started folding all of my clothes and put them in their respective bags. I just finished with my last item when there was a knock on my door. I obviously knew who it was. 'Come in Sexy!' I said. 'Gia! Damn! What if it was Steven or… someone else for fuck's sake?' My dad sat on my bed looking, instantly at what I was doing. Or *had* done, rather. I looked at him, head down, looked up under my eyes and replied, 'I would have talked my way out of it. Like, 'Just kidding' or 'you wish', etc.' He continued to look at me. 'Gia, you have an answer for everything! Damn!' as he laid back onto my bed. I laughed a little bit, still looking at him. 'Like father like daughter. Don't you think?' 'I suppose. God help me.' I laughed again. 'BUT… that's why you love me so damn much. Right?' '*One* of the reasons baby. One of the reason's. What the hell are you doing, love? Moving? Say no.' I glanced at him. He was actually mimicking *my* words. 'Very good!' 'Don't condescend me, Gia.' 'I'm not! I swear, Tata. I am just not used too ***you*** mimicking me, that's all. I love you, as you know. And, if you love someone, you do *not* mimic them. At least not in a condescending way. IF there is another way. Is there?' 'No, not that I'm aware of. But you are trying to get me off track. As you do so well. What are you doing? Seriously?' 'I came up here to separate my entire closet to keep, donate or consign. Depending if they are designer pieces or not.' 'Can we go tomorrow... never mind. I have a dang car! I love you so much, daddy. I really do. In so many different ways, baby. As you know, so *very much…* sexy, sexy, sexy, beast, you.' 'Gia! I *DO* like when you tease me like that, but what if the help hear you talk like that? They are all women and will gossip like 16 year old girls, baby. Even Detail would gossip if they heard you speak to me that way. Anyway. What are you or when are you going to be finished with this mess anyway?' I looked down at the bags that I had just finished filling and I looked back up at him. 'I *am* done, Tata. I am just going to drop them off at the consignment shop and the store that takes donations if they are not designer items. But I'm doing all of that after school tomorrow. Will you follow me into my closet so that I can show you something?' 'Of course.' He replied. As he followed me into my closet, I showed him all of the empty space that was left. I hardly had any summer clothes that fit me left. Everything that I put in the bags were too big for me. 'See? This is where I hang all of my summer clothes. And since it is coming up onto summer, I have, like, nothing to wear. Except maybe 1 or 2 bathing suits and a few t-shirt's. All of my shorts, except the pair that I wear only at home or at the beach with the holes in them?' 'Yes, I know those horrid things, Gia.' 'Well, they are the ONLY shorts I have left. The other ones from last year are all too big for me.' He looked at me sort of stern and asked, 'What size were/are they?' I looked down at my feet for maybe a few seconds. Trying to decide if I tell him the truth or make up a size or two bigger than they really are? No. If he did not believe me, he would dig them out; or have me do it and show them to him. 'Size 1 or a 0, daddy.' He looked incredulous. 'WHAT? And they are *TOO* big for you? MY God, Gia. You are getting WAY too skinny. Now, you know I am all about thin and all of that. But you are telling me that you are smaller than a 1 or a 0?'' I looked at him and wondered if I should tell him the truth about this situation. I *always* told him the truth. But that was because I knew he would find out the truth regardless of what I told him. I didn't know if he had an 'issue' with me being, what 'society' deemed too skinny. I knew I wasn't too skinny. I had a lot of muscle tone and I didn't have any bone's sticking out. Not really, anyway. I answered him the truth. As usual. 'I am a double 0. But, daddy, you've seen me naked. I look good and healthy.

You've even told me that, Tata. I don't feel breakable. I have great muscle tone, etc. Steve would have said something to you sooner, you know? I know for a *fact* that I am not 'anorexic'. Ask Steven what he thinks, ok? He can do a body mass test on me first thing in the morning. And even before I eat. But he needs to do it pretty quick because of my blood-sugar issues. Ok? How's that?' He continued looking at me. 'Alright. I'll call Steven now and tell him to make it an early night so that he can get up at a reasonable hour and give you that test. I want you to be ***healthy***. You should know that, Gia.' 'I do daddy. I really do, sweetheart. Call Steve.' He took a double-take, yet again, when I called him 'sweetheart'. He took his phone out of his jean's back pocket and dialed. He walked over to my bed and sat down. I sat down on the floor in front of my bags and taped one piece of paper on each of them. 'Designer' & 'Other'. I sat there and walked back to my shoe closet. This was going to be the hard part. My beloved shoes. I heard my father say, '…alright, bud. See you around 10AM then. Bye.' As I picked up 5 pairs of my designer shoes that I hadn't worn in 6 months and 10 pairs of other types of shoes. I carried this huge 'tower' of footwear into the middle of my bedroom and dumped them on the floor. As I sat down on my floor again, I sorted them; designer with designer and other with other. As I looked at them, I looked up at my dad and asked what Steve said. 'He'll do it, babe. But let me tell you something. And I am *NOT* mad, alright?' 'Ok, Tata. What is it?' 'If his finding's, per the test, say that you *are* skinnier by more than 50% of other girl's your age and height, I will have to put you on an Ensure program with ZERO exercise. Alright? Promise me. With zero bitching. I cannot have you unhealthy baby.' 'Ok. I promise. *IF* he comes back with an un-healthy reading, I will do whatever you want me too. Just remember, I will become a HUGE fat person.' I looked at him with, I assume, a sarcastic look on my face. 'Gia. You are not going to become a 'Fat person' as you say. Believe me? Do you think *I* want you to look like that? Taking you with me wherever I go? Galas, Openings, Overseas? 'Hello, Mr. So-and-so. This is my fucking fat daughter, Bertha. Hot, yes? Can you actually see me saying that, let alone, *doing* that to you?' I looked up at him from looking at my feet. 'No. I guess not. But I do want to stay in my size 0 or 1's. I would be giving away my most favorite jeans, shorts, *everything*! It would be very personally *devastating*.' 'Honey, I know it would be. We'll just see what Steven's number comes up with. Alright?' 'Ok, Tata. But I do promise you, that I am healthy and a healthy size and weight for my stature. Ok? So, please do not worry about me, father.' 'Hon. Being a father means that I will *always* be worried about you. No matter what the issue may be. You have *got* to understand that, my kitten.' I ran what he said through my mind. Yes, he is my dad and he *is* supposed to 'worry' about me. Just like he said. Even if we were sleeping together. And on a regular basis. So, that would mean that he is worried about me as a daughter *and* a girlfriend. I wonder if *anyone* is in my situation. Well, *IF* they were, I doubt my father would feel comfortable in me talking to them. So fuck that idea. 'I understand daddy. I do. Ok?' 'Alright then. Anyhow, when are you planning on going to these consignment shops?' 'I was thinking about getting some shorts on and a t-shirt and going now, if that would be ok.' 'That's fine, Gia. Just give me enough time to let Lane and two more Detail know you are going so that they can follow you. And no, you won't be able to see them. Or, better said, no one will be able to see them, yes?' I laughed at that. He knew me so damn well, it was scary. Scary good. 'Ok, Tata. I'll find you when I'm ready. In about fifteen minutes I'll come and find you. Do you know where you'll be? Like, in general? It is 12,000 square feet to find your fine ass.' 'Gia! Please. Not that kind of talk unless behind closed doors. Alright? Damn.' I noticed his face was red again. And *very* red at that. 'Yes, sir!' I replied as I saluted him at the same time. He gave me a scolding head shake and walked out of my bedroom. I smiled, grabbed my bags and my purse and walked down the stairs. Making sure my bedroom door was closed. As I hit the bottom of the stairway, I walked towards the back door and dropped my bags on the floor. Thank God it was summer. It stayed light outside later than *any* other 'season'. I opened the back doors that went towards the backyard and the garage and walked towards the garage. As I entered, I saw all of detail either working on their guns or playing poker (way at the end of the garage and behind one of my father's classic Vettes). As soon as they saw me, they all stopped what they were doing and looked at me. Some with looks as if asking themselves, 'Am I in trouble or not?' 'Hi guys! I need the keys to my car please. And no, I will not nark on you if you be nice to me. I never will either. But! Just be on your **best** Detail behavior. And Steve will or should be down here in 5 to 10 minutes, BTW. Last I heard anyway. Just a head's up.' One of the guys, I think his name was Eric, ran over to the key safe, unlocked it, grabbed my key's and tossed them to me as usual. He winked at me. In a professional way of course, and mouthed 'thank you'. I said you're welcome to all of the guys in the garage and got in my car. I put my purse in my lap, took out my make-up bag, unzipped and grabbed my MAC© face powder as well as my lip gloss and applied it. I put my car in drive, pushed the button for my top to go down and drove out into the sunshine. The high today, I checked before I left, said it was going to be 75 and Sunny, with no clouds. As I tossed my bag into my purse, I drove down the driveway at turtle speed. The 'high' so to speak, had passed now. So, I thought, it must be around 70 or 67/68. Something like that. DAMN it was beautiful today. I put my seatbelt on and also took the loose hair band out of my hair, put my sunnies on and looked at myself in the mirror. Pretty damn hot, I thought. When I hit the gatehouse I waved and gave them the thumbs up. The guys opened the gate for me and I took a right out of the gate towards Sunset. As I was driving, with the wind in my hair and the warm, yet cool, ocean breeze in my face, I felt wonderful. And *FREE*. Yes, I knew I had my bodyguard's all behind me. At least until I hit the light for Sunset. Then they would split off and do their thing. But today was my day. In my car. Damn, this was so liberating! I would have to thank my father again for such a fantastic gift. It was more than just the car. It was my *freedom* that was *so* meaningful to me. That was what I had to tell my dad. He would understand that. I was sure of it. As I came to a stop at the light at Sunset, I looked in my rearview mirror. Yep. Detail behind me. And I bet there were 7 more in various places as well. Whatever made my father feel safe. And, I did understand that as well. Nothing was going to ruin my day today. I drove leisurely down Sunset Blvd. To my favorite consignment shop looking around at all the tourists at Mann's and at various 'tourist' places off of the 'famous' street. About 15 minutes into my drive, I turned left onto a little street no one would know about unless they lived here. I found a parking spot and parked, grabbed my bags and got out of my car. I took my handbag and pushed the button on my key-fob that set the alarm on. It was a top-of-the-line alarm to where if anyone got within' 3 ft. from the car, it would make a really loud obnoxious sound. And for someone not expecting it, they would jump out of their shoes. As I walked into the doors, arms full as Hell, I instantly looked for my favorite sales girl. I finally saw her. She was just finishing up her lunch. I had to turn down three other girls until she was finished. She saw me and held up a hand as if to say, 'Please wait for me, Gia!' I kind of laughed and nodded my head towards her. I looked around for a bit. Just to see if anyone had dropped off anything that I would fall in love with. Nada this time. Probably just as well, too. I would like to leave here with some money for once. As 'my' girl finished with her meal, she came up to me. 'How the hell have you been, girl? I haven't seen you in forever!' 'I know. I haven't cleaned out my closet in forever. Plus I have been traveling for a while lately. By myself and with my father.

How have you been? Business good? I HOPE?' She laughed and looked back at me. 'Yes, as a matter of fact. A lot of people are coming in here to actually shop! Can you believe that? I think its people that have just moved here from out of state and finally found us. So, let's see what you brought us? Or me, in case I buy it before I put it on the floor?' I laughed at that because she usually always bought at least a couple of things that I brought in. Every damn time, too. So, we had the same taste. Plus, if she *really* liked something that I brought in, I would sometimes just give it to her. I knew she only made $50,000 + bonus' a year (she told me) and I also knew she would never be able to afford to buy the things that she liked from the things that I brought in. As I followed her into the back room, I saw out of the corner of my eye, the other sales girls give her the 'evil, jealous, eye'. They knew that I gave her shit. Plus, she didn't hide it from her employee's either. She was the manager as well. Plus she gave employee discounts a lot, as well. So these bitches had *nothing* to complain about. As we reached the corner table that was a long-ass table, I dumped all of my bags onto it. I separated my purses from my clothes and put the outfits together that went together. I looked at her when I was done. Her eyes were as big as saucers. I followed her gaze. She was 'drooling' over a Louis Vuitton handbag that I had two of. And it had never been used before. I remembered that it was a gift. 'So, babes. What do you think? See anything that you like first?' 'Um, yeah! She whispered back. What amount of cash are you expecting to leave here with?' 'Well, why don't you add up all of my item's and then tell me the total, like we always do, and then I'll tell *you* what you can have. When I said that, I leaned in and whispered that to her. 'Sure thing chicky! Be right back!' 'Sounds good sweetheart.' Once all of my things were laid out on the table 'just so', I walked a ways from the table to look at their shoes and their accessories. When I was looking inside their glass enclosure that was held for vintage jewelry or handbags, mostly clutches, which I didn't care for at all, I spotted something that I absolutely *loved.* A longish, gold chain; pretty thick, with about an inch and a half long, wide Chanel pendant that, according to the tag attached to it, said it was from the 60's. I WANTED IT *BAD*. Even though I didn't have a credit card in my name, per say. I did have my own black Amex card in my name but had my father's card number on it. So, they were attached together so to speak. Whenever he got his statement, he saw my purchase's as well. I looked at the tag. $2,049 was how much it was. I will wait and see if my friend could give me a 'discount' (usually hers) and if not, I would call my father and see if I could charge it on 'my' card. She walked back to me, (ALL the bitches were staring at us now) and set the calculator down on the glass table. She turned it around to show what I would walk out of the store with that day. I looked down at it. It read $6,875.47. I knew it would be quite a bit, but never that much. Never had I made *that* much from all of my shit that I brought in. 'How did this pile of 'crap', per say, make so much money? Like, where is 'the money shot' in all of this?' She laughed her ass off regarding the 'money shot' comment. 'Well, what really made the value go up were the Louis bags. This simple small Carry-Over-The-Shoulder Vernis bag was the one that really tipped the scales. I believe because they discontinued it. As of… I think… maybe 3 months ago? Oh shit. 3 YEARS ago. Sorry. I am in total brain fart mode today, Gia.' 'That's fine, girl. I have been in Brain Fart mode *all* damn day!' I leaned into her a bit since we had 'The Vultures' watching our every move. 'Follow me for a minute so we can get out of eye-shot of those scabs, k?' 'Sure.' As she followed me, I asked her what bag she wanted the most. I also told her since the bag that made the money scale jump, I couldn't give her since I really wanted as much spending money as I could get because my father was tightening the reins on his cash flow AND allowance to me lately. Especially since he got me the car for my birthday. 'Oh, no problem babe! That wasn't the bag I was drooling over, as you said. It was the MCM handbag. The Visetos Shopper Project that's reversible. It is *so* sought after. And in pink? It tipped the scales babe. Nope. The bag I really, really want, the one that I have been hoping someone would bring in, is the Louis Vuitton Speedy, Stephen Sprouse Edition. In Green. That *is the* bag I've been waiting for babydoll.' 'Really? You will punch me when I tell you this, but I have always been honest with you. So…I got two of them for my birthday last year. And I totally forgot about it until I cleaned out my closet! Today! I am so glad that that is 'the bag' you've been waiting for. Tell you what. I will give it to you, if you give me the amount you showed me on the calculator *and* I was kind of interested in that vintage Chanel necklace you have in the glass encasement? I will even sign a receipt that does not include that bag on it when I brought all of this stuff in. 'Wow, Gia! Really? Give it to me? Let me go and see what we priced that Chanel Gold necklace at. Be right back, k? How does that sound?' 'Sounds good to me sweetheart!' I waited, standing by the table for about five minutes and then she was back. 'Well, babe, that necklace is priced at $3,000! I don't know if I can just give it to you without anyone from the 'Vulture camp' noticing, babe.' She nodded her head in the direction of the other sales girl's. '*Really*? No Shit?' I tried my fucking damndest to keep all of that in a whisper. 'Yes, unfortunately I *am* serious, baby. It SUCKS major!' 'Well, is there anything that you *CAN* do?' I watched her wheel's spinning in her mind as she was trying her hardest to find a way to get me that necklace without the other 'Vultures' finding out. 'I know! Listen, Gia. And tell me how this sounds. I will go over to the counter, take out the CC necklace and walk it over to you. Right in front of the girls and hand it to you. Then, you smile and nod your head or something to that effect. Look at it, try it on and look in the mirror. Crap like that. Like you are considering whether to buy it or not. Then, since I am closing the store today, place the necklace back on top of the counter, take out your wallet and wrap a $1 bill around a wad of white paper, receipts, anything that's trash so that it looks like a big amount of 'cash' but with the 'green' of money on the outside. So they wouldn't know how much the bill was. Get what I'm saying?' I thought about that for a bit and it actually was a brilliant idea. And, since she was closing the store tonight, she would be managing all of the tills too. Counting them out and all of that. 'That is brilliant, babe! You got it! You have *always* been the kindest, most fair girl in here. You know that. So, that bag is yours, also. Ok? As long as you *know* you will never, ever get caught.' 'I will never get caught, Gia. That is why I always bring you to the back table. I just tell the bitches over there that all of your things are worth a lot of money so I like to value your privacy and take you back here. Besides. They aren't really looking at us. They are trying to take a look at all of the stuff you brought IN here. Ok?' She walked up to me, out of eye-shot from the other chicks and gave me the biggest hug she had ever given me. 'Alrighty. Follow me to the cash register and I'll give you your cash and you just sign off on your receipt. And then you're good to go, hon! I hope I don't see you for another 6 months too!' 'Hey! Tell me what you are looking for and I will keep an eye out for those things too. My dad will never know. Especially since I will only do it when I just go shopping for *me*. Plus, this is the only consignment shop I *ever* go too. That way, chances are, you *will* get lucky, hopefully in 6 months' time. Just in time for Christmas! HA!' 'Sounds good to me baby girl!' She punched in some numbers, took out some cash and handed it to me. I signed the receipt she put in front of me, wrapped a $1 bill around some receipts from the gas station and a grocery receipt and handed it to her. She slipped the Chanel necklace in my bag as well. I gave her a kiss on the cheek and then thought about something. I walked back quickly to the counter, before she left it, and gave her my cell number. I wrote it on the back of one of her business cards. 'Call me when you *really* want to go clubbing or to Vegas or whatever floats your boat. We need to go out together. Plus, we're about the same size, so take a look at my closet if you can't find anything you want to wear from yours, ok?' 'Sounds good to me! And thank you *so* much, Gia. You truly are the best.' 'Back at ya, girly!' And I walked out of the store towards my car. All of the other girls then walked to the front of the store just to see if I was driving or if a bodyguard was driving. They must have been listening to Karen and I's conversation. And that I got a new car from my father or something. The bitches. Oh well. Let them be jealous. I promised myself right then and there that I would *only* deal with Karen. Period. As I drove away, out of their parking lot, I wondered what I wanted to do this evening. All of a sudden, at the light I was stopped at, I felt the need to vomit. And now! Right NOW! I frantically looked around for a bag. Obviously there wasn't a bag. It was a NEW CAR! I pulled into the nearest shopping center, stopped, opened my door and wretched right there in their parking lot. Damn! Am I sick with the fucking stomach flu? Great! I slowly drove to a convenience store and parked. Taking deep breaths. I still felt nauseated. I looked up and saw that the convenience store would not have a bowl or pan or whatever to puke in. I looked around the center until I saw an actual grocery store. I drove over to their parking area in a handicapped spot; screw them. I was handicapped right now. I got out and stood there for a minute. I didn't know if I could do this without throwing up. I saw a middle-aged woman walking into the store. I walked up to her, holding my hurting tummy, and asked her if she would please buy me a bowl of some kind and I told her why. She looked at me with pity in her eyes and said yes. I reached in my bag and handed her some money. She refused the money, but I insisted. I told her that I had plenty of money and that I wasn't some homeless person or a prostitute. I even pointed at my car. She finally accepted the money that I was holding out for her. 'I'll be right out, honey. Now go and sit in your nice car, and please hold your head out of the window. *If* you can that is.' 'I will. And thank you SO much, ma'am.' She smiled and walked into the store as I walked, very slowly, to my car. I got in and laid back into my seat. I had to throw up again. Shit!!!! I opened my car door and puked in front of a family of 6 no less. How *embarrassing*!!! I took some tissues out of my bag and wiped my mouth up and closed the door. About 5 minutes later, thank God, the lady walked out of the store as well, walked over to me and handed the bowl over, plus my change. I told her to please keep the change and she did. I was glad that I didn't have to argue that one. I was in no mood too. I put my car in reverse and drove home. Thinking all the way, what in the hell could be wrong with me? Someone probably gave me some stomach virus. But I never got damn stomach viruses. I bet that PIG, at the Grove, gave it to me, I thought. But *IF* he did, I would have received it a lot earlier than now for God's sake. As I was on Sunset, closer to Mulholland, I had to throw up yet again. Oh Damn! Not again!!! I put on my Hazards and pulled over onto Mulholland, opened my door very fast, and then threw up in the dirt. 'Beautiful' I said out loud. Puking on a beautiful Sunday afternoon. As I finally was driving up our driveway towards home (about time, too!), I pulled in front of the door, put my car in park and put my keys in the visor. I grabbed my bag and my purse, closed the door and continued towards the house. When I got out, I walked as fast as my body would allow. I opened the door and walked around the centerpiece and into the living room. I saw Juanita dusting. I said 'Hola' to her and asked, in Spanish, where my father was. She looked at me and smiled. 'He is in the kitchen, mi bambino. How was shopping?' I looked at her like a sick puppy. 'Not so good, Juanita. I have been throwing up *ALL* the way home. Yucky, Juanita. I need to go to bed. Soon. She stopped dusting, looked at me with concern and walked over to me. She felt my forehead and told me I didn't have a fever. But to go into bed and Com her when I was done so she could come upstairs to my bedroom and get me all comfortable. I told her I would as soon as I talked to my dad. ‘Si, mi bambina.’ And smiled that sympathetic smile. As she continued her dusting, I continued walking into the kitchen, looking for my father. I saw him rummaging through the refrigerator. 'Hi daddy!' He looked up from bending over and stood up, closing the door. 'Hi my baby. How was your trip in your beautiful new car? Hmm?' 'The trip was *fine*, Tata. But I think I have the flu or something. Or stomach virus because I started throwing up as soon as I was done at the consignment shop. I feel like crap, daddy.' 'Stomach Virus? Baby, you never have that sort of thing. Are you sure that you didn’t eat something that didn't agree with your tummy, baby?' He walked over to me and felt my forehead. 'Juanita did the same thing, daddy, and said that I didn't have a fever.' 'Hmm. That is awfully strange baby. Did you eat a stranger’s food or eaten *from* a stranger that you have never eaten from before, my love?’ ‘No, Tata.’ ‘Why don't you go upstairs ...' Just as he said that, I held up my hand, touched his arm and ran like Hell to the restroom, puked, and came back out. Ten minutes later. 'Oh, my poor kitten. Let me help you upstairs. Now I get to take care of *you*, yes?' 'Yes, daddy. Please do. I feel awful. He leaned down, picked me up and I put my head against his chest. 'Which bed should I put you in love?' 'Your choice, daddy. Actually, you better put me in mine, Tata. Juanita said she would take care of me and when it comes to sleeping, IF it's a virus or whatever...Oh My God!!!' My father took a step back when I let that shoot out of my mouth. ‘Oh no, father. Can you do me the biggest favor right now? Please?' He looked at me strangely for a second. 'Of course, sugar. What is it?' 'Can you please go and get my calendar for me, Tata? *Please*? I beg you.' 'Hon, you do not have to beg, baby. Of course I will get it for you. I do not know why, but I will.' 'Thank you, daddy. Very much.' 'God, I better be wrong about this' I said to myself. My father put me back on the steps as he went back up them to my room. When I heard my father come down, I scooted over to let him by. I took the calendar from his outreached hand and opened it up. I went to the month we were in now; July. I counted the days since my last period. Then I counted from then to the day we were at now. Oh My God. I was right. I am officially 10 day's late for my period to have started. And I was *never* late. Not once. Daddy, we need to talk. As my father got comfortable on the stairs next to me, he asked, 'What is it, my kitten?' As I was gathering the courage to tell him, he started to get a look of concern on his face. 'Well, Gia. What is it that is so disconcerting, yes?' I put my head up so that I, as usual, could look into his eye's to tell him this, and after I told him, he got this complete shocked, stunned, look on his face. He even let his mouth hang open. Which, to him, was not in his DNA. I would have thought he physically just could not do that. 'Come again? Are you sure? Positive?' I looked at him again and repeated myself. 'Daddy,' I said. 'I am Pregnant. And The Baby Is Yours.' He just slowly leaned back against the stairs and put his head in his hands. Thinking about God knows what. I figured that I was either going to be gotten 'rid' of, or, a coat-hanger abortion on the kitchen table was in order for me. For the first time, since being raped repeatedly by 'The Monster', I was terrified.

Chapter 27

We must have both sat there, on the stairs, for 25 minutes without saying a word. *Finally*, my father turned to look at me. 'We have a lot of work to be done right now, Gia Mahari.' And then he stood up, as did I. 'Why don't you go upstairs, lay down and rest, while I speak too Steve. I will then be up when we are finished.' 'Yes, father.' I replied. I watched him walk slowly back down the stairs and into the kitchen for a second. I then realized that he was talking on the phone too someone. After he had hung up, he walked back up the stairs. But not up to me, but towards Steven's room. I turned around and continued walking upstairs to my bedroom. Still feeling queasy. I took off my current outfit, threw what was dirty in the hamper, 1 item in the dry-cleaning basket and hung the rest up in my closet. When I was standing in the middle of my closet, I had to puke again! Damn this crap! I said out loud. I dropped what I had in my hands and I ran into my restroom. After puking yet again and then cleaning myself up, I slowly walked out of my bathroom, opened my dresser drawer where I kept my nightgowns and put it on over my head. I felt *so* miserable, I didn't even remember if I had put on make-up or not. I just said screw it and walked to my bed and crawled in it, scooted on my butt to where I felt comfortable and buzzed Juanita's Com. 'Juanita?' 'Si, Bambina?' she quickly replied. 'Juanita? Whenever you have the time for that chicken or beef broth? I am in my bed' knowing I sounded pathetic. 'Ok, Gia. I will be right up'. She replied in her jilted English. But *dang* she was getting *so* good at her English! I was so proud of her. I got out of bed, slowly. I saw that when I was outside of my room, my father was not in his office. I was bored and I wanted my father. Someone to comfort me and tell me 'that everything will all be ok.' I walked into his office and sat a little. Then I spotted a document. I started reading this document and realized that it was the first page of a very important document regarding The Illuminati or, rather, The Brotherhood. I quickly picked it up and walked semi-quickly to my room. I crawled back in bed and got myself comfortable. This should make for good reading until my dinner was ready, I thought. As I was reading this one page piece of paper, I was reading all of the names belonging to *THE* Illuminati, and some of the things that they have been doing to the general populace since the early '50's. Damn! I found some pretty interesting shit. I thought to myself. I kept reading until I heard Juanita coming up the stairs, with my dinner probably. I shoved the paper under my covers and laid back down on my bed. 'How you feeling, Miss Mahari?' 'I feel the same, unfortunately Juanita.' 'So sorry, bambina. Please eat or drink this broth slowly. Until you know your tummy is ok after each little big sip (I know. But at least she was *trying*). 'I will, Juanita. And Gracias, Juanita. You are the best!' I smiled really big at her. Well, as big as I could in my present condition. She smiled back at me, told me that she loved me and out she went. Telling me that she would be back to take my temperature. Well, I knew what that temp would come back as. Normal. Hey 'Juanita! I love you, but I'm pregnant! And it's my father's baby, too! Isn't that awesome? My father is even getting me an abortion!!! Sweet, huh?!' Damn, my life was something else, I said out loud. I took out the paper I tucked under the bed and started reading again. Wow, man. My father, after I just read just the *names* on this document, would *not* want me seeing this! Shit! All of the Rockefeller's were in this. Not to mention the Famed and Powerful Habsburg family and Big Time on him/Them! So, I had *all* of the names and a little dirt on them now. *In my* hands, at *this moment*. I turned the paper over and read part of a sentence stating something about what 'They' have done to the whole World, especially the United States, as far as, the Food

Industry. They apparently, too make it short, at least for now; made Fast Food addictive to the human body by adding sugar to *all* fried foods so that all American Men, Women and Children will become addicted to it. Hence, making American's overweight. Well, *now*, ladies and gents… now you know the 'who' whom made the entire fast food nation… Overweight and 'Fat', so to speak. Not only ruining their self-esteem but their health. Plus, many more things that I absolutely *had* to write down. I just knew, in my gut, that this information was important. I had already mentioned the Fitzburgs and the Thurman's. As I continued, I saw The Vandersnipes, The Rushes, and Mr. 'Rick'… Oh My God! 'Reney'?!! No! I just saw him at The Bohemian Grove! As well as a *couple* of Vandersnipe's too! There were a bunch of other names that went back decades. And every single name that I read on that document did horrible things to their own people! Their own country! And, the whole, 'Who Killed JFK thing? Yep! *We* did do it! Our *own* C.I.A. **killed** our own President! I read about half a page on which document all of the details had on that little bit of information, too. I *had* to get my hands on it. And fast, too. I put the page under my covers and listened intently. I still heard my father speaking to Steven. I also heard Juanita making a lot of noise in the kitchen as well. I slowly put my bowl of broth onto my nightstand and slipped out of my bed. Tiptoeing outside of my room. I walked down the hall to my father's office again. I remembered something and quickly walked back to my room, grabbed that piece of paper and went back to my father's office. I made a copy of it and returned the original to my father's desk. Where I had found it. I grabbed the copy, folded it in half and stuck it in my panties. Under my white nightgown. I looked around the top of his desk and finally found the rest of the huge document that this piece of paper belonged too. I stuck it in the copier and pushed print. Since I knew my father was in another room *and* on another floor, he could not hear me. I only had to wait five minutes until the whole document had finished copying. I took the copy and put the original back on my father's desk. As I was walking, quite funny too, since I had an entire 8.5 x 11 document in my panties; sticking straight up! Thank God my nightgown was big or baggy around my entire body. Rather, under my breasts and below. I heard my dad's voice behind me. 'Kitten. What were you doing in my office?' 'Daddy! I was looking for you to tell you that I am still feeling horrible. I can't even walk normal and I am still, occasionally, throwing up.' 'Why don't you eat your broth that Juanita made for you and then come to my room so that we can have a talk. If you feel too bad for that, Com me and I will come to you. Yes?' 'Ok, Tata.' I replied. I wanted and hoped that I sounded normal to him. 'Alright then, my Princess. I will be waiting to hear from you then.' He walked over to me and kissed me on the lips. I kissed him back. Only with a little 'more' than he did. I sort of tried to use my tongue. But when I pulled away from him, I told him that I just felt too bad. I apologized too. 'Hon, you feel wretched. No need to apologize, ok hon?' 'Ok, daddy. Thank you. But it doesn't mean I do not want too. Ok Tata?' 'Of course, my baby. I know that.' He turned and went downstairs to have dinner with Steven. I walked slowly too my bedroom.

Once I was all settled in my bed and had finished my broth, I picked up the document that I copied in my father's office. 'Damn, what a find!' I said softly out loud. I started on page one and didn't stop until I Googled anything or anyone that I hadn't heard of. When I was finally finished, I looked at the clock. It was 10 pm. I only had one interruption. My father telling me goodnight. And that was at 9:30 pm. I had told him that I felt a little better and that I was going to bed soon. He replied, 'That we would talk about my 'little predicament' tomorrow when we woke up.' I sat there and took all that I had read in. Our government was so *evil*! And they ran *our* government, these evil people. Not the President, necessarily. But the people all around him! 'Rick Rheney', whom earlier, I said that I 'liked his intelligence?' Not so much now. Hell, I *hated* him after my trip to The Bohemian Grove! Now? He was a Monster! Plus *all* of the people that I *knew* their last names just because I was always interested in politics, some were never mentioned, and the ones that were? My God! How could they even sleep at night? Rumsfeld? I liked him too because of how he put 'The Press' in their *place* and how smart *HE* was and how funny he *could* be. Now? A fucking *Monster* as well! All of these revered Military Generals? They were the real evil people. After every single war that we had, especially the ones that we had since I had been alive. Mainly both Desert Storms, I was 100% for them. Still am. As is my father (obviously). But everything that they had said about 'waterboarding' and 'us torturing the people that were locked up at Guantanamo Bay'? And how 'The soldiers that tortured all of those that were captured from Desert Storm' should be punished because of 'what they did'? Never were! Why? Because the people that are truly in *power* in our government (not the POTUS)? They are *the ones* that *told* our soldiers *TOO* WATERBOARD the Prisoners if they did NOT cooperate! Sick scumbags! All of them! I then decided that we, the *people* of the USA, have the best Government that ***MONEY CAN BUY***. And, as far as those soldiers that did the waterboarding? They *didn't* get punished at all! The press was *told* that they **indeed** got punished, but they didn't! Hell, they were commandeered! Probably, according to this dossier, given medals and maybe promotions, whatever. All of the torture that these Middle East/Iranians/Iraqis got may be what they deserved compared to what they did too our citizens and The Twin Towers, but the lies that our government gave us is what *blew* my mind. I just could not wait to *write* a *book* about all of this! And, I knew that my father knew **ALL** of it. Every last bit of it. I also knew that **I** *had* to get out of here. Escape. I knew the password to my father's bedroom safe as well. So, as soon as he went to the office? I was going to go into his safe, hoping above *all* hopes that he did *not* change the password, and take a few stacks of money and escape. I slowly got up and stood up straight. Just to see how my stomach felt. It actually felt pretty good. Thank God. I kept the dossier in my room; under the covers to be exact and walked across my room to my bathroom.

I needed to brush my teeth. And *bad*! The more I thought of leaving my home and my father, Steven and Juanita, the more I tried to second guess my decision. Damn will I miss them, I thought. Especially my beloved and first love. *My father*. But I just could NOT stay here. Not with my father being a part in knowing what was/is really going on in our Government. We were the Biggest Hypocritical Country in the world. Yes, I loved my country and did not want to live anywhere else. *But*! I wanted the truth out there. And this dossier was Proof. I had *THE* ***MOST*** important, Most High-Up *signatures* in Washington on this thing. As well as a stenographer's typed documents that stated a *lot* of other Washington Big-Wig's *confessions*; what they did know, what they did order, do, etc. Not to mention 8 United States General's confessions on what they ordered, knew, allowed, etc. Not to mention that all of the documents that I *did* have were notarized. I picked up my toothbrush and started brushing my teeth. As I felt the toothpaste melt into sudsy, tingly, liquid, I made sure (as best as I could, anyway) that I did not swallow any of it. I knew that I would probably throw it back up. As I finished with my teeth, I washed my face and then applied my night cream. No wrinkles was my goal when I hit my 30's, my 40's as well as my 50's and hopefully beyond!! I sort of giggled too myself as I hung up my hand towel. I walked too my bed and crawled into the covers. When my clock read 1am, I was out like a light. I had finally finished *the entire* 600 page document.

Chapter 28

The birds chirping at 8am woke me up. Damn! I didn't remember to close my window last night. OR my curtains. As my eye's got adjusted to the light, I remembered what I *read* last night. My body started to wake up faster than normal for 8am. *Especially* being in the summertime. Where would I go too? Where the Hell would I stay? Shit! I knew that I *had* to get out of this house, this 'Cult'…wow, I thought. This was *the* first time I had called my father's 'religion' a Cult. But, I knew, deep down, that indeed it *was* a Cult. Not just a Cult. But a Satanic/Luciferian Cult. A *very dangerous* Cult that worshipped the Devil, traded women for money, gold, among other valuable things. Tortured these women as well until they were sold. They would rape them as well. The one's that they knew that they could get the *most* money for, they would torture, pour acid on them, brand them, attach them to batteries from cars, anything! Just too scare them! Christ! After all of that? They would practically beat them too death, if they were not dead already. Then there was *The* Bohemian Grove. I knew all about *that* Hell-Hole and 98% of the American public knew *nothing* about that place, I was sure. Especially what **exactly** went on there. I knew for a fact. Just then, laying in my bed, before breakfast that I *had* to leave. And as quickly as I could. Today, if possible. I buzzed Juanita and asked her if breakfast had even been started. She told me that it was almost ready to be served since my father had to go into the office today. I told her that I felt a bit better, I thought, and I would be right down. 'Damn. I better be better. At least to hold something down.' I said out loud too no one. I got out of bed and slowly walked into my closet. I pulled down my

Louis Vuitton Carry-All off of its 'perch' from the top shelf of my closet and carried it too my bed. I walked to my drawers and opened all of them, trying to make as little noise as possible. I knew that I would stop once I heard anyone walk up the stairs to see how I was doing. Meaning only my father and Steven. The only thing that I put in my Carry-All today was 'The Dossier' or the Document from last night. I knew that most likely I wouldn't have much time packing tonight. I would just finish it all tomorrow. While my dad was at work. Once The Dossier was inside, I pushed the bag under my long ball gowns inside my closet. I closed it and then walked out of my room, closed the door and down the stairs I went. My tummy actually did feel better this morning. Thank God. I couldn't be driving far, far, away, stopping every time I had to throw up. That would be absurd. If I *was* as sick as I was yesterday, I would just stay home, pack and then stay in bed and read and nap. Then, when I *was* actually feeling better, and done with this whole 'morning sickness' bullshit, that was when I would escape. When I hit the middle of the stairs, my father saw me and smiled his sympathetic smile and motioned for me to come down to the table. The food smelled so good. I hoped that was a good sign. 'Hi everyone.' I said to Steven and my dad. 'Hello Little GG. How are you feeling now?' said Stev-o. 'Yes, baby. How are you feeling?' My father said as well. 'A little better. I think. We'll see once I start eating. Let's hope that I can keep all of this wonderful looking food down! It looks so dang good!' 'It is, G. It *is* good.' 'Gee. Thanks Steve. Let's hope I can keep it down now. Or I shall beat you!' He looked at me in surprise and then I smiled. He just shook his head after half a minute or so. 'I never know when you are kidding or not, Gia. Never do; never will, I guess.' I laughed a little. 'I was just semi-kidding Steve. You should know that.' As I sat and put my napkin in my lap, I put small portions of food onto my plate. When I was done I just sat there and stared at it. I listened to my stomach, so to speak. No queasiness. Not at all. At least not right now, I thought. I took my fork and put a little piece of pancake on it, as Steve and my father spoke, I put it in my mouth and chewed. Please go down and *stay* down, I said to my tummy. After I swallowed that piece, I took a swallow of milk and then waited awhile. Nothing. No queasiness, none of that horrid 'feeling' you get when you are about to throw up. 'How is everything in there, kitten?' 'So far so good, father. So far so good.' 'Excellent.' he responded. I looked at him and smiled while looking in his eyes. I had a half a smile on my face while he was looking at me. He looked deep into my eyes as well. But… in a completely different way than normal. I secretly wondered if he could see that I was planning on… leaving? Or could tell that something was different...I did not know. Or if I was just being paranoid. 'Something you want to tell me, love?' I swallowed big. 'No, Tata. Just stressed about my food staying *in* my stomach instead of *out*.' 'That is very understandable, Gia. Very understandable. How does your tummy feel now?' 'It feels ok now, Tata. I just better *not* feel stressed or I *will* throw up. Or feel like it anyway.' 'Try to think of something completely different, babe. That way your mind will be off of the whole concept of throwing up or being sick entirely, for that matter.' 'Good idea, father. I'll try that then.' Just to make sure that he didn't think anymore off of the 'beaten path of '*normal'*, I leaned up over the table a bit and kissed him on the cheek. After I did so, he looked over at me and smiled a bit. Not his normal smile. But a smile of love and regret. 'What the Hell am I going to do about this pregnancy all alone when I leave?' I thought to myself as I ate alone in my thoughts. Then I thought of a pretty damn *great* idea. I would make myself have a miscarriage! I will go out as soon as my dad left for work and take a jog for about a mile. And run fast. That should do the trick. And, pretty damn quickly, too. After I was done with my breakfast, I knew Steve and my father were waiting on me anyway. I pushed my plate to the center of the table, looked at my father and told him to have a good day and that I would call him later. He smiled, agreed, and walked with Steven to the front door. 'I will see you when I get home, Princess. He smiled and mouthed 'I love you' and out the door he went. Once I heard the Limo leave towards the gatehouse, I walked/ran upstairs as fast as I could and into my bedroom too. I shut the door, took off my gown, threw it in the hamper and continued to get ready for my 'miscarriage run'.

Once I looked in the mirror of my bathroom, I put my hair up into a high ponytail. I had my Lycra running pants on, my Nike™ sports bra and my hot-pink running shoes on. By Nike™ of course. I opened one of my bathroom drawers and took out a pink headband too. Once that was on, I took one last look and out my door I went. I wondered if I should run on our property or not. Might as well. If I did not, I would have to have my detail follow me. If I snuck out, I would most certainly be caught and told on. Which *was* understandable. I jogged down the stairs, walked into the Foyer and told Juanita, as she was putting away clean napkins, that I was going outside for a run. She looked concerned and I told her that I felt fine. That I must have had a 24 hour bug or something. She looked at me for a second, understood what I said and said, 'Si, bambina! Run Bueno, yes?' 'I will, Juanita! Gracias!' 'Denada, my Gia bambina!' And out of the front door I went. I walked quickly at first, then once I was out of eyesight with my 'personal' Detail, like Lane, who, amongst a few others, that knew me personally. Or knew things about me personally, I started full on running. And, fast. I popped in my iPod before I started running, too. Once I started hearing my favorite song, I looked down, hit the 'repeat' button and ran like Hell.

Once I ran around my father's compound for about 3 miles, I did start cramping. That, in itself was the first sign of a miscarriage. I kept running and ran faster. I figured that I would run as hard for another five more minutes. That's when I would slow down and start my cool off. As the five minutes came upon me and the end of yet another great song, I looked down, slowed down and turned my iPod off. I walked pretty damn fast back towards the house. I quickly looked at my watch and noticed that I had been running about two hours and ran hard for 5 miles. I then could not ignore the ultimate pain in my abdomen.

A miscarriage feels like bad cramps from your period. *If* no one knows that. I hope no one does. But just for informational purposes. As I reached the back end of the garage, I snuck in the Maid's entrance. Detail didn't notice a thing. Or, if they did, they didn't make a big deal about it. No 'Hey, Gia. How was your run?' Nothing like that, thank God. As I got in the house, it took everything I had to not double over. Thank the God's that Juanita was not in the kitchen. I made it to the stairs and grabbed the rail. Just barely, the pain was *so* bad. And for me to say that? It *was* b-a-d. As I made it finally to my room, I crawled in bed and picked up my mobile as I ripped off my running clothes. Once I took off my running leggings, I looked down. Massive blood. I ran/hopped on one leg, grimacing as I went, sat on the toilet and cleaned myself off. I knew I could not take a bath or lay in warm or hot water. It made the bleeding worse. And I did *not* want to end up in the hospital. No way, Jose. I dialed my father as I put on my 'granny panties'. The ones that I usually wore when I *used* to be friends with 'Aunt Flow'. As I got Steven on the phone, he must have heard the 'pain' in my voice or the 'urgency', because as soon as I asked for my dad, he didn't give me any jokes or funny 'back-talk. He told me, 'hang on, babe' and handed the cell too my dad. 'What's wrong my kitten, hmm? Throwing up again, my poor love.' 'No daddy. I am having a miscarriage. Which, I know, is a good thing for us. But it sure hurts. Could you please call Henreick and see what will make me feel better and be healthy too where I can stay home? Please? I don't want to go to the hospital. I *do* know Tata that after all of the pain is gone, I can give myself an, um…cleaning out? So to speak. But I need to hear from some sort of doctor what I can do at home.' Weirdly, my father was quiet during my entire 'speech' too him. 'Gia, my love? Steven is an EMT. He knows all that needs to be done. Let me put him on the phone. And do everything he tells you to do, yes?' 'Oh My Gosh daddy. I completely forgot. Yes, Sir.' I could have kicked myself but I was in such a good mood, I wasn't thinking of anything but getting off of the phone, taking some of my

Vicodin and then packing. Then I will get in bed and read. 'Gia, I am SO sorry that you are going through this.' 'Thank you, Stev-o. But it *is* for the best. Just don't tell my father that. Ok?' 'Ok babe. Now. Take some of your Vicodin. And when I say 'some', I mean two. Ok sweets?' 'Ok.' I replied. Then try to *just* clean yourself up with a warm wash-cloth. No douches or anything like that until the bleeding completely stops. Alright? Got that? And, finally, for dinner, even though I know you'll want to eat with us or your father or whatever, NO sitting up. Just tell Juanita that you need some broth. Preferably beef broth. Call Juanita on the Com and tell her what happened and, believe me, she will be as sad as you probably are, ok darlin'?' 'Ok, Stev-o. You're the best. I'll always love ya. Forever. No matter what. Ok?' 'Hell, I know that, GG. What brought that on?' 'Nothing. I just wanted to tell you so that you will always remember that. Ok?' 'Well, ok love. Now go and take care of yourself. Love ya and see you when your father and I return from here. Ok?' 'Ok, Douche.' I replied. 'Kiss my Butt, Bitch'.' 'My father isn't sitting there is he?' 'He wasn't, no. Now he is and I'll tell him you said that. See ya later babe.' And we hung up the phone. I sat/leaned there on my bed. Or, against my bed. I then very slowly walked into my bathroom and grabbed two Vicodin and washed them down with a glass of water. I had, by then, taken off everything and put on my 1 remaining pair of Granny Panties. I then thought that can still get those messy, if you know what I mean, so I went and also got a small panty liner thing.

Chapter 29

I picked up my Princess phone and called Maria instead to tell her the truth. She picked up the house phone and I told her who I was. I then proceeded to tell her what happened with my pregnancy. She almost started crying! My God! How Catholics treat pregnancy is unbelievable!! Crying? Geez! 'But I will keep trying Juanita. I will. I promise, ok? Please don't cry. Si?' 'Si, bambina, Si. No more crying. You have much thinking too do and too heal, Si?' 'Si. I do, Juanita. I will. And I shall relax.' 'Bueno, Gia. Bueno. I will bring broth now, Si?' 'Yes, please do. That will make me feel so much better. Ok?' 'Ok. I will bring it up in fifteen minutes.' And we hung up. I felt hardly any pain at all. We must have been on the phone for quite a while. Damn! Plus, speaking with Steve and my dad. I pulled out my Carry-All™ and walked around my room. Just packing the essentials. Two pairs of my favorite jeans, four great t-shirts and one pair of tennis shoes, three pairs of my *favorite* heels, Christian Louboutins™, Giuseppe Zanotti™, Louis Vuitton™ (of course) and last but *not* least, Celine™. Now for the extra hard part. Handbags. Looking at the room that I had left in my LV Carry-All™, I had to pack sparingly. I could only pack so much. THIS was the ONLY bag that I was going to take with me in my escape. I would count the bag I was carrying *as* a handbag as one of them, of course. I decided on that one being the obvious choice. My Louis Vuitton Lockit MM. I would pack my Bottega Veneta Marco Polo Tote, my Proenza Schouler PS1 Medium and finally, another tried and true favorite of mine, my Fendi Medium Peekaboo Bag. After I got them out of my closet and slipped them into their dust bag's and arranged them too not scrunch each other too bad, I knew I had to go and pack, sparingly, my hair products. Once all of my bathroom articles were packed, I was exhausted. I decided to take my Denim Dolce & Gabbana jacket with me just in case I was chilly wherever I ended up. I KNEW it wasn't going to be nowhere damn freezing so that ruled out the Central U.S. and back East. So, it looked like I was going to stay in Cali or Washington State or Oregon. Oh yeah. Granola Eaters. But, I doubted my father would look for me there. At first he would call Michelle and she would say nothing because I was not going to tell her nothing. I made sure not to get any of my friends in trouble. No way. I then realized that I hadn't thrown up in forever. No more being Pregnant for ***Me***! Fan-Fucking-Tastic!!!! My Com went off and, as usual, scared the Hell out of me. 'Dinner's about to be served, bambina. You feel ok to eat? Down… um… stairs?' I stifled a laugh and told her 'I'd be right down'. I slid my Carry-All under my bed and walked out of my room. Closing the door behind me. As I walked down the stairs, my dad looked at me in both eyes. As usual, obviously. But, since I was taking off tonight, it made me paranoid for some reason. I just decided to play it cool and try my hardest to act normal. 'What's up everyone?' 'We are good, Gia. How are *you* feeling? Yes?' 'A lot better than I was earlier today.' I also decided to act a little 'down' from having a miscarriage. But not too obvious. That just wasn't me. Too ask for sympathy like that. My father knew that if something was really bothering I or I was sad over something, that I always grieved in private. 'Well good then, my Princess. Let's eat, shall we?' He smiled as he put his napkin in his lap. I looked over at Steven, smiled, and then at my father and smiled. Plus winked at him. He smiled and winked back. Once Juanita set all of the plated onto the table, we all dug in. Me, because I hadn't had a decent full meal in two full days. As we were all eating, talking about just day to day things, in the back of my mind I started to get sad. I was going to miss my father immensely as well as Steven. Even Juanita and her entire family. After everyone was done talking about 'nothing' really, my father turned to look at me and said, 'Gia, would you listen to me for a bit?' 'Of course, Tata. What is it?' 'Harris called me at the office late afternoon and told me that there was a Ritual this evening. Now. Before you go on telling me that you don't want to go or can't go, I have already taken care of that job for you. For the first time ever, I think, you do not have to go. But. You *do* have to go during the Fall Solstice, yes? You, yourself know, that this is a very big, important, Ritual that would require your appearance as well as attention by being there. You understand?' 'Yes, sir. And thank you for not making *him* make *me* go tonight. I don't think I'd be able to stand, let alone preform, my duties there this evening. I am still… well, for Steven's sake, I won't say it. But I just cannot physically go.' 'What is this 'keep it from Steven condition, love? He is a big boy now. I think he can take it, don't you think?' 'Well, daddy, I would think so. I am still bleeding and pretty heavily Tata.' I glanced at Steven and not a phased look was on his face. Duh! I thought to myself. He is a damn EMT for fuck's sake! Why would he even care about THOSE words? 'See, love? Nothing. Now. IF you are indeed bleeding quite a bit, why don't you be excused from the table and get your cute little ass in bed and do some reading? Also, don't forget to take 2 more of your Vicodin™ before bed, too, baby. I'll be up in 45 minutes or so to give you a tuck-in, ok now?' 'Thank you, daddy. I love you so much. You too, Steven. I really do. Please don't forget that, ok?' He looked up from his 'feast' and said 'and why would I forget that, Lil G? You're the best!' And then he winked at me. I got up from the table, said, out loud, 'Thank God for Vicodin.' And went and kissed my father's cheek and then Steven's cheek. 'Good night all' I said as I walked towards the stairs. They half-waved at me as they started into another conversation. As I took the steps 2 at a time since they were not looking at me, I reached my room in record time. Almost like normal, I thought. I closed the door behind me and decided to stay in bed and read until my father walked into my room to kiss me goodnight. I was holding back my tears since the middle of dinner. Shit, how in the Hell was I supposed to keep it together when my father came in here to tuck me in? 'I know!' I said out loud, I will pretend that I'm asleep! My dad will knock, there will be no answer and when he finally cracks the door open, he'll see me sleeping with my book half-assed on my stomach. Or, even on the floor. I will just fold it really well when I heard him ascend the stairs. I went and did all of my business in my restroom, took my 2 pills and then crawled into my bed. I made sure by looking that my bag could in no way be seen from my bedroom door; it couldn't. As I started to read, I didn't even remember if my dad came in my room or not. Obviously he must have before I folded my page, because my book was indeed on the floor upside down. And, the most telling, was my bedroom door was completely shut. I remember I had left it open just a crack when I came into my room earlier. I looked over at the clock on my night table. 2:30 am. I better get going, I thought. I slowly got up, went to my closet and looked inside my handbag. Yep! My car keys were right where they were supposed to be. So was my smallish photo-album. I took put my Celine sweatpants and pullover and put them on. I took out a pair of socks and my day-glow pink Nikes ™, put them on and was good to go as far as clothes went. I took out my wallet from my purse and took it in the bathroom with me. As I fixed my hair into a pony tail, I counted the money that was *in* my wallet that I put in there a few days ago. $4,000.00. That should get me to where I need to go, I thought. I smiled to myself. I walked to my socks/ panties/lingerie drawer and dug around until I found my gun. A 45 Glock. A sweet piece and the only pistol that I would *ever* use. Plus I had a license to carry too. So, all good there. As I put my piece in my purse, I closed it and twisted the top flap that closed the top of my purse entirely. I zipped up my LV Carry-All and picked it up, holding it in my left hand, my handbag in my right; along with my car keys. I opened my door very slowly. All was super quiet. As it should be at this hour. I woke up at around 2:30 am and now it was 3:22 am. I walked down the stairs one at a time. Listening very, *very* carefully. So far so good, I thought. As I reached the front door, I slowly opened it and scooted out. Sideways with my bag. God, please, please, do *not* let my father catch me! He would kill me! Beat me *first,* even! As I walked out the front door, I saw that there were zero cars parked in the cul-de-sac around the fountain. Good. I took the key that opened the garage and put it firmly between my thumb and pointer finger. When I was right in front of the door to the garage, I saw my finger's trembling a little. I took 2 deep breaths and continued to put the key in. I turned the lock, it clicked and I was in. I rushed to the alarm, put in the code and all was d-o-n-e! Now for the hard part. Getting the car *out* of the garage. I pushed the button to lift the far west garage door and walked back to my Ferrari. I opened the trunk and put all of my things in it and closed the trunk. I tossed my handbag onto the passenger seat. I reached back to the gear shift and put the car in Neutral. I walked to the very back, put 1 hand on the small spoiler and the other onto the lower backside of the car. As I pushed as hard as I could, the car did move. And, moved pretty damn fast, too. Without making a sound. *That* was the best part. I quickly skipped over to the front of the car and turned the wheel in the correct direction, went back behind the car and kept pushing.

Chapter 30

After three fucking hours of sweating, falling and scraping my knee's on the carpet (thank God there is carpet) I was *out*. I turned around, put the car back in park, looked back at the house and pushed the security code to the garage. As I got into my car, watching the garage door slowly and silently (thank God) close, I smiled at my father's out-of-site bedroom, mouthed 'I love you daddy' and drove off, tears slowly falling from my eyes. My head then turned, facing forward and I put my car in drive. But too where?

I HAD NO IDEA.

www.ingramcontent.com/pod-product-compliance
Lightning Source LLC
Chambersburg PA
CBHW050451270326
41927CB00009B/1692

* 9 7 8 1 7 7 0 7 6 5 3 8 2 *